# The Career Coaching Too

*The Career Coaching Toolkit* is a practical guide to 34 effective and relevant career coaching techniques to help practitioners encourage, stretch and clarify their clients' thinking. Structured around ten of the most common career dilemmas clients bring to their coaches, this book provides clear advice to coaches about when to apply the right technique to address all of these problems.

With a dual focus on theory and practice, each chapter explores the links between the coaching technique and the scientific research on which it is based. The book explains how and why the technique works, giving the reader a real appreciation of the underlying mechanisms that make these techniques effective. Written specifically for career coaching, this deepened understanding will enhance confidence when working with clients.

A practical toolkit for practitioners and students alike, *The Career Coaching Toolkit* will add depth to the practice of anyone working with clients facing a career crossroads, or conducting research into occupational identities and career decision making.

**Julia Yates** has worked in the field of career coaching for over 20 years, as a career coach, trainer and writer. She is currently a Senior Lecturer at City, University of London, where she runs the MSc in Organisational Psychology and conducts research into the impact of non-conscious processes on career decisions.

# The Career Coaching Toolkit

Julia Yates

LONDON AND NEW YORK

First published 2019
by Routledge
2 Park Square, Milton Park, Abingdon, Oxon OX14 4RN

and by Routledge
711 Third Avenue, New York, NY 10017

*Routledge is an imprint of the Taylor & Francis Group, an informa business*

© 2019 Julia Yates

The right of Julia Yates to be identified as author of this work has been asserted by her in accordance with sections 77 and 78 of the Copyright, Designs and Patents Act 1988.

All rights reserved. No part of this book may be reprinted or reproduced or utilised in any form or by any electronic, mechanical, or other means, now known or hereafter invented, including photocopying and recording, or in any information storage or retrieval system, without permission in writing from the publishers.

*Trademark notice*: Product or corporate names may be trademarks or registered trademarks, and are used only for identification and explanation without intent to infringe.

*British Library Cataloguing in Publication Data*
A catalogue record for this book is available from the British Library

*Library of Congress Cataloging in Publication Data*
Names: Yates, Julia, author.
Title: The career coaching toolkit / Julia Yates.
Description: Abingdon, Oxon ; New York, NY : Routledge, 2019.
Identifiers: LCCN 2018014711| ISBN 9781138057296 (hardback) |
    ISBN 9781138057302 (pbk.) | ISBN 9781351675581 (epub)
Subjects: LCSH: Career development. | Personal coaching. | Executive coaching. | Vocational guidance.
Classification: LCC HF5381 .Y3746 2018 | DDC 650.1—dc23
LC record available at https://lccn.loc.gov/2018014711

ISBN: 978-1-138-05729-6 (hbk)
ISBN: 978-1-138-05730-2 (pbk)
ISBN: 978-1-315-16492-2 (ebk)

Typeset in Times New Roman
by Swales & Willis Ltd, Exeter, Devon, UK

 Printed in the United Kingdom by Henry Ling Limited

To Ted, Jack and Hugh

# Contents

| | | |
|---|---|---|
| | *Acknowledgements* | ix |
| 1 | Introduction | 1 |
| 2 | Where do clients get stuck? | 6 |
| 3 | How can I make sense of my career so far? | 12 |
| 4 | What do I want from a job? | 33 |
| 5 | What jobs would suit me? | 48 |
| 6 | What job do I want to do? | 66 |
| 7 | I want to go for it, but I am just not sure I am good enough | 83 |
| 8 | Part of me wants it, but part of me wants something else | 96 |
| 9 | It is what I want, but my family aren't so sure | 111 |
| 10 | What's the point in trying? I am never going to make anything of myself | 123 |
| 11 | I just can't decide between these options | 143 |
| 12 | I am not feeling very motivated | 152 |

| 13 Multi-purpose tools | 166 |
|---|---|
| 14 Conclusion | 171 |
| *Further reading* | 175 |
| *References* | 179 |
| *Index* | 194 |

# Acknowledgements

Thanks first go to Christian for suggesting that I should compile these techniques into a book. My students, both at UEL and at City, have always been an enormous inspiration to me, and I would like to thank them for allowing me to try out all the techniques on them, for providing valuable feedback and for making the career choices that they themselves have made. I had a fabulous group of reviewers to whom I am most grateful: Christian, David, Janet, John, Ian, Paul, Rob and Rosie, who made sure that each chapter made sense. Thanks go to my darling boys, Jack and Ted, who occasionally let me practice on them, who keep me cheerful and whose lives remind me why this is important, and to my mother, who showed me how to combine a career with motherhood and who helps me make it work. And, most of all, my love and gratitude to Hugh, for being supportive and encouraging throughout the process, reading every word, keeping my semi-colons in order and bringing me endless cups of tea.

# Chapter 1

# Introduction

Our clients are complex people and often come to us with complex stories. As career coaches, we are committed to doing our best to move them forwards and helping them to identify and meet their goals. Many of us have a number of tools and techniques that we have developed and mastered, and that add value to our clients. But sometimes it can seem as though we are not making progress and it is frustrating to feel that we are not supporting or stretching a client enough.

In the pages ahead I will be introducing a variety of tools, techniques and approaches that have been shown to be effective at resolving career dilemmas. Some you may have come across before and others you may not feel are quite suitable for you, your professional context or your clients. But I hope that there will be some that strike a chord, that you like the look of and that you come to enjoy using.

The book is structured around the most common dilemmas that our clients bring to us. I have described the techniques as *career coaching* tools, but my priority was to find techniques that would work and, as a result, the tools have not all been drawn from coaching. Acceptance and commitment therapy (Chapter 10), for example, is not a mainstream coaching approach, and the five ways to well-being (Chapter 10) isn't really a tool at all. I make no apologies for this. If the techniques could answer our clients' questions and if they have been shown to work I was keen to include them, regardless of the field from which they originated. Clients are multifaceted and career development is complex. If we restrict ourselves as practitioners to one perspective, we are limiting the support we can give our clients. The tools in this book therefore are drawn from a wide range of relevant disciplines.

The description of each tool is accompanied by two boxes. The first one, 'Why it works', links the technique with theories. This explains the underlying processes but doesn't necessarily prove how effective the tool is. The 'What's the evidence?' box highlights empirical research that aims to (and sometimes does) actually demonstrate that a technique makes a difference. An understanding of the theory is important because it enables you to understand how to use the tools and manipulate them to make sure they are effective for you and your clients in your context. It allows you to know what to hold on to and what you can lose, how to describe and explain things and how to change what you are doing to suit the occasion. The theory boxes also offer some insight into how all the different kinds of approaches, ideas and constructs tie in together and this enables you to start to build up an overall picture of psychological behaviour and career choices. Alongside an indication of whether the tool actually does what it claims to do, the evidence boxes give some idea of the clients for whom it has been shown to be effective and the contexts in which it has worked. It is worth stressing that the findings from the research should not take the place of your professional judgement, but should be one strand of evidence that feeds into it.

Each and every tool introduced in this book has an empirical evidence base. Each technique has been put into practice, its value assessed through a thoughtfully designed study, and the quality of the research has been peer-reviewed and published in an academic journal. This doesn't necessarily mean that the technique will work, for every career coach, and each client, but it does, perhaps, mean that the tool is worth considering. The quality of the evidence base varies from one technique to another. For some more well-established tools there are enough studies published to put into a meta-analysis, which combines the results of multiple individual studies into one statistical package and can provide very credible data. Some tools too have been widely evaluated with a range of different participants whose situations and dilemmas may be similar to those of your clients. The evidence base for other approaches, however, is less comprehensive and there may be fewer smaller studies that perhaps look at the impact the tools have on a population that differs from your typical clients.

An evidence base will never be perfect, and within a field as intricate as ours it will always be difficult to run randomised control trials that isolate the specific aspect of people's experience that has made a difference. The research should always be interpreted with caution, and even the most robust and large-scale study should never be thought to 'prove' that something works, let alone to ascertain that it will work for you. But given that we want to offer the most effective service that we can, techniques that have at least some claim to offering demonstrable benefits to clients seem like a good place to start.

I have thought a lot about how much information to provide in this book. My priority is to introduce you to a range of different tools from which you can pick and choose. Inevitably, then, I can only offer an overview, but there should be enough depth to enable you to put the techniques into practice straight away. How confident you feel about trying out any particular tool will vary. You may find that some of the techniques will chime with your natural coaching style and you can incorporate them into your practice fairly easily. For those that seem a little more alien it might be useful to do some more reading, and you could look for online demonstrations or talk to practitioners who already use these techniques. For the most part, you will develop your expertise by trying things out, reflecting and trying again. If you can find a colleague (or even a willing friend or family member) to team up with then you can always practise these ideas on them first, but at some point you will just need to give it a go.

For the most part the tools have been described accurately, faithful to the original papers in which they were first introduced, although occasionally the descriptions have been slighted adapted to make the tools more suitable to a career-coaching context. It is, however, useful to remember that the specific details of how to implement the approaches are not set in stone. As professional career coaches, you are in the best position to know exactly what is going to work for you, with your clients, in your context. You might want to implement the approaches as they are outlined here in the first instance, but then you can adapt and improve them and make them your own.

One important aspect of ethical practice that might be useful to raise before you start putting the tools into practice is the issue of boundaries. The issues that our clients come to us with can encompass and influence all aspects of life. We see people who are struggling with their identity, their relationships, their health, their life purpose and their finances. The tools introduced in this book enable us as practitioners to engage with all of these aspects of our clients' career development but we need to be mindful that these issues can be profound, deep rooted and long lasting, and we must acknowledge that sometimes our clients might need the support of a professional with more specific training and expertise. As such, it may be useful for you to give some thought to how you would respond if a conversation takes an unexpected direction and goes further than you feel comfortable with, or reveals issues that you don't feel that you are well placed to help with.

One mechanism for coaches who feel that they need more support with their practice is supervision. Supervision is not a mainstream part of professional practice in the UK, but the more we understand about our clients' decision-making processes, and the better and more tailored our techniques become, the more important it is that we have systems in place to ensure our continued ethical and effective practice. Supervision is an aspect of professional practice that originated in counselling, and in that professional arena it is considered vital. The purpose of supervision is to protect the client's best interests by ensuring that the coach is performing at their best. Supervisory conversations allow a coach to reflect on their own practice and explore ideas and concerns that have come up within their practice. They provide a safe confidential space in which to reflect on professional performance and ethical issues. Supervision can take different forms. At one end of the scale, you could have a supervisor who is trained and experienced as both a career coach and a supervisor, and whom you see regularly, every six weeks or so, to discuss your professional practice. This is the gold standard, and if you are doing quite a lot of coaching and you are finding that your coaching conversations often touch on difficult issues, then this might be appropriate. An alternative is to have a looser arrangement with a supervisor, in which you meet up less frequently, or perhaps on an ad hoc basis, contacting them when you feel that it would be useful to have a conversation. Peer group supervision can work well too. You could form a group with a number of colleagues and meet regularly to discuss your experiences. The key thing here is to be aware that your coaching conversations can have an impact on you, and that this could then have an impact on your coaching, and to have a plan in place to minimise any negative effects.

The assumption for most of the techniques introduced in this book is that you will be working in a one-to-one context. A lot of career interventions are delivered in this way, but increasingly career practitioners are being asked to deliver their sessions in groups or online. Both of these additional modes of delivery bring their advantages in terms of convenience and cost, but they differ in terms of the value they can add for clients. Working in a group context can allow clients to learn from each other and derive reassurance or affirmation from seeing others in a similar position and sharing their stories. I have included some suggestions for ways that the tools can be adapted to a group context, and I do urge you to find your own ways to make them work in larger forums. I've tried pretty much every technique out in a group setting with my long-suffering Masters students and, as long as the instructions are clear, I have found that they can work well. Adapting the tools to an online context I think is harder. The tools in the book for the most part will really benefit from the interaction with an advisor and, in my experience, it is during this collaborative reflection that the expertise of the career practitioner comes into its own, pushing the client's thinking and taking them further than they could get on their own. The exercises can certainly be introduced online – you could offer clear instructions and identify suitable online formats – but the challenge is to find a mechanism for the debrief that will allow the client to crystalise and capitalise on the insights gleaned from the exercises.

It has dawned on me as I have collected these techniques, tried them out and reflected on my practice, that I am not a fan of the quick fix. There are quick fixes available – well, there are exercises available that are quick to do. But, in my experience, they are rarely a substitute for some serious hard thinking and I remain a little dubious about their ability to 'fix' anything. The techniques introduced in this book are designed to encourage clients to spend some time digging deep and dredging up ideas, making links, reframing, creating new pathways, building bridges and designing personal futures. The exercises can start the process, but it is the conversation with you that can take the threads of the ideas and weave them into a realistic, achievable and positive future.

There are numerous different approaches to coaching that can vary, according to Eric de Haan (2008), along two continuums: from confronting to supporting, and from suggesting to exploring. The career coaching approach that underpins most of the ideas in this book is a person-centred one, which provides high levels of support from the coach and offers an emphasis on exploring rather than giving suggestions. This approach (outlined in more depth in Chapter 8) acknowledges that individuals are best-placed to solve their own problems, and assumes that they have the resources and capabilities to do so. Coaching can help them to work out what it is they want, what might be holding them back, and what they need to do to move forwards. The role of the coach is therefore a facilitative one, aiming to enable clients to work out their own opinions and identify their own best solutions.

This book will not teach you how to coach. There are other introductory handbooks you can read or courses you can take that provide a broad overview of the basics of career coaching. This book is aimed at those who are already coaching but who are looking to go beyond the basics and to enhance the value they can offer their clients. It offers a range of different techniques that can be incorporated within your career coaching practice and can help to make sure that your career conversations are more easily tailored to the particular needs of each client.

Career coaching is a privilege and a challenge. We make a difference to people's lives and this is a responsibility that is, and that should be, taken seriously. We owe it to ourselves and to our clients to be the best coaches that we can be, and I hope that adding a few new techniques to your professional practice will enable you to add a little more value to some of your clients.

# Chapter 2

# Where do clients get stuck?

This chapter will explore the nature of the challenges that our clients face. The focus will be on the stumbling blocks that our clients might encounter, and the chapter offers a close look at the specific aspects of the career decision-making process that commonly cause problems. Prior to homing in on the challenges, I thought it might be useful to highlight some of the research that tells us a bit about the process of career choice. An understanding of how the process works when it is working well can help us identify and explain what is going on with our clients when it is proving difficult.

## How do people make career choices?

The traditional career theories that dominated the field during the 20th century held that the process of career decision making was straightforward. People simply needed to develop good self-awareness, learn about the job opportunities around them, and apply true reasoning to find the perfect match. Considerable theoretical and empirical work has gone into the field since Frank Parsons made this claim in 1909 and, whilst his model still resonates in some ways, the different elements of it are now understood and interpreted in a more complex and sophisticated way. There are myriad, diverse career theories that can help us to understand the processes. Some focus on one or other specific aspect of the process, some acknowledge the wide range of factors at play and others claim that one particular factor dominates. Looking at the theoretical landscape as a whole, there seem to be four different elements that are generally considered crucial to the process (Yates, 2016).

1 **Identity**. The notion that people need a good understanding of themselves has never wavered, but this is now understood as the more holistic and multi-dimensional concept of 'identity'. Rather than the more traditional understanding of self-awareness as a combination of skills, values, personality and interests, identity is far broader. Identity incorporates past, present and future (where I come from, who I am now and who I want to be in the future), and combines a wide range of elements including

lifestyle, broad questions such as life purpose and demographic factors such as sexuality, gender, race and class.

2   **Understanding of the environment.** Awareness of the world of work still matters, but this is now seen as a more complex set of interactions as people also need to understand how they can influence the environment around them and how the environment influences them. This includes the impact of politics, the media and one's family, as well as the labour market and the career opportunities available and the role that chance plays in our lives. We now embrace the idea that perceptions of reality are more important than reality itself, and so how people see themselves and their perceptions of jobs are more relevant than what things are 'actually' like.

3   **Decision making and research skills.** Decision making is seen as an important aspect of the process but, in conjunction with the value placed on rational logic, we now understand that gut instinct is invariably influential and often helpful in our decisions. Alongside decision making, another skill that is increasingly important is that of research. Google provides us with all the information we could ever need at the touch of a button, but this explosion of information brings its own challenges. Finding the right information and interpreting it in such a way that it is meaningful for a particular context is a complex skill that needs to be honed.

4   **Personal attributes.** Finally, there is another set of factors whose influence is significant. Research has shown that we are not all equally equipped to make good career choices or all equally able to put our plans into action. Those with higher levels of confidence, resilience, optimism and the ability to set goals have a distinct advantage in their career development and, whilst we may have different levels of these skills naturally, they can be enhanced through specific tailored interventions.

These then are the four aspects of career development that are consistently highlighted in current career literature. In general, if people are clear about and comfortable with their identities, if they have a good understanding of their environment, if they are good decision makers and researchers, and if they have a strong battalion of the right personal characteristics, their path to a good career decision is likely to be fairly straightforward. Unfortunately, not many of us are so blessed. I will now turn to a brief overview of what the research community can tell us about the kinds of challenges our clients are most likely to face as they work towards finding and securing the right role for them.

## Where do career decision makers get stuck?

There have been a number of analyses of career decision-making difficulties published in the last 20 years or so. One of the largest was conducted by Gati, Krausz, and Osipow in 1996. They contacted career practitioners across the globe and asked them to keep a diary for one month, recording the details of the nature of the queries or problems that their clients brought to their career sessions. Gati and his colleagues analysed the results and identified ten key questions, which they categorised within three themes: lack of readiness, lack of information and inconsistent information. Lack of readiness included lack of motivation, indecisiveness and dysfunctional myths. Lack of information focused on information about the self, the world of work and the process of research and applying for jobs. Inconsistent information covered internal tensions (part of me wants one thing and part of me wants another), conflicts with significant others (I want to do one thing but my parents want me to do another) and conflicting information from unreliable sources.

A year later, Chartrand and Robbins (1997) developed the 'career factors inventory', which divided career decision-making difficulties into two categories, classifying them as either down to a lack of information or the result of what they describe as *affective impediments*, which include anxiety about making choices and general indecisiveness.

Kelly and Lee (2002) conducted some further research into the area, examining these two taxonomies of career decision-making difficulties alongside an earlier one, the Career Decision Scale (Osipow, 1987), and testing the different factors with a large cohort of students. They concluded that the challenges facing this population could be explained under three headings:

- lack of information
- indecision
- disagreement with others.

*Lack of information* was, by far, the most significant challenge the student participants faced. This was a broad category and incorporated a lack of information about the process of research, applying for jobs and making career decisions, about occupations, and unreliable information. Lack of information could also incorporate lack of information about the self. In particular, Kelly and Lee found that some people were struggling with 'identity diffusion', which describes those whose understanding of how they could and would want to fit into the work place was not crystalised. People experiencing this identity diffusion might not be able to see how their strengths could be used in a work context, or how their values could be realised within their work.

The category of *indecision* encompassed two challenges. First, *trait indecision*, which refers to people who just struggle to make decisions. As a 'trait', the indecision is not limited to career choices but is an aspect of personality and can strike at any time. Indecisive people might struggle to choose which sandwich to have at lunchtime, where to go on holiday or what to watch on television, and this indecision can also take its toll on career choices. The second kind of indecision was described as *choice anxiety* and refers to those who may find it relatively easy to make choices in most aspect of their lives, but who feel particularly anxious about putting their career plans into action in case things do not turn out well. Given the huge investment that can accompany a career choice, this is not an uncommon or indeed an irrational position to take.

The final aspect, *disagreement with others*, is a decision-making difficulty that manifests itself after a career plan has been formulated. It refers to situations where family and friends do not agree with or support the choice that has been made, whether because they feel that it reflects on them in some way or (more commonly) because they feel that the choice is not likely to bring their loved one the fulfilment they are looking for.

## Who gets stuck?

Saka, Gati and Kelly (2008) took the direction of research a little beyond the 'what' to explore the 'why', and reviewed the literature that examines the kind of personalities that tend to lead to a state of career indecision. Their model suggests that there are three clusters of characteristics that can make things tricky: pessimistic views, anxiety and issues about self-identity.

Pessimism is the tendency to focus on the negative aspects of a given situation and to anticipate negative outcomes. In terms of career decisions, a pessimistic view of the world of work, a limited belief in the degree to which one can control one's own career paths and a negative view of one's ability to make positive career choices, will all have a negative impact on the ability to make a career choice. Those who feel pessimistic about the world of work might believe that unemployment rates are high, the chances of getting a job are low, redundancies are commonplace, and robots will, soon, leave us all out of work. People who engage in this kind of thinking will be less motivated to expend their energy on career research and job hunting as they can't see that it will come to any good.

This idea that energy invested in proactive career behaviour will be a waste of time is also seen in those who have an external *locus of control*. Your locus of control describes your perception of who or what is in control of your life (Rotter, 1966). If you have an internal locus of control, you will believe that what happens in your life is, at least in large part, within your control. You believe that if things have gone wrong that is because you did not try hard enough, or did not focus your energy in the right way. If things have gone well, that is because you worked hard and made good choices. An internal locus of control is, generally, shown to be positive because it motivates people to make more effort. They believe that their effort will make a difference and therefore believe that it is worth their while to work hard. This then has the knock-on effect that they are then more likely to succeed in any given context, whether making a decision or putting a plan into action (Santos, 2001). Finally, pessimism about one's own ability to research and apply for jobs, often described as a lack of *career decision making self-efficacy* (Taylor & Betz, 1983), has been shown to lead to career indecision as people do not feel confident in their ability to get it right so they will not commit to one option (Osipow & Gati, 1998).

The second cluster of characteristics that tends to make career decisions more difficult is anxiety-related. This can take many forms and includes perfectionism, fear of commitment, high self-criticism, low tolerance for ambiguity, fear of failure and even fear of success (DeRoma, Martin & Kessler, 2003; Leong & Chervinko, 1996; Serling & Betz, 1990). Saka and colleagues identify three different aspects of anxiety that have particular relevance to career indecision. First there is anxiety about the process of career development, often linked specifically to perfectionism. This anxiety can be manifest both before the process has started and during the research or application phase, as individuals worry about not choosing the right (or perfect) option. Second, there is anxiety that is sparked off by the uncertainty of the future, and this manifests itself as anxiety about being undecided. Third, there is anxiety linked to the fear of getting it wrong: what if your perfect career plan, which has been so lovingly and painstakingly crafted, leads you to a job that you actually do not enjoy?

Finally, there are characteristics around one's own identity that can make the whole process more challenging. The issues here highlight people's difficulties in developing or identifying a clear sense of who they are and who they want to be with regards to their career. Young people in particular can struggle to work out where their family's identity stops and their own identity starts. As a child, identity is very much determined by family but, throughout adolescence and early adulthood, young people gradually break free from this as they start to conceptualise themselves as individuals in their own right, influenced by, but independent from, their parents. For some this developmental process happens smoothly, but for others it is more of a rocky ride. Finally, self-esteem is contained within this cluster of identity issues. Self-esteem is often very tied up in occupational choices as people opt for jobs that reflect their beliefs in their own abilities.

## Implications for career coaching

The literature, then, gives us some insights into the career choice process when it works smoothly and some indication of the types of challenges that people commonly face. The next step is to explore some approaches that career coaches can adopt that might be able to support clients in the face of these challenges.

This book is structured around the issues identified in the literature above and aims to provide you with some new approaches that can help support clients as they face common career dilemmas. The chapters that follow offer tools and techniques to address ten questions that, based on the research, represent some of the key challenges that our clients face. The issues identified in the literature above are not all addressed in this book. I have omitted those that concern information about the process and about career options. These are, of course, important issues for our clients and therefore important issues for us, but they tend to be more fact based, so the need for the kind of techniques offered in this book, which provide an alternative approach to delving into cognitive stores and awakening creative thinking, are not as relevant. Leaving these career challenges aside then, the other issues described above have been distilled down to ten key questions.

- How can I make sense of my career so far?
- What do I want from a job?
- What jobs would suit me?
- What job do I want to do?
- I want to go for it but I am just not sure I am good enough.
- Part of me wants it, but part of me wants something else.
- It is what I want but my family aren't so sure.
- What's the point in trying – I am never going to make anything of myself.
- I just can't decide between these options.
- I am not feeling very motivated.

The people we work with and the situations they find themselves in are complex, and the career challenges that they face are often multifaceted. I am not suggesting that all career dilemmas can easily be reduced to one of these ten questions and that the simple application of a new technique will solve their problem. But sometimes it can be helpful to try and unpick the complexity of their lives and I hope that the tools offered in these pages can help you to work out new ways to address some of the facets of their dilemmas.

There are over 30 tools described in this book and, before you start reading about them, it might be worth pausing to consider how you might make the decision to opt for one rather than another. The tools have been categorised on the basis of the client questions they are most suited to addressing but, for each career quandary, there are two or three different approaches offered. The tools in each chapter will vary on the basis of the nature of the tool, the cognitive processes they tap into (creative, verbal, conscious, unconscious), whether they extend back to the past or ahead to the future, how long they take and the level of demands they place on the client. I would suggest that you make your choices based on a combination of pragmatism and preference. Pragmatically, it's down to the tools that you think would work for your clients in the contexts in which you work. You might want to focus on the techniques that work effectively in groups, or which seem particularly suited to career changers, or which you could manage within 15 minutes. Alongside a focus on the tools that you feel are most likely to be effective for you, it is worth considering which tools you think you will enjoy using. There is some evidence that the coach's commitment to their particular approach is more important than the nature of the approach (McKenna & Davis, 2009) so, for your clients to reap the best rewards, you should opt for tools that make sense to you and that you feel you will enjoy using.

# Chapter 3

# How can I make sense of my career so far?

In this, the first of the techniques chapters of the book, I start with a series of tools that are aimed at helping clients to make sense of their careers so far.

Sometimes a client's inability to move forward in their career planning is rooted in things that have happened in the past. It is not uncommon for people to make a 'false start' in their careers, and they can look back and wonder why they spent so long in a position or organisation that was wrong for them. At other times, when they look over their story so far, the whole career path can seem disjointed and piecemeal. Clients can feel confused about why things went wrong, or why they made the choices that they made, and they may need to understand this in order to feel confident that they are not going to make the same mistakes again. This dissatisfaction with an apparently chequered or incoherent history is acknowledged in the career literature. There is some evidence that people need to be able to tell themselves a convincing story about their history, and to link up different episodes from their past and present in order to plan their future (Haynie & Shepherd, 2011). This continuity helps people to make sense of who they are and this is important to self-esteem. It can be, then, that in order to move forwards, clients need to make some sense of their past.

In this chapter I introduce three techniques that are useful for clients who are looking back and trying to make sense of their story. The first one is a personality questionnaire. This identifies four personality traits that can help people understand why previous roles didn't suit them. The second tool introduced in this chapter is the career construction interview. The interview consists of five different questions that may seem a little unexpected at first glance but that are surprisingly revealing and can help clients to identify life themes. The final technique in this chapter is the career genogram, in which people are invited to think about the different work roles that they have been exposed to within their family and to consider the impact this range of jobs may have had on their own choices or expectations.

## Personality traits

### Introduction

The notion of *personality* is an enormously complex one. There is no generally accepted definition as such, but it is widely agreed that personality consists of a blend of habitual behaviour, thoughts and emotions, and is developed through a combination of genetic and environmental factors. Over the decades, many academics have tried to break personality down to specific components, trying to work out what it is, where it comes from and what impact it has. The result is a complex web of dozens of different frameworks of personality types, traits and states that both complement and contradict each other. There has been considerable research that has tried to link personalities to careers and it seems clear that there are some strong associations. Certain personality types are more likely to be found in particular jobs and some personal characteristics are associated with different styles of job search and different levels of success.

Personality questionnaires are sometimes used to help individuals to identify suitable career options, but their value as a way to generate job ideas is questionable. Whilst this kind of approach can spark off some interesting ideas, it could imply that there is one single personality type that fits a particular job and this limiting approach is not helpful to either the individual or to the overall diversity of any given profession.

The questionnaire below is offered as a tool that can help individuals to make sense of their own narratives. In particular, it aims to help individuals to develop an understanding of why their previous jobs did not work out for them. Developing a clear understanding of the factors at play can be important in reassuring clients that they won't make the same mistake again and in restoring their self-esteem, as they see that the problem was the result of a misalliance and not a fundamental personal flaw. Jobs can fail to work out for many diverse reasons. Often the cause of the problem is clear to our clients – if it is a difficult boss, or a relentlessly boring set of tasks, or a job that lacked meaning, people are usually able to identify and articulate the reason for the mismatch. But, in other cases, it can be harder for an individual to crystalise exactly what went wrong. An incompatibility between an individual's personality and the ideal personality for the job often seems to provide an explanation for a job that just did not work out.

This tool, devised by Brent Donnellan and colleagues in 2006, is known as the Mini-IPIP scale (International Personality Item Pool). The authors describe it as a 'tiny yet effective' measure of personality. It looks at four personality traits, drawn from Costa and McCrae's framework of personality (1992), and identifies at which end of each scale an individual is most likely to feel comfortable. They are described here as the need for interaction, the use of imagination, the need for harmony and the love of planning, and are linked to Costa and McCrae's factors of extraversion, openness to experience, agreeableness and conscientiousness.

This tool is not intended to provide a comprehensive account of how people actually behave. Our actual behaviour is based on such a wide range of different factors that this would be a prohibitively difficult task. It looks instead at the behaviour that comes most naturally and most easily to someone. This distinction is important because, whilst an individual may train themselves to behave in a particular way, perhaps to fit in to a role or an organisation, if this style of behaviour doesn't come naturally to them they may find it hard to sustain and enjoy on a long-term basis. People are often able to perform well in their less-natural style, but choosing this behaviour will come at a cost.

14   How can I make sense of my career so far?

### How to use

#### Step 1: the questionnaire

There are four personality traits that this explores and there are four questions for each. You can ask your clients for a straight 'yes/no' answer, or offer them a scale of 1–5.

A NEED FOR INTERACTION

The first personality feature is often described as introversion and extraversion and examines the degree to which an individual needs and thrives on interaction with others.

|   | Disagree............................................Agree |
|---|---|
| 1  I am the life and soul of the party | 1............2............3............4............5 |
| 2  I do not talk a lot | 1............2............3............4............5 |
| 3  When I go to a party I talk to a lot of different people | 1............2............3............4............5 |
| 4  I like to keep in the background | 1............2............3............4............5 |

Extraverts, those who need more interaction, are more likely to describe themselves as the life and soul of the party, and to talk to a lot of different people (higher scores for Q1 and Q3). Introverts, in contrast, are more likely to indicate that they tend to talk a little less, and may prefer to keep in the background rather than enjoying the limelight (higher scores for Q2 and Q4).

Whilst most of us will enjoy interactions and find work is much improved by the addition of some like-minded colleagues, introverts and extraverts tend to differ in how much interaction they need and what impact contact with others has on their overall levels of energy. Extraverts are more likely to find interactions energising and therefore seek them out more, and Introverts are more likely to find too much socialising a little draining, so might prefer a more contained level of interaction.

In a work context, extraverts can favour an open-plan office, will enjoy some office banter and tend to like to feel part of a team. They may enjoy working on a number of different projects at once and may find they get bored easily.

Introverts, in contrast, prefer a calmer and quieter office environment and probably find they can concentrate better in an office on their own. They can be great team players, but often find that they get their best work done when they have a project that is their own and that they can work on independently. They tend to like being able to finish one project before they start the next.

THE USE OF IMAGINATION

The second scale discriminates between those who enjoy using their imagination and those who are better with practicalities.

|  | Disagree....................................Agree |
|---|---|
| 5  I have a vivid imagination | 1............2............3............4............5 |
| 6  I am not interested in abstract ideas | 1............2............3............4............5 |
| 7  I have difficulty understanding abstract ideas | 1............2............3............4............5 |
| 8  I do not have a good imagination | 1............2............3............4............5 |

People who describe themselves as having a vivid imagination (higher score on Q5 and lower scores on Qs 6, 7 and 8) are what is described in Costa and McCrae's model as *open to experience*. This also has a strong link with the preference for *intuition* in the Myers Briggs Type Indicator (Myers, 1962).

Those at the imaginative end of the scale are interested in and skilled at strategic thinking, creative ideas and possibilities. They do not tend to be terribly good at detail and can find minutiae both tedious and difficult, but they thrive in environments where they are allowed intellectual or creative freedom.

Those at the other end of the scale (low score on Q5 high scores on Qs 6, 7 and 8) flourish where attention to detail is needed and a step-by-step approach adds value, but may feel less at home in changeable environments and may struggle to see the relevance of very abstract ideas.

A NEED FOR HARMONY

The third scale examines the degree to which an individual values and needs harmonious relationships.

|  | Disagree....................................Agree |
|---|---|
| 9  I sympathise with others' feelings | 1............2............3............4............5 |
| 10  I am not interested in other people's problems | 1............2............3............4............5 |
| 11  I feel others' emotions | 1............2............3............4............5 |
| 12  I am not really interested in others | 1............2............3............4............5 |

Those who strive for harmony above all will sympathise with others' feelings and feel their emotions (high scores on Q9 and Q11), and those for whom harmony is less important are likely to indicate that they are not so interested in others and their problems (higher scores on Q10 and Q12).

Those who value harmony tend to be happiest in a working environment that is thoughtful and sensitive, and where people pull together in a team. They might particularly thrive in an organisation that is values-driven. They can deal with criticism and may be as ambitious as the next person, but it is of paramount importance that they are valued and are made to feel so.

Those who have less interest in people's problems and emotions may be a bit more task-orientated and prefer a working environment that is goal-driven. They are very likely to value good working relationships but may also enjoy a healthy dose of competition and feel frustrated when emotions slow things down.

A LOVE OF PLANNING

The final set of questions explores whether an individual likes to plan or prefers spontaneity.

|  | Disagree.....................................Agree |
|---|---|
| 13 I get chores done straight away | 1............2............3............4............5 |
| 14 I often forget to put things back in their proper place | 1............2............3............4............5 |
| 15 I like order | 1............2............3............4............5 |
| 16 I make a mess of things | 1............2............3............4............5 |

People with a love of planning tend to prefer to get all their jobs done before they can start to have fun and appreciate a degree of order (higher scores on Q13 and Q15). Those who prefer to be a bit more spontaneous are less troubled by whether things are in their right place and can be comfortable leaving their chores to the last minute (higher scores for Q14 and Q16).

Those who prefer a planned existence like to be able to work at a predictable pace, with deadlines and lists and spreadsheets and Gantt charts. They can work fast and hard, but work best when they know what they are dealing with. Those who prefer spontaneity can find a predictable workplace a bit stifling, but tend to thrive in environments that are volatile and can cope, and even perform at their best, when the goal posts change or in a crisis.

*Step 2: the conversation*

As we will see with many of the tools introduced in this book, it is not so much the answers to the questions that are insightful but the conversations that stem from them. Once you have elicited the answers from your client, you can then, together, try to see whether there is any light that the answers can shed on their previous experiences.

Once your client has identified their own personality type, invite them to reflect on the context in which they have been working and to identify the personality type of the organisation, team or role in which they have been working. It may seem a little odd to think about an organisation or team in terms of a personality type but, with a bit of encouragement, people are usually able to pinpoint some aspects of this and it can be a revealing exercise. If they are finding this difficult, the following questions might be helpful prompts:

### THE NEED FOR INTERACTION

- Is it usual in your team to talk ideas through together before reaching any conclusions (*high*), or do people tend to think about things on their own and then bring their ideas to a meeting (*low*)?
- Would you describe it as a lively, sociable organisation (*high*)?

### THE USE OF IMAGINATION

- Is it an organisation that values ideas and creativity (*high*), or is it more important that ideas are realistic and practical (*low*)?
- Does the team approach projects in a step by step methodical way (*low*), or is it more likely to leap in anywhere and hope that the details sort themselves out as the project goes on (*high*)?

### THE NEED FOR HARMONY

- Would your colleagues in general choose to sacrifice quality for the sake of good relationships (*high*), or sacrifice good relationships for the sake of quality (*low*)?
- Is it a values-driven organisation (*high*)?

### THE LOVE OF PLANNING

- Does your boss like to make a plan and stick to it (*high*)?
- Is the team good at firefighting (*low*)?

Once your client has identified a mismatch between certain aspects of their natural style and the style that might fit in best in their role, team or organisation, spend some time identifying the impact of this misalliance, exploring how it manifested itself, what emotions it engendered and what impact it had on your client, the team and the work.

When you feel that this has been explored in sufficient depth, you can turn the conversation towards the future and ask whether there are any lessons to be learned from these new insights that might help your client's future choices. If your client has a particular career idea in mind, you could think together about whether this option is likely to suit them and what mitigating action they could take to make sure the impact of any mismatch is lessened.

## *In practice*

A mismatch between you and the prevailing culture, your boss, your colleagues, or the work itself can have quite an impact and leave you feeling isolated. But it is important to remember, and to share with your clients, that there is no one single personality type that works for one job. You might be more likely to find detail people in law firms but imagination can play a valuable part in a legal career too; empathy is enormously important in nursing but a task-orientated nurse could be a great asset to a team.

This approach is probably best used in one-to-one contexts as the conversations that help people to analyse how the personality traits influenced their work can need the support of a professional, but the questionnaire can be used as a general tool to enhance self-awareness in a group context. The four aspects of the tool are presented together here, but you may also find that it is useful to just raise one of the personality traits with your client. If you hear something in their story that alerts you to the possibility that there may have been a mismatch on one of the personality dimensions, then you could simply identify that one characteristic and see whether it, on its own, contributes to your client's understanding of their experiences.

This is one of the few techniques in the book that are not so suitable for clients who are making their initial career choices, as the focus is on what has happened in the past more than what will happen in the future. As such, it resonates more with people changing career.

| | |
|---|---|
| One to one | ✓ |
| Group sessions | ✓ |
| Within the session | ✓ |
| As a self-directed intersessional task | ✗ |
| Initial career choice | ✗ |
| Career change | ✓ |
| Suggested timing | 20 minutes |

## Case study

Clare came to see a career coach because she was unsure of her next move. She had just resigned from a prestigious retail graduate training scheme, which really hadn't worked out for her and the failure had hit her hard. She had always managed to make a success of things before and still couldn't see why it hadn't worked out. She had tried hard and had wanted to succeed, but somehow she just hadn't been able to perform well and wasn't happy. This lack of clarity was making her feel enormously anxious about making any other choices. How could she be sure she wouldn't make the same mistake again?

Looking at her personality, it became clear that she was an extravert who had a great imagination, loved harmony and liked to plan. The extraversion and planning aspects of her personality worked well in the retail context but, as she talked, it dawned on her that her imagination and love of abstract thoughts were accompanied by a lack of interest or engagement with process and methodological detail. She remembered a cliché she had heard numerous times at work, 'retail is detail', and it occurred to her that working in a retail environment where precision is valued and procedure is important was always going to present her with a challenge. Succeeding in this field would inevitably be an uphill struggle for her. The love of harmony also did not really seem to fit with the environment that she had come from, where profit margins were tight and empathy seemed in short supply.

These clashes between two aspects of Clare's natural style and the dominant culture in the organisation did not mean that she could never enjoy retail nor that she could not make an excellent retail manager. But it did indicate that it might be easier for her to achieve success and fulfilment in another environment. And, more than that, it explained things. It explained that her struggle and sense that she did not fit in was no failure, it was just a mismatch.

Armed with this new insight, Clare found that she was better able to make her peace with her previous job experience and felt more confident that she would be able to make a better choice in the future.

## Why it works

Traditional career development literature suggests that we should be aiming for a good 'person environment fit', where the features of the individual match the requirements of the role (Holland, 1959). Research in the 21st century highlights that this *congruence*, as it is known, makes only a limited contribution to good career development, and we now understand that career choice and the world of work is more complex and fluid than the traditional approach might indicate. But the notion of congruence is still acknowledged to have a part to play, and finding an organisational culture or a kind of work that suits your personality is most certainly a good thing (Sampson, 2009).

One piece of relevant research to have emerged more recently is that the construct of incongruence is more significant than congruence (Dik, Strife & Hansen, 2010). What this means is that, whilst finding a perfect match between an individual and their work place is not essential to job or career satisfaction, avoiding incongruence is really important. Whilst a reasonable match between the individual and the environment is usually good enough, an out-and-out mismatch is quite likely to cause real problems at work. This explains why an approach such as this, which allows people to identify or reflect on the causes of a mismatch, can be so insightful.

## What's the evidence base?

There are two sets of literature that we can draw on here. The first is the literature that validates measures of personality. Personality is a really tricky thing to pin down. Our personalities are complex and are influenced by many different factors, and the idea that a fully rounded evolving person can be reduced to four specific elements is of course nonsense. But that is not what this tool is aiming to do and it doesn't mean that this kind of personality analysis will not be of value. This approach makes no claims to summing up a personality, but it can hone in on some particular aspects that have been shown to be fairly stable. There are many different scales that measure different aspects of personality. These Mini-IPIP scales have been fairly well validated (Donnellan et al., 2006) and the authors themselves, alongside other researchers, have shown that these scales have fairly good reliability (which means you are likely to score the same each time you take the test) and validity (which means that it correlates pretty well with other more elaborate tests that purport to measure the same things). This suggests that if you think that a personality questionnaire might be a useful addition to your professional repertoire then this would be a good one to choose.

The second set of literature that is of interest here is that which examines whether these personality traits have any bearing on career choice or job satisfaction. Considerable research attests to the links between particular personality traits and satisfaction at work. Judge, Heller & Mount (2002) conducted a meta-analysis of 163 separate studies and found that extraverts, those who love to plan and those who strive for harmony are more likely to be happy at work than others. The links between extraversion and the love of harmony and satisfaction are accounted for by the sociable nature of most work contexts: if you enjoy developing harmonious relationships with people then the office is quite likely to be a satisfying place for you to be. Those who love to plan are shown to have higher levels of *work engagement*. They are the ones likely to be composing tomorrow's to-do list on the bus on the way home from work and waking up in the middle of the night with the solution to a thorny work problem, and it is this focus on work that seems to make the planners satisfied in their jobs.

This shows, then, that there are some lucky people who are predisposed to being happy at work. More relevant to career coaching, however, and more useful to our clients, is the notion of the match between a personality and the environment in which they find themselves. Here, the evidence isn't entirely unequivocal.

There are clear links between person–environment fit and well-being (Assouline & Meir, 1987), indicating that being well-suited to your role does lead to feeling happier at work. The notion of *person–environment fit* used in this study includes personality alongside a number of other characteristics, but the numbers don't reveal how important *personality* is on its own. Other studies have shown that workers whose personality was more congruent with the dominant personality in the organisation had higher levels of self-esteem and showed less inclination to look for a new job (Marcic, Aiuppa & Watson, 1989), and that a personality congruence with one's line manager leads to higher levels of job satisfaction (Zaman Bin Ahmad, 2008). But other studies have found no significant correlations between personality congruence and job satisfaction (Rahim, 1981; Tokar & Subich, 1997).

The evidence is therefore a bit unclear. Personality definitely has an impact on job satisfaction, but the match between personality and job satisfaction is less assured, although there is some evidence to suggest that a mismatch between the individual's personality and the organisation's prevailing culture or the demands of the role causes dissatisfaction.

## Career construction interview

### Introduction

Mark Savickas and colleagues pioneered a new approach to career counselling in 2009 that they called 'life design' (Savickas et al., 2009). They describe this as a new paradigm in career theory. The dominant thinking amongst career theorists up to this point was that career decisions were made once and that, barring a set of unusual circumstances, people stuck with their choice until retirement. Savickas et al. suggest that this approach to career choice is no longer appropriate in a workplace that is characterised by rapid change, and that a new way of working with clients is required. In the name *life design* are two key messages. The first is that making a distinction between *career* and *life* is neither useful nor realistic. In practice, career choices are enormously influenced by other aspects of our lives: family, geography, hobbies and health all can play a significant part in career choices. Equally, other aspects of our lives are influenced by our career choices, as we cope with work stress, live within our means and accommodate out-of-hours work or take advantage of travel opportunities. The second implication in life design is that we should all be taking some ownership of our own career development and pro-actively designing our career paths ourselves, rather than waiting for our organisations or society more broadly to dictate our career plans.

Alongside this idea of careers as an integral and important part of our lives, Savickas stresses the importance of meaning making: the idea that individuals need to develop an in-depth understanding of their own experiences, because only then can they start to identify the meaning and purpose of their lives overall. Constructing narratives, or telling stories, is a great way to make sense of experiences and the approach introduced here, the career construction interview, offers an interesting framework to help you enable your clients to tell their stories and work out how they make sense of their lives.

The career construction interview is a series of questions that a career coach can ask a client to help them make sense of their story so far. The questions on their own do not immediately seem particularly careers-orientated, but it is in your discussions with clients that you can help them to identify the links and use their answers to better understand what has been going on within their career history, and even link this to their career futures.

The questions can help individuals to see things in a new light and to make connections between different elements, and it can be particularly useful for clients who are struggling to make sense of their own histories or whose understanding of their own stories seems narrow.

### How to use

The career construction interview consists of five questions. Savickas suggests going through each of the questions one by one, but each question can take some time to explore in depth and you may find that one or two are sometimes all that is needed to stimulate a new direction of thinking.

*Step 1: the questions*

1   Who did you admire when you were growing up?

This question is all about role models and should lead to a discussion about values. You should try and elicit three role models ideally from your client's childhood. It is common for people to first think about their parents in response to this question; parent/child relationships are so complicated and so real that they are not as useful for this exercise as role models who were a little more removed from their everyday lives, so do encourage your clients to think more broadly. Having identified the three individuals, you should explore each one with your client to find out a bit more about who these people were and what it was that your client admired in them. You could ask what they have in common, and in what ways they see themselves as similar or different from their role models, and how this makes them feel. You could ask them if those are still people or qualities that they admire and, if not, what has changed.

This could then lead to a discussion about their values and the qualities they admired in their role models. Once these have been identified, you could invite your client to reflect on how these values have manifested themselves in their career paths so far.

2   Do you subscribe to or regularly read any magazines?

This question allows your client to talk about their interests. Interests are a core part of numerous career theories and many interest inventories exist online to help individuals work out what is important to them. Rather than asking clients what kinds of things would interest them, this question identifies the things that actually do interest them by asking them about the choices they make in their leisure time. It is useful to get three examples and you could ask about television programmes or websites if that is easier for your client. It is the analysis that is valuable rather than the choices themselves. You should ask your client what it is they like about their choices, what it says about them, and what links they can see between their answers and their careers.

3   Currently, what is your favourite story from a book or a movie?

Stories from books and films can sometimes reveal ideas for plans or strategies that an individual might be able to use to help them move to the next stage in their career. Encourage your client to tell you the story in four or five sentences. You could ask about the key characters and their motivation, and ask how they are feeling and why they have made those particular choices. And then, again, ask whether they can see any links between the elements you have identified in your discussion and their current situation. How would it be for them if they were to adopt the same kinds of strategies as the characters in the story?

4   What is your favourite saying?

A favourite saying (or motto, or bumper sticker, or the message you would have printed on a t-shirt) tends to sum up your own approach to life. Savickas describes it as 'the best advice the client has for himself or herself' (2015, p. 34) and it can be a powerful way to allow your client to see whether or not their behaviour or story so far lives up to their hopes for themselves.

5   What are your earliest recollections?

Try to elicit three different stories from your client here and make sure that your client is recalling specific incidents rather than general memories. Memories of early childhood can provide insights to the current self as they can expose some core aspects of a person's identity. Ask your client to retell the story, focusing on how they felt about the incident then and how they feel about it now as they recall it. Ask about the ways their four-year-old self was the same or different from their current self and, again, ask them to find some links between their stories and the situation they find themselves in now.

### Step 2: the debrief

Asking the questions should be fairly straightforward and, during this first part of the conversation, you will be drawing on your coaching skills as you listen to your client's story, using open questions to encourage your client to tell their tale and using summaries and paraphrasing to help to clarify their meaning. The more complicated skill is needed in the debrief, when you help your client to draw out the themes from their answers and make links between these themes and their current career concerns. This aspect of the interview needs to be practised but the best advice is for you to not put yourself under pressure to find the 'right' answer for your clients. Your role is to ask the questions that lead your client to the insights and to make sure that they have the time to explore their ideas.

The first step is to encourage your client to talk about their answers in a bit more depth. The prompts you use to get them exploring their own answer will obviously depend on the particular question you asked them and the nature of the answer they give. You should aim to support them to paint a vivid picture, and to talk not only about what they mean but also how they feel about it, generating some analysis alongside their descriptions.

The next step is to ask your client to try to identify any links between their response and their current work situation: 'how do you think this answer relates to your current work situation?' It is important that you hold back at the start and allow them the space to think. If nothing comes to their mind, this could be a good time for a silence and then, if there is still nothing forthcoming, you could ask the question again, using different words: 'what connections are you making?' You could ask more specifically about whether one particular element might be linked for them or you could highlight any connections you yourself have identified, making sure that you put these forward tentatively, owning them yourself: 'one thing that struck me when you were talking was how important control seems for you. Do you think there might be anything useful to unpick in that?'

Once a link has been established, you should allow time to explore it and consider whether it adds anything new to their understanding of the past or the future.

## *In practice*

This technique needs to be carefully set up. As mentioned above, the questions, on the surface, do not appear to be very related to careers so a preamble can be useful to set the scene. Your belief in the technique is probably the most convincing signal of credibility, but some well-chosen words can help to make the technique effective.

This is a great technique for working collaboratively with your client. The value in the task is in the links that are identified between their answers and their current career dilemmas, but these associations may not be easy to spot and may need to be teased out and identified by means of trial and error. Your role is to gently push your client's thinking, using open questions and silences, but I find that a collaborative approach – almost treating it as an experiment – can make this process more smooth.

These are the kinds of words I would use:

> There is a technique that I think might be interesting to try with you today. The idea behind it is that trying to find some common ground between your current situation and other aspects of your life and your history can help you

to understand things better. The technique involves asking some questions about things in your life that have meant something to you, and then trying to see if we can see some links to what's going on now. The questions can seem a bit left-field when we start, but sometimes it can lead to some really interesting discussions. What do you think? Are you interested in having a go?

This can be quite a powerful tool. The questions are personal and are intended to unearth some quite fundamental issues. The unconscious nature of the links that can be uncovered can mean that the ideas that emerge can come as a surprise to your client. It is useful to make your client aware that the outcomes can be a little unpredictable and, for you, it is good to be prepared, whichever direction your client takes the conversation.

This tool is quite versatile. It was originally designed for use in one-to-one contexts and that is still probably the best way to get the most out of it. As described in the box below, however, there is some good evidence that it works within group contexts too, although it may be that in group contexts it works better with adult clients who have developed a degree of self-awareness and who are motivated to push themselves to identify the links during the debrief section. One option, if you are working with small groups, is that the debrief is done collaboratively with the whole group facilitated by the career coach: one person at a time tells their story and the whole group provides some support as the individual identifies their own themes and relates them back to their current career dilemma. The atmosphere and relationships within the group need to be conducive to this kind of approach and there needs to be enough time to make sure that each story is properly explored, but the views and support of the group can make this quite an effective and potent use of the technique.

| | |
|---|---|
| One to one | ✓ |
| Group sessions | ✓ |
| Within the session | ✓ |
| As a self-directed intersessional task | ✓ |
| Initial career choice | ✓ |
| Career change | ✓ |
| Indicative timing | 15 minutes per question |

## Why it works

One of the psychological processes that underpins this is the concept of attentional bias (Fiske, 1980). This is the phenomenon that makes us pay attention to some things more than others, by determining what information we notice, how we interpret it and what we remember (Bar-Haim, 2010).

*(continued)*

*(continued)*

In particular, we become particularly aware of things that are on our minds: when you buy a new car, you are far more likely to spot cars of the same make, type and colour than you ever noticed before; when we are preoccupied with our careers, we notice similar dilemmas in the books we read and the films we watch.

In the career construction interview, the questions provide a framework within which an individual can spot links between their current career dilemma and other things that mean something to them. These links between the current situation and other things that matter emerge as life themes.

It is probably worth noting that Savickas's ideas have not gone uncontested. Whilst it is hard to argue that the current workplace is not characterised by rapid change, some of the writing about the new era of career has failed to produce much empirical support. The much-vaunted notion that a job for life is a thing of the past, for example, seems to be somewhat overstated in the literature: jobs for life were not always the norm and they do still dominate in many industries (Rodrigues & Guest, 2010). The idea of 'agency' too has ruffled a few feathers. One of the most dearly held principles in our profession is the notion of social justice (Hooley & Sultana, 2016), and there is something in the idea of encouraging people to take ownership of their own careers that assumes either that we can't change the social structures or that we do not want to.

## What's the evidence base?

This approach was introduced by a number of high-profile academic researchers and, as such, you might reasonably assume that there would be a considerable amount of empirical evidence to back it up. It certainly appears in the career literature frequently and has garnered widespread credibility.

A fair few papers have been published that provide some empirical support for the approach, and these offer some convincing evidence that the approach can work and can lead to transformational insights in clients (for example, Cardoso et al., 2016; Pouyaud et al., 2016; Taylor & Savickas, 2016). The limitation of these studies is that they are very small scale – often just single case study examples. This approach to research is completely in line with the philosophical position of life design, which holds that people's individual experience of life is so personal that the kind of sweeping generalisations that large-scale quantitative research claims to make are meaningless. Whilst I admire the consistency and authenticity displayed, and can appreciate the richness and depth in these papers, I am still itching to find some research with a larger sample size that could convince me that this approach would be likely to work with a wider range of clients.

In a rare quantitative study, Di Fabio and Maree (2012) used the approach in a group coaching context, working with a group of 38 clients, and found that it increased their confidence in their ability to make career decisions and decreased their career decision-making difficulties.

Exploring the use of the career construction interview from the perspective of career practitioners, Hazel Reid and Linden West (2011) conducted a research project with eight career practitioners working with young people in the UK. They asked the practitioners to use the career construction interview with clients and then recorded and analysed their views of the process. The results indicated that the practitioners genuinely saw considerable value in the approach and the young people found the process enjoyable and insightful, but there were concerns that the time the process took was prohibitive within the constraints of the public-sector context in which they were working.

## Career genogram

### *Introduction*

Traditional career development theories, in the West at any rate, advocate that career decisions are best made by the individual. There is some wisdom in this. There is evidence, for example, that young people who aren't sure which options to pick at school end up opting for those that their friends have chosen, and this may not be the best basis for a major life choice. There is, however, more and more evidence emerging of the widespread and mostly positive role that other people play in our career choices. All sorts of different people in our lives seem to have an impact on our career decisions: teachers, friends, colleagues, characters from books and films, role models. But the group that influences us the most is our family. Studies have looked at the important role that parents, siblings and even deceased relatives can have on our understanding of the world of work and our career choices. It is our family who shape our values, introduce us to a range of occupations, develop our understanding of what it means to work and what we should give to and get from our careers, and it is family who show us what kind of jobs are thought to be realistic for 'people like us', in terms of our gender and class.

The influence of family is broad, pervasive, often (but not always) helpful and frequently happens below our conscious awareness, leaving us with a conviction or a feeling that we can't quite identify or trace back to its source. This could indicate that these family influences could have a valuable part to play in career conversations, as career coaches can help clients to work out what their influences are and decide how they want to respond to them. The 'genogram' is one tool that can help clients to identify some of the family influences on their opinions, assumptions and choices about careers.

### How to use

A career genogram is, in essence, a family tree of careers in which the different occupations of those closest to you are mapped out. It is drawn out just like a standard family tree but, alongside the names of the various relatives, details about their jobs, careers or education are added.

Typically, the family tree used will cover three generations but you can encourage your client to set the parameters and decide how far and wide to go – depending on who they think may have been influential. Alongside blood-relatives, it is common to include those within the family who are related by marriage but other key figures who have been influential could be included. Your client too can make the decision about how much detail to include: job title is the usual place to start, but it could also be interesting to explore industries or educational levels, and discussions afterwards could also focus on aspects such as levels of job satisfaction or attitudes towards work.

### Step 1: drawing

It can be useful to give your clients an example of the kind of thing you are envisaging. You could just sketch one out there and then in front of them or have a couple of pre-prepared examples to hand. The case study below offers an example of how a career genogram might look. Ask your client to draw their own version and make it clear that they can choose who to include and what information to highlight.

### Step 2: reflection

Once your client has completed the family tree, the next task is to try to encourage them to identify patterns. It is usually best to get your client to come up with their own themes as they will inevitably have a much clearer idea of the kind of thing that might be relevant and meaningful to them. Your client might want to have a few moments in silence to reflect on their diagram or might prefer to talk their thoughts through out loud. Do make sure that you leave enough time here for your client to really reflect properly. If it helps, you could be explicit about what you are doing, saying something like 'it can sometimes take a little while for the patterns to become clear, so do take a few moments just to look at it and see what emerges', and this can give your client the licence to take their time. When you feel that your client is ready, you could check this with them and then ask them to talk to you about some of their thoughts.

## Step 3: discussion

At this point your job as the career coach is to see if you can push their thinking by encouraging them to explore their thoughts in more depth. The discussions can go in all sorts of directions, exploring values, attitudes to work, levels of job satisfaction, what 'career success' looks like in their family and issues about gender.

Here is the list of questions used by Malott and Magnuson (2004) in their intervention study with undergraduates. These are, of course, just suggestions. They seem to have worked for Malott and Magnuson's clients but, as with all of the techniques in this book, you should practise, play around and work out which ones work best for you and for your clients.

### SUGGESTED QUESTIONS FOR REFLECTION AND DISCUSSION

1. What in your family was seen as women's work/men's work?
2. What jobs were admired/scorned by members of your family?
3. What are your family members' attitudes about fun or leisure activities?
4. What are your family members' attitudes about money/spending/saving?
5. How do members of your family define success/failure?
6. Who in your family do you think is or was successful?
   What makes them successful?
7. To whom in your family are you most similar?
   How are you similar to that person or those persons?
8. Who in your family would you like to be like?
   What do you admire about that person?
9. What do you perceive as your biggest block or barrier to achieving qualities of your role model?
10. What do you perceive as your biggest block to making a career choice?
11. In what ways are you similar to your family?
    In what ways are you different from your family?
    In what ways do you want to be similar to other members of your family?
    How would you like to be different?
12. In examining the diagram of your family, what repeated patterns have you seen?
    What seems most significant?
    How has this recognition affected you?

## In practice

The studies described in the evidence box indicate that the career genogram is a versatile tool and seems to add value to a range of types of clients and in a range of contexts. The approach described above assumes a one-to-one context but, if you are working in groups, this can be effective too. The recommendation for group settings is to take it slowly, using two or three sessions to get as much as possible from the exercise, doing one of the steps above each week. Some research suggests that combining groups with one to ones can be a good approach, with steps one and two taking place in a group context and step three reserved for one to ones.

## Case study

Sam had been working in HR since she graduated. It was a profession that suited her quite well and she had been fairly successful, rising to a senior level in a large management consultancy firm. She also felt that the sorts of roles she had been given had allowed her to use some of her best skills.

But now Sam was facing redundancy and, whilst the firm had offered to give her a new role, she wasn't sure that this was what she wanted. Sam came to see a career coach to explore alternative ideas. She had already considered four or five options, wondering about setting herself up as a freelance consultant, perhaps finding another job in a more niche consultancy firm, or maybe even taking some time off to support her children with their upcoming exams. But, as the career coach commented, none of these options seemed to make Sam's face light up.

Sam had alluded to the careers of a couple of family members during the conversation and the coach suggested that a career genogram might be interesting to try.

As Sam reflected on her family's career paths and the influence this may have had on her choices, she noted that there were two typical paths: stay-at-home mum and high-level commerce. It seemed that the messages Sam had

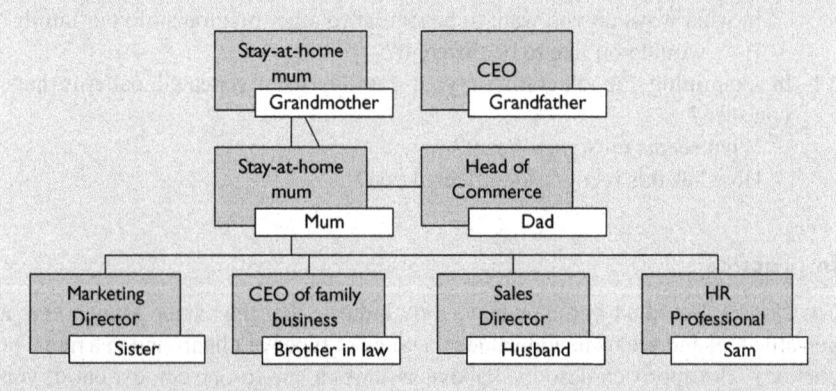

*Figure 3.1* Sam's career genogram

received were that women either had no career outside the home or had a successful career in business. Sam herself had opted for the commercial route but, on reflection, wondered if there might be a middle course, which might suit her better. The coach encouraged her to reflect on her work day-dreams and she talked about a local charity she had come across recently that offered support to refugee children in the UK. As she started to describe this to her coach, Sam herself noticed that she was becoming animated and passionate in a way that she rarely did when discussing the HR issues in her consultancy firm. Although she still couldn't quite identify the specific role that she might play in this kind of organisation, the career genogram had enabled her to broaden her options and consider a whole new sector, which she felt resonated with her values and interests.

| | |
|---|---|
| One to one | ✓ |
| Group sessions | ✓ |
| Within the session | ✓ |
| As a self-directed intersessional task | ✓ |
| Initial career choice | ✓ |
| Career changes | ✓ |
| Indicative timing | 20 minutes |

## Why it works

It will not surprise you to hear that there is quite a lot of convincing evidence that family members have a significant influence on people's choices. The influence is exerted in different ways. First, families provide a significant amount of occupational information, both in terms of the jobs that family members have chosen and the information about other careers that they have amassed and share (Whiston & Keller, 2004). Then families make a contribution to the decision-making process by suggesting suitable career options and through re-direction, as people are put off a career idea because of influence of one sort or another from family. Parents' unfulfilled dreams can have an impact on their children's career choices (Jacobsen, 2000), and family members will get involved in career decisions even when they are not asked or asked not to (Chope, 2002).

On top of information and ideas, family members often can offer tangible support – social, financial, practical or through access to networks

*(continued)*

*(continued)*

(Schultheiss et al., 2001). This support can be of great value but can seem to come at a price – implicit or explicit.

Clients can place a heavy reliance on advice from the family for two reasons (Chope, 2002). First, through their own lack of confidence. Career decisions can feel daunting and making sense of the world of work can be overwhelming. Falling back on the advice of those whom you trust and who love you can feel like a good solution. The second reason is the idea that the career choices of an individual may well have a direct impact on their nearest and dearest; choices can have an impact on the amount of money coming into the family, the time available to spend with the family and the degree of reflected glory.

## What's the evidence base?

The family genogram has been fairly widely tried and tested in the career literature, with a range of qualitative studies suggesting it is an effective strategy for career coaching. Clients find that the discussions around the genogram are insightful, allowing them to understand themselves better, and giving them the chance to think about where their ideas about and attitudes to work come from. Evidence has been gleaned from a range of types of clients. The technique has been shown to benefit children at primary school (Gibson, 2005), undergraduates (Malott & Magnuson, 2004) and adults. Studies have been conducted both in group contexts and within one-to-one career coaching, suggesting that this is a usefully versatile tool for career practice. The evidence is primarily qualitative, with researchers interviewing clients after they have completed the genogram exercise and asking them how they found it and what they felt they learned. This constitutes valuable and rich data but is, inevitably, subjective and we cannot be sure that it is generalisable. As I will keep reiterating throughout the book, there is a dearth of large-scale randomised control trials, which is what we need to state with greater certainty that this is a technique that works and that works better than others.

Chapter 4

# What do I want from a job?

Before someone can make a decision about the kind of job they might want to pursue, it can be useful for them to gain some clarity about the aspects of work that they consider desirable and attractive in a job. Generating a list such as this can be a useful process in itself as it is likely to enhance and refine an individual's self-awareness – helpful for career decision making and for the application process. Once complete, the list can act both as a starting point for discussions that might generate job ideas and as a checklist for opportunities that are under consideration.

The three tools presented in this chapter each enable your client to think about the topic from different angles. The first one focuses on job satisfaction and uses past experience to help individuals to sculpt their ideal role. The second, drawing, makes use of a technique from art therapy that uses people's emotional response to both their past experiences and their future aspirations to clarify their thinking. The third tool, the personal constructs model, can allow a client to produce an insightful overall picture of the aspects of a job that are most important to them.

## Your personal job satisfaction model

Job satisfaction is something of a holy grail for career coaches; it lies at the heart of our practice and is something we very much want to help our clients to find. But identifying or predicting the exact role that will make a particular client happy in the workplace is quite a task. Job satisfaction is a measure of subjective well-being at work and research has uncovered the kinds of factors that lead to job satisfaction for the population in general. This is a good place to start but, on its own, this kind of evidence is not enough – each of us have such different requirements that generalisations are only useful to a point. This technique uses the empirical evidence as a starting point but encourages individuals to identify what is going to work for them.

The academic literature highlights seven key areas that tend to lead to higher levels of job satisfaction (Roelen, Koopmans, & Groothoff, 2008):

1   **Task variety.** This one comes up at the top of almost every piece of research into the topic. Having a job that you consider to be varied has been shown

time and again to lead to satisfaction, but quite what constitutes 'variety' can be subjective. One call-centre operator might see their job as interminably repetitive, answering calls about heating problems all day, every day. Another might see it as incredibly varied as they never know who is going to be on the other end of the line and what their story is going to be.

2 **Colleagues**. Perhaps not surprisingly, the people you work with have a huge impact on your daily experience. Organisational research has shown that having a like-minded team with shared goals and commitment, and having a boss who is engaged and appreciative, makes a big difference. More important than that though is having someone you would describe as 'a best friend' at work (Rath & Harter, 2010).

3 **Working conditions**. This covers two groups of factors. First the term refers to the physical conditions: a pleasant office, a reasonable commute to work, a nice canteen for lunch. Alongside this the term also covers something about the ethos of the organisation. You are likely to be happier at work if you are involved in an organisation that promotes positive qualities such as creativity and collaboration.

4 **Work load**. Job satisfaction is hard to get if your work load isn't right. For optimum work well-being you need to have enough but not too much work.

5 **Autonomy**. It is important to feel that you have some control over your job. This autonomy could cover a wide range of factors. It could be to do with flexible working and being able to manage your work around your other commitments; it could be about which projects you take on, which colleagues you work with and when your deadlines are.

6 **Educational and development opportunities**. It is important for individuals to feel that they are growing and developing. It is such a widespread desire that many scholars see this need for personal growth as a universal trait and a part of the human condition (Deci & Ryan, 1992; Maslow 1943; Rogers, 1962). For a job to be truly satisfying an individual needs to feel that they are making some progress, learning new skills and becoming competent. This could be achieved through external training courses or educational qualifications, but can as easily be achieved within the daily job if the conditions are right.

7 **Congruence**. The literature talks about a concept called 'person–environment fit', which is the degree to which there is a good match between the individual and the environment in which they are working. The academics have not quite come to an agreement as to which particular elements need to fit to achieve person–environment harmony, but three have emerged fairly conclusively as quite important. First, strengths. Strengths will be defined in more detail in the next chapter but, broadly, your strengths are things you do well. The evidence is clear that if you are able to use some of your key strengths at work you are likely to be happier (Litman-Ovadia and Davidovitch, 2010). Second, values. If you feel that the things that matter to the organisation are also things that matter to you, this is likely to increase your satisfaction levels. Finally, identity. If you feel that you can be yourself in the workplace, you are more likely to be happy there.

## What do I want from a job? 35

### How to use

It can be easy to conflate the factors that make a job impressive with those that make a job satisfying, but the point of this exercise is to make a distinction between 'what I imagine will make me feel good' and 'what has actually made me feel good in the past'. People's lists of 'what I want from a job' are often weighted towards the aspects that make them feel good *about* the job, at the expense of those that make them feel good *in* the job. This tool can be particularly valuable when working with clients who are looking for a job that will make them fulfilled but who seem focused on the extrinsic factors such as pay and location.

### Step 1: what has led to job satisfaction in the past?

Ask your client to identify the best and worst jobs they have ever had. 'Best' and 'worst' should be defined in terms of their levels of job satisfaction rather than their levels of success. Starting with the one that they enjoyed most, ask your client to tell you what made it such a great job. The discussion should centre on their personal experience – you are not after a list of what made it a good job objectively but an exploration of why they felt good on a daily basis and what made them positive about going into work on a Monday morning.

This should generate a list of perhaps half a dozen qualities. You could have a discussion at this stage about whether these qualities constitute a good model for their personal job satisfaction. It is important to stress here that you're not trying to devise a list of the qualities they are looking for in a job; it is strictly focused on their experience of psychological well-being in the workplace.

### Step 2: the empirical evidence

The next stage is to present your client with the seven-factor job satisfaction model, based on the empirical research outlined above. Have a look together to see which of the factors on the research-driven list have been covered already in your conversation, and whether your client's understanding of each aspect is in line with that described in the model. Then focus on those that have not been identified so far and explore the reasons for their non-appearance: it could be that these factors are not important to your client or just that they weren't particularly notable in the experiences discussed. This could lead to an exploration about whether these factors may or may not be significant to them in future roles.

### Step 3: a personal list of job satisfiers

When you have explored this in sufficient depth you should bring the two elements of the discussion together, asking your client to articulate their own list of factors that are likely to make them happy or fulfilled in their future roles. Invite them to list the key factors that they believe will have the most impact on their future work well-being, making sure that they have articulated exactly what they mean by each term.

This list then could feed into a broader discussion about what your client is looking for in a job, or could be used as a checklist to help them analyse the relative merits of the occupational or job ideas they have.

## *In practice*

The key to this tool is making sure that you establish clearly that this is all about happiness at work and not about how 'good' a job is. If your client is focused on the external trappings of a particular role, it may be worth spending some time making sure they are clear about the difference and stressing that you are not suggesting that they disregard the other factors, just that they should put them to one side for this particular exercise.

I like to be quite explicit with clients about the research that underpins the technique. As long as you make it clear that you are not implying that their experience is bound to mirror that described in the research, I think that sharing the evidence on which it is based can add to your credibility and can encourage the client to believe that the technique may have something valuable to add.

| | |
|---|---|
| One to one | ✓ |
| Group sessions | ✓ |
| Within the session | ✓ |
| As a self-directed intersessional task | ✓ |
| Initial career choice | ✗ |
| Career changes | ✓ |
| Indicative timing | 20 minutes |

## How it works

There has been a lot written about the notion of 'career success' and this is a concept that can be useful to discuss with your client as a precursor to this exercise. Career success in the academic literature is generally divided into objective and subjective career success. The former, objective career success, is defined in terms of the facts about someone's career that can be spotted and assessed from the outside, and which can be easily compared with other people's careers. It is usually described in terms of level of pay, seniority and the prestige of the occupation chosen. Determinants of objective success are levels of intelligence, education, training and the hours that you work (Ng et al., 2005). Objective success is generally described as being the result of either *contest mobility*, in which you simply need to out-perform your competitors, or *sponsorship mobility*, where you are given a helping hand by someone further up the ladder. Sponsorship mobility accounts for the success of those in graduate training schemes, those privileged through their social networks, and those who have a lucky encounter with a senior colleague or mentor who can put opportunities in their way.

Subjective career success is defined by the individual themselves and is made up of their perceptions of their objective success (for example, where objective success would be measured by how much someone earns, subjective success would be a measure of how well the individual believes that they are paid) and their levels of job satisfaction. A meta-analysis examining the factors that lead to subjective perceptions of success found a whole range of influential factors, including dispositional traits (in particular self-esteem), motivation, support from their supervisor and from the organisation. But, by a mile, the key factor was shown to be expectations (Ng & Feldman, 2014). Regardless of how prestigious, senior and well-remunerated an individual is, if their position surpasses their expectations they will feel that they are successful and, if they feel that they have fallen short of their expected career success, they will feel like a failure.

## What's the evidence base?

Job satisfaction is one area of the careers field that has been really well researched, but it is interesting to note that the research all gives slightly different messages depending on the agenda of the researchers. Organisational psychologists are particularly interested in the work factors that predict job satisfaction as these are the things that organisations may be able to control. Much of the evidence described above comes from this kind of research (for example, Roelen, Koopmans, & Groothoff, 2008). Other groups within psychology are more interested in the kinds of personality traits that tend to be associated with job satisfaction – there is some evidence that certain types of people are more likely to be happy at work. I haven't mentioned these aspects above as I do not feel that they are as relevant to our work, but do have a look at Judge, Heller, & Mount (2002) if you are interested in finding out more.

Research has given us some interesting insights into the role that money plays in our sense of well-being at work and concludes that it has a minimal link with job satisfaction (Judge et al., 2010). Money, it seems, is mostly a measure of how valued you feel both within the workplace and within society broadly, so, if you are paid less than a colleague doing a similar job, this will really hurt; not because the lower salary in itself is making your work any less fulfilling but because it is a clear and tangible sign that your bosses do not value you.

## Drawing

### Introduction

Creating images is something that humans have evolved to love. It is an innate human tendency and since the earliest signs of human life we have been drawing. Art therapy is a form of psychotherapy that capitalises on this ability and uses art as a tool for helping clients to express themselves. Through this expression, the approach aims to help people to understand and reconcile their feelings of confusion or distress. The technique described here draws from this tradition and invites clients to create a visual representation of some aspect of their career-related emotions or thoughts. The process can help them to make sense of their past and present, and to envisage their future.

These kinds of visual tools are particularly effective when clients are struggling to put their feelings into words. It may be that their feelings aren't entirely clear to them, or perhaps they can't readily identify and communicate labels that describe their emotions. This can happen when the feelings are buried deep, when their thoughts and emotions are complex or when the words do not come easily, perhaps working with a client whose first language isn't English or who may be a little diffident when it comes to sharing their emotions.

There are three stages, each of which brings distinct benefits to the client.

### Step 1: creation

In the first stage the client creates their picture. In the art therapy literature this part is known as 'art as therapy', highlighting the intrinsic therapeutic properties of producing a piece of art. For many clients the actual process of creating an image is pleasurable and can lead to a state of *flow*. Flow is the feeling you get when you are so absorbed in a task that you do not notice the time passing and aren't aware of anything around you. The time it takes to produce a drawing will vary widely from one client to another. If left to their own devices, clients can take anything from half a minute to an hour to finish their picture. You might want to have a think beforehand about the timing and how to negotiate this with your client. One option is to ask clients to create their image at home, but this might add some pressure on clients to produce a beautifully crafted work of art so, if you decide to suggest something more self-directed, you could ask them to produce a collage or something else that relies less on their raw talent. One other approach is to ask the clients to start their image within the session, spend some time together discussing what they have done and then suggest that they might want to finish it, or do another, at home. Alternatively, you could just explain that you only have five or ten minutes for the task and suggest that they produce something very simple in this time.

### Step 2: reflection

In the second stage, the client gets the chance to reflect on their work. This will often happen in silence, although clients do sometimes find it helpful to do their thinking out loud. The client may be surprised by what they have drawn and how it makes them feel, and they may need some time to process this and make sense of it.

## Step 3: discussion

In stage three, the coach, for the first time, gets actively involved and intervenes to push the client's thinking a little further. You might open this stage of the conversation by asking your client to talk to you about their picture. It is important to be clear here that your role is not to interpret the drawing; your job is to help your client interpret their own image. You can help them do this by making some gentle observations, along the lines of 'there is a lot going on in this picture' or 'I notice that the top half is really empty compared with the bottom half'. If you have some slightly more personal reactions to the images that you think might be useful prompts to get your client to explore their own thoughts you could voice these tentatively, owning the views, and explicitly asking your client for their opinion: 'I am struck by the vibrant colours in your image – is that significant to you, do you think?'. Open questions too can stimulate your client to think a little deeper, 'tell me a bit about this part of the picture', 'what does this represent to you?', and you could ask your client to talk about their picture in emotional terms, 'what emotions would you say you have highlighted in this image?'.

Once you feel that the conversation has gone as far as it can, it is time to link it back to their current career dilemma or the overall goal of your session together. Again, you can ask your client to make the links, encouraging them to consider what light the discussion has shed on their current situation and identifying any action points that they might now think are suitable.

## In practice

Some of us love to draw and feel fairly secure that the product of our endeavours will at least vaguely resemble the picture in our minds. For others, drawing can strike fear into the heart. Memories of the public humiliation of art classes at school can be vivid and the idea of having to expose a sheer lack of talent to a relative stranger can engender a considerable amount of disquiet. This, however, does not mean that you shouldn't use these techniques with this kind of client. In fact, a bit of discomfort has been shown to play a useful part in stimulating new thought, but it is useful to be aware that drawing, or painting, or creating in this way might be far outside some clients' comfort zone. It is, therefore, important to think about how to set up the exercise to ensure maximum impact and minimum distress.

First, it is important to consider the specific words you use. You could use a few different phrases that mean the same thing, just at different levels of formality. You might start with 'draw a picture', using a very clear and accessible phrase to ensure that your client is in no doubt about your meaning. But then follow up with something a bit less prescriptive such as 'sketch something out' and finish with 'or just make a few marks on the page' to highlight that you are really not expecting anything polished or even recognisable. You could then spend a few minutes explaining why it works as a technique and what to expect within the coaching session. It might go something like this:

> Sometimes if you find it difficult to find the words to explain something it can be because the emotion is stored in your brain in the form of an image. People sometimes surprise themselves by finding it easier to draw how they feel than to put it into words. I am not going to be interpreting the drawing in any way – we'll just have a look at it together and you can tell me about it. It is your image and only you can know what it means, but I do find that it often sparks off some quite interesting thoughts and conversations. What do you think? Shall we give it a go?

If a client is still resistant you might see whether another kind of visual technique might be better – perhaps they could describe the picture in their mind's eye or think about it in terms of a metaphor. Or you could suggest that the drawing could be something they might like to try on their own at home.

I mentioned above that drawing can be useful any time a client struggles to put their feelings into words. It can be particularly useful to help clients raise awareness of what is going on for them in the present moment, but you could also ask clients to use visual images to help them consider what kind of a future they might want – this works particularly well when you can get clients to compare two images, their current state and a future state. And, rather than asking them to generate a whole new drawing, you might just want to ask them to make changes to their first image. You could also get people to draw their conceptualisations of different jobs if they are struggling to make a choice between two options, or invite them to draw a picture of their vision of themselves at work in the different roles they are considering.

One final thing to consider when working with art tools is ethical practice and your own boundaries. These tools can be surprisingly powerful and it is important that we keep in mind that we are not trained as art therapists or counsellors. It can sometimes be valuable to alert your client at the outset to the possibility that the technique may reach surprising depths and then the two of you can monitor the emotions of the client and decide to change tack if needed.

One final point is to highlight that this technique could be one that could be used with clients who have particular difficulty in expressing themselves verbally, such as those with learning disabilities.

| | |
|---|---|
| One to one | ✓ |
| Group sessions | ✓ |
| Within the session | ✓ |
| As a self-directed intersessional task | ✓ |
| Initial career choice | ✓ |
| Career changes | ✓ |
| Indicative timing | 15–30 minutes |

## How it works

The magic of a technique such as this lies in its ability to connect unconscious thoughts directly with the page. Most of the information we store is not within our conscious awareness at any given moment. Some information that we have stored in our minds can be accessed simply by focusing our attention on it, but other information is more difficult to unearth. It is thought that information in or very close to our conscious awareness is stored in the form of words, so is usually easy to articulate verbally. Information stored a little deeper is represented in the form of images. It is this, in part, that makes it more difficult to discuss, as the images first need to be translated into words. For some issues with some clients, this extra layer of cognitive processing is prohibitively demanding and they find that it can't be done. But, because the ideas are stored as images, drawing is a way that people can use to externalise this kind of information, getting it out of their heads and down on paper, without having to go through the step of translating the ideas into words.

Once the image in their mind has been represented in some way on the page, the artist has the chance to look at their ideas out in the open and can start to make some sense of them.

## What's the evidence?

Drawing and other forms of visual creation have been shown to have quite a wide ranging impact on clients. The evidence breaks down into two spheres. First, art tools have been shown to increase self-awareness. It is this that has led to their inclusion in this chapter as these tools can be used to help clients to crystalise their thinking and clarify their own aspirations, and they have been shown to enhance people's ability to self-express (Slayton, D'Archer, & Kaplan, 2010).

The second tranche of evidence suggests that art tools can increase psychological well-being. Although not at the heart of this chapter, tools that can boost self-esteem can be of great value in career coaching. There are clear links between positive well-being, career decision making and successful job hunting (Lent, Brown, & Hackett, 1994). Art tools have been shown to increase positive mood, a sense of confidence and self-efficacy, they can promote self-awareness and self-acceptance, lessened anxiety and increase general psychological well-being (Coiner & Kim, 2011).

## Personal work constructs

### Introduction

Career theories have long recognised that each of us has our own unique set of values, skills and attitudes. Personal work constructs takes this idea of an individualised approach to careers one stage further, acknowledging that we each interpret the world in a different way: even when two people have access to the same information about a job or an occupation they will notice and focus on different details. This approach suggests that each of us has a set of 'personal constructs' that act as a filter when we are taking in information, leading us to see some aspects of the world around us in sharp focus whilst others remain a little blurred.

This is a useful tool to aid self-awareness and is particularly valuable for helping clients to understand how they view the world of work and to identify what is important to them.

The tool is based on George Kelly's 'personal construct theory' (Kelly, 1955), and his theory fits in well with the current thinking in career development, which acknowledges that everyone's experience and interpretation of events is different. In order to identify our own list of personal constructs, Kelly suggests that we should compare different items (or different occupations) to see what differences we home in on. Kelly stresses the value of comparing things in groups of three. Whilst people might find it difficult to identify one personally meaningful difference between two occupations, as soon as a third occupation is added it becomes easier to identify one quality that two of the occupations share and one doesn't.

Kelly proposed a particular technique for identifying particular constructs that he called the 'repertory grid', which offers a framework to structure the thinking process. The tool introduced below is based on Kelly's repertory grid and aims to increase awareness. As with so many of these techniques it can be used in a number of ways, and you could play around with it a bit in order to work out what works for you and what works for your clients. The approach can be used to identify your personal constructs in any element of your life – you could use it to identify what matters to you in friendships, in holidays or in yourself. But, in a career context, it can be used to get clients to think about how they conceptualise the world of work and what matters to them in a job.

### How to use

#### Step 1: identify the occupations

In this technique clients take a number of different occupations and, by comparing their views of the roles in question, they gradually build up a list of their personal work constructs. The occupations used for the exercise are usually generated by the client, although when you are using this technique with large groups it may simplify the process if you provide the job titles yourself.

If you are working with someone who has already had some experience in the workplace you could invite them to use the job titles from their previous occupations. Alternatively, you could suggest that your client picks six occupations that they think might be quite attractive. The choice of occupations is less important than the process itself so, really, any meaningful job titles would do.

The total number of occupations you select for the exercise depends in some part on the context in which you are operating. If your client is doing this as an intersessional task you might assume that they have a good amount of time to devote to this and so a dozen or so occupations might be suitable. Within the session itself you may find that six is a more manageable number.

### Step 2: identify the personal constructs

Having identified the occupations, the next part of the process is to put them into groups of three. There are no rules about this, you just need to go through all the possible combinations of the occupations. The client then takes the first triad and is asked to identify a characteristic that two of the occupations share and one doesn't. They need to ascribe a clear label to it and write it down. For example, if the three occupations are nurse, police officer and web designer, your client might think that nurse and police officer are both *physically active* jobs. It is important to stress that there is no right or wrong answer. Each of us will have our own take on it, and it is this individuality that the exercise is trying to capture. Your client should keep going until they have run out of triads, or until the same kinds of labels or qualities seem to be coming up time and again. This will then constitute a list of your client's personal work constructs.

### Step 3: reflections

At this point you should ask your client to reflect on this list. Are these qualities all important to them? Are some more crucial than others? Are they all positive or are some important as aspects to avoid in a job? Are there any key things missing? Does this feel like an accurate reflection of the way they view the world of work or are some important qualities missing?

The conversation here will be dictated by the particular context of your client. The list can be used to help your client reflect on their previous roles and consider if the constructs can help to explain why particular jobs did or did not work out for them. It can be used as a starting point for generating job ideas. If a client has identified 'intellectually demanding' as a label, the two of you could have a discussion about the kinds of work that they might find challenging in this way. The list could also be used as a checklist for any job ideas already identified, analysing the extent to which any ideas under consideration reflect the list of qualities identified.

## In practice

### Case study

This is an example of how personal work constructs have been used in a group context. The occupations used in this example were common destinations of psychology graduates in the UK and these occupations were presented to a group of final-year psychology students. The students were given a handout to complete individually (Figure 4.1) and considered: counsellor, clinical psychologist, occupational psychologist, primary teacher, social worker and researcher.

Students were asked to think about different combinations of the jobs (six different combinations are shown here in Figure 4.1, but in practice it might be possible to show all possible combinations). The students were asked to work through the handout and, for each triad of occupations, to identify a characteristic (any kind of feature they associate with the jobs) that they associated with two of the occupations but not the other.

The completed handout (Figure 4.2) is based on the personal work constructs of one particular psychology student, Jamie. When considering the triad of counsellor, clinical psychologist and occupational psychologist, Jamie felt that two of these were jobs that had a high social status and one was not. When thinking about the triad of clinical psychologist, primary teacher and social worker, he thought that two of the jobs involved one to one work and one did not.

When the students had all managed to complete their own handouts they were asked, in small groups, to compare their responses, and they were surprised to see that people's conceptualisations of the same jobs were so different.

Each student was then asked to look at their own personal list and consider whether the list felt like a good reflection of the way that they see the world of work. They were also asked to reflect on the degree to which the constructs that they had identified were features that matter to them. For Jamie, then, his work constructs were: social status, one to one or group work, calmness, formality of dress code, political leaning and availability of jobs. Jamie found that these were a useful starting point for identifying what makes a job appealing to him. He concluded that high social status was important to him and this was linked, in his eyes, to jobs that were difficult to get (i.e., those that did not have plenty of job opportunities). He also found that he was drawn to working in an environment that was relaxed and calm, and would prefer to be surrounded by colleagues who shared his political views. On reflection, he felt that whether the occupation involved one to one work or work with groups was not important to him.

This analysis then gave Jamie a useful starting point for his research and, when exploring different job ideas, he was able to pay particular attention to these factors that he had identified as being particularly meaningful to him.

| Triads of elements (any combination, in any order) | Characteristic that two share |
|---|---|
| Counsellor, clinical psychologist, occupational psychologist | |
| Clinical psychologist, primary teacher, social worker | |
| Counsellor, social worker, researcher | |
| Occupational psychologist, primary teacher, researcher | |
| Clinical psychologist, occupational psychologist, researcher | |
| Counsellor, primary teacher, social worker | |
| Further combinations of the six occupations… | |

*Figure 4.1* Handout.

| Triads of elements (any combination, in any order) | Characteristic that two share |
|---|---|
| Counsellor, clinical psychologist, occupational psychologist | High social status |
| Clinical psychologist, primary teacher, social worker | One to one work |
| Counsellor, social worker, researcher | Calm |
| Occupational psychologist, primary teacher, researcher | Relaxed dress code |
| Clinical psychologist, occupational psychologist, researcher | Left wing |
| Counsellor, primary teacher, social worker | Plenty of job opportunities |
| Further combinations of the six occupations… | |

*Figure 4.2* Completed handout.

This technique can be quite transformative for clients who are finding it hard to make sense of their reality. The challenge is in explaining the underpinning concepts. It can seem a bit abstract and will be more effective as a tool if the client can see its value. To this end, it is worth spending some time honing your introductory spiel and an example or two can help make the abstract a little more concrete.

| | |
|---|---|
| One to one | ✓ |
| Group sessions (might need to be simplified) | ✓ |
| Within the session | ✓ |
| As a self-directed intersessional task | ✓ |
| Initial career choice | ✓ |
| Career changes | ✓ |
| Indicative timing | 30 + minutes |

## Why it works

Here is another technique that finds a way to access your unconscious knowledge. There is a body of literature that explores the notion of tacit or implicit knowledge (Polanyi, 1966). This represents the information that we know intuitively but that we might find hard to verbalise. This is the kind of knowledge that allows us to say confidently and accurately 'that job did not work out for me', but wouldn't always allow us to articulate what was so bad about it or might lead us to feel sure that 'that kind of job wouldn't suit me at all', without being able to identify exactly why not.

Key to understanding how this technique works is that the information is stored not verbally (which is why it is hard to put into words) but as patterns of data. We make sense of the world by recognising similarities or differences between one situation and a host of old examples. Schön (1987) highlights how we can recognise and describe deviances from the norm far more easily than we can describe the norm itself, and it is this process that allows the triads in this technique to be so effective. Whilst it is hard for us to put our fingers on the most meaningful aspects of any one job, as soon as we put it in a triad the similarities and differences become easy to identify. Using triads (groups of three) rather than dyads (groups of two) is thought to bring a more robust analysis – less of description and more of discovery (Ford & Bradshaw, 1993).

## What's the evidence base?

This approach has been mainstream in the psychological literature for over 50 years and, during that time, it has been used in a wide variety of contexts. The literature offers some support for its value in different settings, with different populations, looking at different kinds of outcomes. In terms of its effectiveness in therapeutic settings, numerous studies have been reported. It has been shown to reduce anxiety (Karst & Trexler, 1970), to reduce phobias (Epting & Nazario, 1987), to increase self-esteem (Sheehan, 1981) and to increase confidence (Viney et al., 1985). More recently, Metcalf, Winter and Viney (2007) conducted a meta-analysis of 23 separate studies that examined the impact of personal constructs interventions. They found that the interventions improved a wide range of outcomes including quality of life, parent/child relationships, anxiety, shyness, sociality and even attendance at an exercise class.

Beyond these positive stories of its value in therapeutic contexts, the value of this approach within career coaching has also had some empirical support. This idea of using personal constructs (or vocational constructs as the literature sometimes calls them) in career practice was suggested by Kelly himself in his original 1955 monograph, and some case studies illustrate how it can be of value to adult clients (Neimeyer, 1992) and young people (Chusid & Cochran, 1989). Beail (1985) noted that the Rep Grid could be used to explore perceptions of school studies and the selection of degree programmes, and Neimeyer (1989) suggested it would be useful for analysing career-related information and values. More recently, Paszkowska-Rogacz, & Kabzinska (2012) have provided some much-needed quantitative evidence that the approach can add value in career practice in their work with a sample of over 136 university students.

# Chapter 5

# What jobs would suit me?

In the previous chapter we explored techniques that can help people to work out what they want from a job. In this chapter we focus on other aspects of self-awareness, looking at three techniques that can help people to identify things that they are good at and things that they value and then link these to job ideas.

Traditional approaches to career development held that the secret to a fulfilling career lay in a simple formula:

self-awareness + understanding of the labour market + a rational decision = career fulfilment

As we know from our own experiences, the stories of our clients and the research that we read, the real formula is much more complicated. But, whilst we now see that career choices are enormously complex, the basic elements of self-awareness and occupational information are still relevant.

The first two techniques described in this chapter could both be seen as 21st- century versions of traditional tools. The first, which helps clients identify their strengths is, in essence, a skills exercise and the second, the values exercise, adds a new dimension to traditional values exploration techniques that many of us have used in our practice.

One key difference between these two techniques and more traditional exercises lies in who takes responsibility for generating the lists of the characteristics under discussion. Traditional skills and values exercises tend to provide pre-written lists of possible skills and values, and clients are invited to assess their own abilities or preferences against each item on the list, generating a final analysis of their top skills and key values. In the two exercises presented in this chapter, your clients are expected to come up with the constructs and qualities themselves. This is, inevitably, more challenging for them, as they need to do a considerable amount of work themselves, but is, equally inevitably, more valuable as they have had the opportunity to push their own thinking further.

The third tool introduced in this chapter is Schein's Career Anchors, which explores work motivation, identifying eight different *career drivers* that can help to steer people's career paths. This tool is more general than the first two, combining abilities and values to identify underpinning work motivations.

## Identifying strengths

### Introduction

Strengths are one mainstay of the positive psychology movement. Positive psychology promises to contribute significantly to career practice and, as such, I am going to introduce it in a little depth here before going on to talk more specifically about strengths.

In 2000 two American psychologists, Martin Seligman and Mihaly Czikszentmihalyi, published a seminal paper that launched a new paradigm in psychology. Traditionally, the authors argued, psychology had been what they described as *pathology driven*. Its focus had been on the sick or on those who were failing and the aim had been to improve their status or mental health to ensure that they could have a reasonable quality of life. Psychology was all about making sure that everyone in society reached a minimum acceptable standard. Seligman and Czikszentmihalyi acknowledged the importance of this position but suggested that, alongside it, there was a place for an alternative approach – a more positive version of psychology – that focused on those who were already living adequate lives and that aimed to find ways to help them to live a good or a great quality of life.

The discipline of positive psychology has given rise to some interesting strands of research that seem to offer some promise for career practice. One of these is strengths.

Put simply, strengths are things you are good at, but the positive psychology definition stresses that strengths must also be things you enjoy. Positive psychology literature has introduced the notion of 'flow', which is a concept you may have come across before. It is the feeling you get when you are so entirely immersed in an activity that you do not notice anything around you and you aren't aware of the passing of time. In general, the feeling of 'flow' is achieved though using strengths, and the presence of both strengths and flow (see the box below for details) has been shown to have a positive impact on work.

There are pre-existing lists and questionnaires that can be used in career coaching but the technique, used in the way it is described below, will push your clients further because they are asked to generate their own strengths.

### How to use

It is useful to spend a bit of time at the start explaining the notion of strengths and highlighting the links between using strengths and job satisfaction (explained in more depth in the Evidence box below). As this is a technique that encourages people to generate their own strengths, it is also worth establishing the idea that your client should feel free to interpret the notion of strengths personally. There is no set list that they should be thinking about and the ideas that they come up with might be quite different from the sorts of skills and competencies that employers claim to be looking for. It is also worth pointing out that strengths are not necessarily work-based. This is a technique that aims to identify and articulate the things that people are good at and enjoy and, whilst some of these might be easier to link to job descriptions than others, the focus should be on your clients as whole people and not just on their work-selves.

It is great if you can find a few different strengths – three or four is often a good number to work with. It may be that the process described below generates more than one strength or you may need to reiterate the process a number of times, using different incidents from your client's experience.

*Step 1: articulating the strengths*

In the first instance, ask your client to recall an occasion where they felt *in their element*: when they felt that they were performing well, enjoying themselves and felt entirely at home with the activity. It could be a work-related incident but might well be something they have done in another part of their lives. Ask your clients to describe the event, what they did and how they felt. Then invite them to identify what they did well and then to take it one step further and crystalise what it was about them that made them good at it. During this section your aim is to get your client to funnel down to a specific characteristic or quality, and it may take a little time to get there. The box below gives an example of the kind of conversation that you might have.

An alternative or additional approach you can use is to ask your client to tell you about the last time they remembered being in a state of 'flow', and ask them what it was they were engaged in doing and see if you can find a strength from that example.

## Case study

Shaimaa was originally from Egypt but, over the last 15 years, she had moved all over the world with her husband's career. She had given up work altogether when she had her first child and, now that her youngest had started school and the family had settled in London, she was beginning to think about what kind of job she might enjoy. Having been out of paid employment for 12 years and never having worked in the UK, she felt very unsure about how she might fit in to the workplace. As part of a series of coaching sessions, her coach suggested that she might think about her strengths. Shaimaa was a little hesitant as her lack of recent experience in the workplace meant that she wasn't readily able to identify work-related skills, but her coach reassured her that they would be drawing on activities from any aspect of her life.

CAREER COACH: Tell me about an occasion where you have really felt in your element.

SHAIMAA: I recently organised a party for 12 six year olds. I was dreading it, but actually, I put loads of work in to the planning, and it went really well.

CAREER COACH: What was so good about it?

SHAIMAA: Well, first of all, I think we got the space right. It was a bit of a faff, but we took basically everything out of the ground floor space so the kids could run around and we weren't worried that they would break anything, or injure themselves. It made it feel more relaxed.

CAREER COACH: What else?

SHAIMAA: I'd put quite a lot of thought into the games. It is not terribly hard to work out games that six year olds are going to enjoy, but I guess I'd thought about making sure there was a bit of variety, and that there were enough prizes for everyone, and something organised for those who got 'out' early on in each game.

CAREER COACH: Anything else?

SHAIMAA: I guess then there was something about the way it was run – the way I ran it – the atmosphere we created.

CAREER COACH: Tell me more.

SHAIMAA: Well, I think we all had a really good time. I think the kids really enjoyed it, and part of that was because I was really enjoying it and made it clear to them that I was happy to be there with them.

CAREER COACH: Anything else?

SHAIMAA: I think I really managed to engage with each child personally, you know, individually, one to one. I got all their names. I think I managed to develop a personal relationship with each of them, and I think this meant that they were more engaged with the activities, and, I think, probably much easier to manage – they were actually really well behaved.

CAREER COACH: Summing that all up, what made the party go so well?

SHAIMAA: I guess two things: planning and then I guess you might call it interactions with the kids.

CAREER COACH: And drilling down to you, and what this tells us about you, what was it about you that made you do this so well?

SHAIMAA: OK, so in terms of planning, actually, it wasn't just about being well-organised, it was more about maybe empathy, really. I thought about the kids, and what they would like and what might go wrong, and how to help ensure that they enjoyed themselves.

*(continued)*

*(continued)*

CAREER COACH: So what might you call that?

SHAIMAA: Um, what about, strategic empathic planning? Or empathic strategy?

CAREER COACH: Great! Empathic strategy. And what about the other part?

SHAIMAA: That was about the relationships, and I guess it was down to seeing and treating each little person as an individual. So, I guess it is empathy again, isn't it? But something about using empathy in different ways – in planning and in groups?

CAREER COACH: So what do you think is the strength we're talking about?

SHAIMAA: I guess it is the ability to use empathy in different ways and different contexts, to manage situations, events and groups.

Shaimaa found this process both insightful and affirming. Without much prompting from her coach she could see how this strength could be of value in the workplace, and felt very much encouraged to see how her home life allowed her both to develop and identify work-relevant skills.

There are myriad roles in which empathy might be valuable. Shaimaa and her coach then spent some time together brainstorming a list of career areas or roles in which this could be an asset. They considered roles in which one-to-one connections are important (such as in counselling or in medical roles), but also jobs where you need to develop relationships with groups (teaching or management roles), where you might use empathy to persuade people to behave in certain ways (marketing and sales), or where you need to organise events that are going to appeal to people (such as an events co-ordinator or wedding planner).

Once this process was finished, Shaimaa's coach suggested that she should think of a different activity that she had enjoyed and they went through the stages again, twice more.

At the end of this session Shaimaa hadn't quite managed to identify her perfect job, but she left the session feeling that her options were open. She could see that she had a range of things to offer an employer, and she could identify a range of different kinds of roles in which she could make a genuine contribution to the workplace.

*Step 2: links with career ideas*

When your client has a few different strengths identified, the next stage is to try and link each one to specific jobs. Ask your client to write one strength in the middle of a blank sheet of paper and then invite them to brainstorm all the roles that they can think of in which this strength could be an advantage. Encourage them to be as wild and free as they want at this stage – it is just a way to get ideas down and they are not going to be committed to anything. It is fine at this stage for you to make any contributions – you may be able to think of some job titles that haven't occurred to your client and, as long as your client is happy for you to include these, they might spark off a train of thought that had not previously occurred to them.

Aim for about ten different job titles for each strength, although, with some, it might be possible to find many more.

Once you have completed this for one key strength, move on to another and, again, try and identify ten or more job titles in which this strength could be used. Repeat this process with up to four of the strengths discussed.

At this point you might have 40 or so job titles to look at. This is not a definitive list of jobs to which your client would be suited but a starting point to spark off thoughts. There might be some jobs that are repeated in more than one list. These might be the ones to notice first. You could then ask your client to identify the jobs they have considered before and those that are new ideas, or to think about those that they are instinctively drawn to and those that they intuitively shy away from. It is the analysis that is likely to bring value to your clients, so do encourage an open and thorough discussion of the job titles that have emerged.

## In practice

I explained in the introduction that part of the value of this exercise is that it is the client who is generating the ideas but, of course, there will be clients for whom and contexts in which this becomes a prohibitively difficult challenge. If you are working with clients whose experience of the world of work is such that they do not really have a concept of what work-related skills and values might be, then it may be that a pre-existing list is a useful starting point. You can always branch off into client-generated ideas later on. Similarly, if you are keen to try an exercise such as this within the context of a group setting, then you may find it easier to predict and control a group who have a pre-existing list to work with. Seligman and his colleagues have conducted considerable research to identify universal strengths. They have identified six virtues that, they suggest, transcend age, gender and culture. These are wisdom, courage, humanity, justice, temperance and transcendence, and they have identified 24 strengths that are linked to these virtues. These are all described in the Values in Action Inventory of Strengths (VIA-IS), which you can access free of charge from Seligman's website authentichappiness.com, and there is a questionnaire that can help you to identify your key strengths. The full VIA-IS is 240 questions long, but there is another that consists of just 24 questions, which may be a little more palatable to your time-poor clients. There is also a version that has been validated for work with children. This too has 240 questions so may prove challenging for the more easily-distractible youngsters.

Another alternative is to invest in some 'strengths cards'. These are packs of 24 postcards, each of which has an image that depicts one strength and a description

## 54 What jobs would suit me?

of the nature of that strength on the back. You can give the packs of cards to your clients and ask them to go through the pack one by one and identify three or four of the cards that reflect their particular strengths. Clients often quite enjoy using the cards as they are usually nicely produced with appealing images, and having a prop such as this can take the pressure off the one-to-one interaction, which can be useful if you are working with clients who feel uncomfortable in the spotlight. The cards also work well if shared in small groups of three or four. There are a number of different versions of strengths cards that you can find online.

| | |
|---|---|
| One to one | ✓ |
| Group sessions (better with strengths cards) | ✓ |
| Within the session | ✓ |
| As a self-directed intersessional task | ✗ |
| Initial career choice | ✓ |
| Career changes | ✓ |
| Indicative timing | 20–30 minutes |

### Why it works

Many of the concepts and ideas put forward by the positive psychology movement are not new – the search for happiness has been a major concern to the human race for millennia.

Positive psychology draws from the Greek ideas of hedonic and eudemonic pleasure (instant gratification and longer-term fulfilment) and is influenced by the ideas underpinning person-centred approaches (Maslow, 1943; Rogers, 1962). In particular, the person-centred assumption that people are predisposed to personal growth and naturally striving towards becoming a fully-functioning person is reminiscent of positive psychology's understanding of flourishing. Within organisational psychology too there are synergies. Cooperrider and Srivastva (1987) developed an approach called 'appreciative inquiry', which aims to improve the way that organisations function by focusing and building on their strengths rather than identifying and trying to fix their weaknesses. There are clear parallels with positive psychology's approach to strengths here.

### What's the evidence base?

Interesting links between positive psychology and careers are emerging. A large-scale international study (Rath & Harter, 2010) identified career satisfaction as one of the five key contributors towards a fulfilled life (alongside social, financial, physical and community well-being), and the data suggested that out of these five aspects of life, career was the most important one, with those thriving in their careers being twice as likely to be thriving in their lives overall.

There seems to be a fairly clear link between strengths and both job satisfaction and overall well-being. The evidence suggests that our job satisfaction is higher if we are able to use our strengths, and particularly our key strengths, on a daily basis (Peterson et al., 2007; Mongrain & Anselmo-Matthews, 2012). Making frequent use of our strengths has also been shown to reduce the symptoms of depression and increase work engagement. These effects increase with the second, third and fourth additional strength that we use each day (Litman-Ovadia & Davidovitch, 2010).

## Implicit values

### Introduction

The notion of values in career work has been core to career development and practice for decades. Our values represent the things that matter to us and, as such, a very broad range of concepts and constructs comes under this banner. There is a distinction made in the literature between 'expressed values' and 'implied values'. Expressed values are those that people explicitly and consciously associate themselves with. It is expressed values that would usually emerge as the answer to a direct question such as 'what are your most important life or work values' and these values are often very influenced by context, family, upbringing and peers and may be linked to social identities. Typical expressed values might include respect, autonomy and fairness.

Implied or implicit values are often more hidden and people will usually need some support to try and identify them. Implicit values are more personal and more individual, and tend to influence or govern choices at a more unconscious level. Expressed and implicit values can have much in common but, when they offer different guidelines for behaviour, they can make career choice more difficult. A conscious awareness of this influential but hidden value system can be a great asset to the career decision-making process.

This technique uses interests as a way to help people to identify their implied values. Interests are chosen here because, in general, people have a pretty free hand in deciding how to fill their leisure time. People engage with their hobbies because they enjoy them, and they stop doing them when they stop enjoying them. In contrast, people's reasons for choosing and sticking with jobs tend to be more complex, and so interests can reflect something closer to an individual's true implicit values than other choices they make in life.

The approach described here is based on a technique called the Depth Oriented Values Extraction (Colozzi, 2003). The words *depth* and *extraction* highlight that this technique goes beyond the surface, and that identifying these values and bringing them into conscious awareness is not necessarily easy. Colozzi describes the process as being akin to peeling the layers off an onion, with the career coach pushing the client to understand themselves in more and more depth.

## How to use

### Step 1: identify the interests

The first stage of the process is to ask your client to list their top ten interests, or things that they enjoy doing or have recently enjoyed doing. Ask them then to tell you about them – explaining what they do, why they do it, how long they have been doing this and how they first decided to get involved. For each interest they are then asked to write down what it is about the activity that they like. Your client should be encouraged to come up with as many reasons as they can. The reasons need to be as thoughtful and specific as possible – general statements such as 'it is fun/interesting/enjoyable' are not going to be very useful. You may need to work with your client here, stretching their thinking and repeatedly asking them 'what is it that you actually enjoy?' or 'why do you enjoy it so much?'. Mindful of the advice that you are helping your client to peel back the layers, do take your time over this stage and work collaboratively with your client, encouraging them to explore their feelings and reactions to the ideas that are coming up.

### Step 2: extract the values

By the end of the first step, your client might have identified 20 or 30 reasons behind their interests. In the next step, the two of you undertake an analysis of these reasons, trying to narrow them down to perhaps four or five overarching themes. In the first instance you should look to see which reasons are repeated frequently – these are likely to be some of your client's core values. Then it might be possible to group some of the ideas together, perhaps under a more overarching label. The box below illustrates the themes that might be identified from three particular activities.

| Hobbies or interests | Reasons for enjoying the interests | Recurrent themes |
| --- | --- | --- |
| Volunteering for a helpline | Feeling connected with other volunteers<br>Hearing stories<br>Understanding more about the world<br>A sense of pride from doing some good for others<br>Contributes to having a varied life | Connecting with others<br>Stories<br>New or different experiences |

| Local book group | Feeling part of a local community<br>Being introduced to new things to read<br>Having a good excuse to prioritise reading<br>Feeling quite intellectual | Activities that lead to a desired identity |
| A recent visit to a local museum | Feeling of discovering something off the beaten tourist track<br>Hearing stories of local residents in the past<br>Becoming more knowledgeable about the town | Enjoyment of learning |

Once you have established a handful of values that have emerged from the reasons, ask your client to reflect on them. Does this feel like an authentic analysis? Would this list be similar to the list that they would have produced had they simply been asked 'what are your most important work values?' If not, what is different and why are the lists different?

*Step 3: linking values with job choices*

In the final stage, you need to bring the focus back to your client's current career dilemma. You could ask them whether their current role or the career they are considering are congruent with this list of values. And, if your client is still looking to identify new occupational areas, you could take each of the values (much as you did with the strengths exercise described earlier in the chapter) and identify a range of job choices that could be congruent with each value.

*In practice*

This process can be surprising and sometimes a little painful for people as they discover things about themselves that they hadn't been conscious of and may not always like. Expressed values are much more straightforward to deal with – these are the values on which people base their conscious choices and therefore that tend to reflect the aspects of their identity and self-concept that they like or at least have made their peace with. Implied values may take more time for individuals to understand and accept. As a coach, your non-judgemental approach and unconditional positive regard for your client will be crucial here as it may be important to your client to see that your respect for them doesn't change when they reveal new aspects of their character.

Beyond the unconditional positive regard that needs to infuse the whole process, the attitude of the career coach here should be one of curiosity. Your aim is to work with your client to find out what their experiences and responses are, and being genuinely curious about this will ensure that you ask the right questions and go far enough.

This is another tool that works better in a one to one than in groups. The process is a little complex, which can make it more challenging to explain in a group context, and the values can take a little teasing out of your clients, which can rely on the expertise of the career practitioners.

The literature suggests, as described above, that clients might find it useful to identify ten separate activities or hobbies and examine each one. It may be that you find that ten are not necessary and that four or five seem to bring good results.

| | |
|---|---|
| One to one | ✓ |
| Group sessions | ✗ |
| Within the session | ✓ |
| As a self-directed intersessional task | ✗ |
| Initial career choice | ✓ |
| Career changes | ✓ |
| Indicative timing | 20 minutes |

## Case study

When she graduated, Paula did not really know what she wanted to do and, having finished a degree in maths, she decided, in the absence of any other particular steer, to train as an accountant. Five years down the line she made the decision that this kind of work did not suit her value system and she felt that a role that allowed her to help people would be much more fulfilling. She found herself a job in an FE college, providing learning support within classrooms. But, although this felt like a much more socially responsible and altruistic thing to spend her days on, she still wasn't happy. She came to see the careers adviser at the FE college and they worked together to try and identify her implied values.

Through the exercise it became clear to Paula that her sense of fulfilment came from feeling appreciated. It did not so much matter whether the work itself was contributing to the greater good, what mattered more was that the people she was working directly with appreciated her and communicated their appreciation in a clear and fulsome way.

Paula was initially a little resistant to her discovery. She had always thought of herself as someone who valued altruism and doing good, and she wasn't sure how she felt about this new version of herself as someone who just liked to be appreciated. But, as she reflected, her new insights filled Paula with relief. In her quest for an altruistic job that she hoped would lead to deep career fulfilment, Paula had sacrificed a number of other things that were also important to her, including a job in smart offices in central London. Armed with her new-found self-awareness, Paula was able to look for a job that had a focus on service.

She now works in the hospitality industry, helping corporate firms to entertain clients. She is aware that this is not fundamentally making the world a better place, but she loves the relationships she builds up with the corporate firms and with their clients, and really likes to feel their appreciation for her care, expertise and hard work.

## Why it works

Theoretical explanations of the power of value congruence (the degree to which your values match those of the role or the organisation) examine its impact on the career choice process and on job satisfaction.

In terms of the career choice process, values are powerful because they work on a number of different levels: cognitive, emotional and behavioural. They influence the choice of career goals and can enhance motivation for career-related behaviour. Thus, a clear understanding of your own values makes it easier for you to work out what jobs you want to do (setting your own career goals) and more likely to put your plans into action.

In terms of their link with job satisfaction, Edwards and Cable (2009) developed a theoretical model that seems to explain why value congruence works. They examined value congruence from a subjective perspective (i.e., the degree to which people believe that their values are similar to those of the organisation) and found that its impact seems to work in three ways. The most important impact of value congruence is trust – if you feel that your organisation's values are similar to yours, you are likely to trust your managers and co-workers. You will have confidence that the leaders have a good sense of what is right and wrong and you will be more likely to support and embrace their ideas and vision. They also found that value congruence with the organisation led to people liking their colleagues more and working more harmoniously together because they have a shared sense of which goals to strive for and how to achieve them. Value congruence also leads to more pleasurable interactions at work because conversations with those who share your values are likely to affirm your beliefs. The final significant explanation for the positive impact of value congruence is in what it does for internal organisational communication, and this has an impact both on the content and style of communication. Value congruence means that your organisation is more likely to communicate about the kinds of issues that are of interest and that matter to you (Erdogan, Kraimer & Liden, 2004), and it indicates that the style of the communication that you receive is likely to suit you (Kalliath, Bluedorn & Strube, 1999).

*(continued)*

*(continued)*

Examining the evidence base as a whole, it is clear that values play an important and significant role in career decision making and development. If clients are able to identify their values and see how they can be reflected in a work context, this can help with career goals and with motivation to put these plans into action, and working in an environment that is congruent with your values leads to greater levels of trust, better relationships at work and more effective communication.

## What's the evidence base?

Values have been shown to play a part in career development (Brown, 1996; Super & Sverko, 1995), and have been discussed widely in the theoretical literature more recently in the light of Hall and Mirvis's 'protean career model' (1996), which suggests that we should all be aiming for a values-driven career path. Despite the enthusiasm with which this theory has been embraced in the career literature, the evidence base for this approach is not as compelling as might be imagined (Inkson et al., 2012).

There is some strong evidence though that clients appreciate and gain from a values-driven component to their career interventions. A recent meta-analysis, which took the results of a range of different smaller-scale studies and amalgamated the data, suggested that career interventions that included a values exercise were some of the most effective overall (Whiston et al., 2017).

Value congruence has been shown to lead to a number of positive outcomes, and the one most relevant to our work is job satisfaction (Kristof-Brown, Zimmerman, & Johnson, 2005), although it has also been shown to link to intent to stay in an organisation and organisational identification (Kristof, 1996; Meglino & Ravlin, 1998; Verquer, Beehr, & Wagner, 2003).

## Career anchors

### Introduction

The final technique in this chapter explores motivations and is drawn from Schein's career anchors (1978). Edgar Schein was an American professor of organisational development and his model of career motivation has been widely adopted in organisational psychology and career coaching worldwide. Schein based his anchors on observations of career paths and he concluded that people's career motivation could be categorised in eight different ways, which he described as *drivers*. He conceptualised these as facets of personality that become increasingly stable over the course of a career path and suggested that finding a job that is congruent with your particular motivation is likely to lead to a fulfilling work life. The anchors combine talents, motivations and values, and it is thought that each of us has just two or three key drivers.

Schein's anchors are:

- **Technical competence**

    Those who are drawn to technical competence base their work identity on their professional expertise. This is also where they derive their satisfaction from and are at their most fulfilled being able to make full use of their particular skills and being known and valued for their expertise. Ongoing career fulfillment comes from the opportunity to apply specific skills at a high level, and developing further expertise is more attractive than climbing a conventional career ladder.

- **General managerial competence**

    People interested in developing general managerial competence are born leaders. They are at their happiest running a team, taking responsibility for the direction and outcomes of the team as a whole, and aiming to bring out the best in each individual they work with. They may start their careers developing technical expertise, but are keen to develop their careers into a more general management role as soon as they can.

- **Security and stability**

    For many of us, a degree of security and stability is important, but for those whose primary driver is stability and security the desire is particularly strong. They may be technical whizzes or gifted managers, but their main goal in seeking promotion or in developing expertise is to get to a point in their career where they feel that their position, their role in the organisation, their salary and their future are guaranteed.

- **Entrepreneurial creativity**

    Those driven towards entrepreneurial creativity want to use their own skills, ideas and talents to create something that is identifiably their own. They may spend some part of their career learning the ropes in another organisation, but are keen to branch out as soon as they can and create something that they can call their own. Their desire for financial success is as a badge that shows the success of their venture.

- **Autonomy and independence**

    For those whose key anchor is autonomy and independence, the most important aspect of work is the freedom to make their own choices. This could mean choosing their own projects, working in the way they want, and setting their own goals. Maintaining this sense of autonomy is more important than other aspects of work and people can end up rejecting promotions or other desirable opportunities if they fear that their freedom might be compromised. They can be drawn to setting up their own businesses, but their

motivation differs from the entrepreneurs described above in that their goal is to retain independence and be their own boss.
- **Service and dedication to a cause**

  Those with a strong career anchor of service are driven by an outward-looking value system that makes them strive to make the world a better place. They may be drawn to roles that help people directly, in which they are campaigning or fundraising for issues that matter to them, or working towards making the planet more sustainable, but, whatever direction their values take them in, they will always want to feel that their work is making a contribution to a more positive world.
- **Pure challenge**

  The *challenges* here can come in any shape or size, but those driven by pure challenge are keen to solve the unsolvable, move the immutable and beat the invincible. They are excited by novelty and will become bored as soon as something becomes easy. They can work in a range of different environments but tend to like variety.
- **Lifestyle**

  Those who value lifestyle above all else tend to see their careers as just one part of their life jigsaw. They may be enthusiastic and dedicated workers, but their main concern is their life as a whole. Whether this means that they prioritise living in a particular location, having enough time to devote to their scuba diving or am-dram, or making sure they can pick the children up from school every day, their career choices are made holistically. Success, for those whose primary driver is lifestyle, is defined in terms of their whole lives, not just their careers.

### How to use

#### Step 1: introduce the anchors

Explain the concept of career anchors to your client and then, one by one, talk through each of the possible drivers. Your clients could read the descriptions themselves or you could describe them yourself. Then, for each one, ask your client to reflect on whether it strikes a chord or has any meaning for them. There will usually be one or two anchors that stand out, but it is quite possible for an individual to be drawn to a number of them to differing degrees. It may be interesting to urge your client to consider where their preference for particular anchors comes from. Why is it, for example, that they are so keen on security, or why are they so drawn to the idea of running their own business?

#### Step 2: reflect on the links

For clients who are already working, it can be interesting to ask them to think about whether their current role meets the needs of their particular combination of career anchors. If they are motivated to develop technical expertise, are they getting the opportunities for skill development they want; if they are looking for security, is their current organisation able to provide this for them? This could then be followed up with a discussion about the options. If the demands of their drivers are not being met in their current context, is there anything that could be done to change things at work? Or are they going to need to change organisation or career in order to meet their needs?

### Step 3: consider the implications

For clients who are not currently working, or for those who are keen to move on, a valuable discussion could be had around the implications of their particular driver for their career management. What kind of organisation or role is likely to meet their needs, and what will they themselves need to do to ensure that their drivers are satisfied in the long-term future?

### In practice

The questions below could be used as the basis of a conversation, or could be answered by your client between sessions, ready for discussion.

For each career anchor your client should consider:

- How important is this to me?
- Why does this matter to me?
- What implications does this have for my career choice or career path?
- How does this match with my current or planned choice?

Schein developed a 40-item questionnaire that aims to help you identify your particular profile of career anchors. The questionnaire includes questions that link closely to the anchors above, for example: 'I dream of starting up and running my own business' or 'I am at my most fulfilled at work when I feel I have complete financial security'. As I have suggested with the two techniques already described in this chapter, questionnaires, as an approach to enhancing self-awareness, should be used with caution as they usually do not push people as far as they can be pushed and can set up a more passive approach (*'it told me* that I value technical competence'). But, having said that, people often like a quiz. It is something they can easily do at home between sessions and, as long as you have the opportunity to discuss the results with them, that can be your opportunity to encourage them to take some ownership of their results and stretch their thinking within your conversation.

This is one of the few techniques in the book that doesn't work well for initial career choice. It may be of some value to ask young people to imagine what their career drivers might be, but Schein was clear that our drivers develop though our experience of work. As such, it is a tool that may resonate more and add more value with career changers.

| | |
|---|---|
| One to one | ✓ |
| Group sessions | ✗ |
| Within the session | ✓ |
| As a self-directed intersessional task | ✓ |
| Initial career choice | ✗ |
| Career changes | ✓ |
| Indicative timing | 20 minutes |

## Why it works

One of the appealing things about this model is its breadth. Whilst some of the other tools described in this book focus on one particular kind of characteristic – skills, or values, or motivation – career anchors comprise all three. In some ways this makes them less easy to test or validate empirically (see the box below) but it also means that they can be quite potent in practice. If one of these anchors speaks to you, then it may well be quite insightful as it may bring your abilities, values and motivations together in one neat but hard-hitting package.

## What's the evidence base?

The evidence base is a bit mixed, but there is some empirical evidence that supports the usage of this approach in career coaching. The evidence seems clear that the eight anchors are all distinct from each other and are real constructs (Steele & Francis-Smythe, 2007). The questionnaire too has been shown to be a reliable and valid way for people to identify which career anchors fit them best (Igbaria & Baroudi, 1993). There is also a fair bit of research that indicates that people with certain drivers are more likely to be seen in certain roles: a large number of practicing nurses are likely to be driven by the *service* anchor, where nursing managers are more likely to have the *general managerial* anchor, and professionals in information technology have been shown to be driven by the *technical expertise* anchor (McMurtrey et al., 2002). This could give some support to the use of career anchors as part of a career choice process and suggests that it could be a technique that is valuable to incorporate in career coaching practice.

But there are two caveats that should be mentioned. First, that there does not seem to be much evidence of how effective anchors are as part of a career coaching programme and, second, that the evidence linking career anchors with job satisfaction does not give a clear message. There are some studies that offer clear correlations between anchors and job satisfaction, and then others that do not (La Lopa, Beck, & Ghiselli, 2009; Willis, 2012).

This equivocal evidence is likely to be a result of the complex nature of career anchors. As explained above, anchors are derived from a combination of values, motivation and skills, and it is difficult to unpick such a complicated construct in the way that you need to for empirical research.

On balance, the evidence suggests that this is a tool that can generate interesting discussions and make a valuable contribution to career choice, but provides only one piece of the jigsaw.

Chapter 6

# What job do I want to do?

The question 'what job do I want to do?' lies close to the heart of the book. It is one of the dilemmas that is most often brought up in career conversations and is one that, in my experience, career coaches find most difficult to resolve. There are dozens, probably hundreds, of approaches or techniques that purport to lead people to the answer to this question. In fact the whole 'trait and factor' matching approach that so dominated career research and practice in the 20th century aimed to provide a magic bullet that linked people's characteristics with suitable jobs. The previous chapter provided some tools that aim to answer 'which job would suit me' and, in one way, this is a much easier task because it is so much more contained. In this chapter we are wondering 'what job do I want to do?' and that is a much bigger question, incorporating all sorts of different aspects of life and identity. The most challenging thing though is that it is entirely subjective. However much you might feel that you know the right move for your client, and however much they might want you to tell them what to do, you simply can't answer this one for them.

Here are three tools that encourage clients to explore their own thoughts from a new angle. The first one invites people to imagine themselves in a particular context in the future – to evoke a 'possible self'. The second tool helps people to capitalise on the process of daydreaming. The final one is adapted from John Holland's influential hexagon of career interests and helps people to consider the kinds of jobs that they might find interesting. All three tools aim to enhance self-awareness and help clients to make a start on identifying or assessing the suitability of specific job ideas. Each tool in this chapter allows clients to formulate a hypothesis – a proposition of a future in which they have chosen one particular job or another – and then provides an opportunity to test the hypothesis out, to try it on for size and see whether it might work. With possible selves, the client is invited to imagine themselves quite consciously in a particular role in the future and they are encouraged to think quite broadly about all aspects of a future that might be associated with that particular choice. With the daydream journal, clients take advantage of their ideas about the future from their unconscious, which makes a fleeting appearance in the conscious mind in the form of daydreams. The exercise uses this unconscious information to provide an idea of a possible future and then allows the client to analyse its suitability. In Holland's Hexagon, the job ideas are offered on the basis of a taxonomy of jobs that are thought to be suitable for particular personality types. Again, the client is offered the chance to reflect on the attractiveness of the options and to start to crystalise their preferred future on the basis of their analysis.

## Possible selves

### Introduction

A *possible self* is an idea of the person you might be in the future. It is an image or idea of one possible version of a future you. Possible selves can be positive or negative, expected or fantastical, feared or desired, work-related or home-based. We can all conjure up numerous possible selves. Your expected possible self would be you in five years' time, assuming that things carry on pretty much the same as they are now. The feared possible self could be you if you fail to get a promotion, or if you are made redundant, or if you become ill. The fantastical possible self could be you winning the lottery, getting to the finals of *Bake Off* or being asked to present a regular career-clinic spot on daytime television.

There is plenty of evidence that vivid and well-realised possible selves can have quite an impact on behaviour and motivation and, pertinent to the topic of this chapter, they can help us to identify what we want from the future. For a possible self to be most meaningful, in terms of career planning, it needs to be vivid. The literature talks about the notion of 'pre-experiencing' the possible self, which highlights that your clients need to imagine their future possible self so clearly that they are almost experiencing how it would feel to actually be that version of themselves.

A client then needs to envisage their possible self in great detail. The story they tell could cover all sorts of things but anything that can make the picture come alive is useful. It might include colours, shapes, people, activities and clothes. Emotions are important as they have particular motivating properties, but really the possible self can be extended in any direction.

### How to use

This tool is straightforward to use but does take a little bit of setting up to make sure that your clients get the most out of it. It is important that clients realise that this is a way to stimulate their imagination, so do stress that they can be as creative as they like. You are not expecting a plan and are not going to make them commit to anything they say – it is just a way to help them explore some things that may matter to them.

*Step 1: identify a range of possible selves*

The first stage is to encourage your client to identify a number of different possible selves. This is most effective when a client writes them down. At this stage the goal is to urge your client to be as open and creative as possible and you can be quite explicit about this, perhaps suggesting that they consciously choose a range of possible selves – some realistic and some fanciful. These are often drawn on branches on a tree but a mind map would work as well (see Chapter 13).

The next step is to ask them to choose one to work on. They can choose any possible self they want, for whatever reason – it doesn't need to be the one that they feel they ought to be aiming for, just one that they would like to explore further.

Possible selves work best when they are in image form, but the client also needs to translate their image into words. It is important that you give them enough time for the picture in their mind's eye to take shape and come into focus first. You could suggest that your client closes their eyes to imagine the scenario, and you should give them a little time to get the image clear before you ask them to verbalise the image and the feelings.

*Step 2: evoke the possible self*

When your client has decided on the specific possible self they are going to focus on, and when you feel the possible self is clearly pictured in their mind's eye, the next step is to ask them questions that encourage them to make the image in their mind deeper and broader and clearer. There is no prescribed sequence of questions that you should use and, as you practise this with your clients, you will start to devise your own list of the questions that you find are most evocative for your clients, but the questions below may be a useful starting point for you.

- Tell me about this future you?
- What are you doing? Where are you working? What's the atmosphere like?
- Who are you working with? What are your relationships like?
- What do you find fulfilling about your work?
- What do you wear to work?
- How do you feel about going into work in the mornings?
- When you tell people what you do, how do you feel?
- What are your weekends like these days?
- What do your family think about your new job?
- How do others see you?
- What is the thing that's most different from your current you?
- Tell me about the corresponding feared self?

The goal here is to encourage your client to bring their future possible self to life. It doesn't much matter in which direction you take them as it all contributes to building up a rich picture, so you should feel free to take the narrative wherever your client leads.

### Step 3: crystallise the learning

When you feel that you have taken this as far as you can, invite your client to open their eyes and ask them to reflect on the process. Did they enjoy it? Did they find it easy? Did anything surprise them? You can then use their visualisation as the basis for a discussion about what matters to them: which aspects of the future life seem to be particularly important and which are less so. Some clients may have chosen a positive and realistic possible self. For these clients, the discussion could focus on what they liked about their future and could then move on to a conversation about their next steps. Other clients may have envisaged a future that was less positive or less realistic and, for these clients, it is particularly important to spend time working out what their possible self can tell them. Are there some aspects of the future they envisaged that they could use as the starting point for a career goal? Perhaps there were some elements of this possible self that have allowed them to ascertain what they definitely don't want from a future. It may be that there are some aspects of the future that are clear, but questions still remain over the exact nature of the role or the job title. It may be that the next stage could be a collaborative brainstorm. A client might, for example, have worked out that they want to be working in a smart office with plenty of client contact and a strong team ethos. This next part of the conversation could open up some practical ideas of the kinds of jobs that might be able to fulfil these criteria, as the two of you spend some time together brainstorming the kinds of job titles or types of organisations that might be suitable.

### Step 4: next steps

Finally, to capitalise on all this useful thinking, your client could consider what they need to do next in order to get closer to their desired future. There is something in the process of clarifying the overall end goals that allows people to identify the first steps they need to take. In this part of the conversation you can take advantage of this newly acquired clarity to encourage your clients to set themselves some clear action points, and to think through what factors could help or hinder them as they try to achieve this.

### *In practice*

This technique can be a powerful one to use for clients who are feeling stuck. It can unlock ideas and opinions that can be difficult to access, but it relies on your clients being open to this kind of guided visualisation and to stray a little from the usual career topics that focus on job duties and skills. Some clients might need to be persuaded that this could be of value, so it is another technique where you might need to encourage your client to have a go – even if they do not seem particularly sure that it might be useful, you could urge them to be a bit playful and just let their imagination take over. Make sure that they understand that you are not planning to hold them to the plans that they describe, but that they might just provide a new angle from which to think about things.

This technique can be used both in one-to-one sessions and in groups. In a group setting, the approach works well as far as getting individuals to think about their own desired possible selves. With large or small groups, you can present the approach step by step and ask each individual to close their eyes and gradually build up a picture of their future as you run through the list of questions. The second part, where clients are encouraged to crystalise the useful thinking and make plans for the future, is more tricky in groups, but asking people to discuss their future selves in pairs afterwards, perhaps with some clear prompt questions from you, can work well.

One group of clients who seem to respond positively to this technique is older workers. With the abolishment of retirement ages, the challenges with pensions and with an ageing population, it seems clear that older clients will increasingly become an important group for career coaching. As yet, the career researchers have not come up with a wide array of techniques that are particularly suited to this client group, but this is one that seems to have some resonance with this population.

| | |
|---|---|
| One to one | ✓ |
| Group sessions | ✓ |
| Within the session | ✓ |
| As a self-directed intersessional task | ✗ |
| Initial career choice | ✓ |
| Career changes | ✓ |
| Indicative timing | 20–30 minutes |

## Why it works

There are a few different theories that possible selves draws from, and it is useful to have a clear understanding of these as this will ensure that you know how to use this technique to best effect.

Much of its power lies in the way it facilitates goal-setting. There has been a significant amount of research that has unpicked how and why goals help (Locke & Latham, 2002). First, goals help to direct focus: if you have established that you are aiming to go into publishing, you are not going to waste your time reading about careers in teaching or wondering what it would be like to be a journalist, so all of your energy and attention can be devoted to finding out more about the job area you have settled on. Second, goals help people to identify the small steps needed. As soon as you identify 'publisher' as your career goal, it becomes blindingly obvious that you first need to pop into that publishing firm that you pass every day on your way to work to see if you can arrange a chat. Finally, a clear goal has been shown to help with motivation. If they have the end goal in sight, then it seems that people end up responding more positively to set backs, are not put off and are able to identify more and more creative solutions.

On top of that, there seem to be two additional features of a possible selves intervention that can help and that set possible selves apart from other approaches that encourage people to visualise the future. They are what are known as *episodic future thinking* and *pre-experiencing*. The idea with a possible selves intervention is that the client should imagine, quite specifically, a particular episode in the future (episodic future thinking), and that this image should be imagined in such vivid detail that the individual almost feels that they are experiencing it (pre-experiencing). A general idea of the future, for example, for a PhD student, would be an era when their PhD is completed and they are working as a university lecturer. A specific episode could be the day that they graduate or their very first lecture when they introduce themselves to their new cohort of students as Dr Sam Simpson. The pre-experiencing could happen as they imagine walking across the stage at graduation, seeing their parents in the audience and hearing the audience applaud their achievement; or as they imagine that sense of pride that they might feel as they say the words 'Dr Sam Simpson' aloud to their students.

The episodic future thinking helps the individual to make strong links between the person they are today and the person they could be in the future. This encourages people to make a clear connection between the behaviour they choose today and the outcome they will emerge with in the future and, as a result, people expend more effort and are more focused on useful activities. The power of pre-experiencing lies in the emotions that it conjures up. Emotions have been shown to have a more powerful influence on motivation than cognitions, so a thought about the future (I am graduating) will not have the same motivating effect as a thought that is linked to an emotion (I am graduating and I'm bursting with pride).

## What's the evidence base?

Since Markus and Nurius first proposed the idea of possible selves back in 1986 there has been considerable research on their role and their value in a range of contexts, including education, smoking cessation and homelessness. The

*(continued)*

*(continued)*

evidence base for using possible selves in careers work too is quite good and growing. There is evidence that interventions that encourage clients to consider their possible selves do result in clearer goals, a clearer understanding of the steps they need to take (Hock, Deshler, & Schumaker, 2007), and increased motivation (Robinson, Davis, & Meara, 2003). A study of university students in 2013 showed strong links between the possible selves intervention and both clear career goals and proactive job search (Strauss, Griffin, & Parker, 2012). There is good evidence that both middle school students and high school students gain better academic grades if they can develop clear and relevant career possible selves (Beal & Crockett, 2010; Destin & Oyserman, 2010). Taber and Blankemeyer (2015) demonstrated that salient possible selves led to better career planning and more proactive skill development and proactive networking.

## Daydream journal

### Introduction

We all love to daydream. It has been shown that typically we spend between 30% and 50% of our waking hours daydreaming (Killingsworth & Gilbert, 2010) and it is thought that daydreaming is the mind's default position – it is what we do, automatically, whenever our minds are not actively engaged with doing something else (Mason, Bar, & Macrae, 2008). Current issues and problems are often the subject of daydreams and, as such, it is no surprise to learn that people thinking about making career choices will often daydream about their work future. Daydreams are usually in the form of images, sometimes quite vivid ones, and are defined as spontaneous trains of thought. Their prevalence hints at the idea that we may have evolved to daydream because daydreams serve a useful psychological function. It is thought that they are valuable tools for allowing us to organise internal information and plan complex future events (Stawarczyk et al., 2012). In this technique their power is harnessed to help with career planning.

Clients are invited to keep a work-related daydream journal, in which they record a number of the work-related daydreams that they notice during the course of a few weeks. The diary entries are then discussed and analysed collaboratively by the coach and client and the themes are interpreted in the light of the career dilemma facing the person.

### How to use

#### Step 1: journaling

This is an exercise that is set up during a coaching session, carried out in between sessions and de-briefed in the following session.

Clients are asked to write down the details of any work-related daydreams that they have noticed between one session and the next. It is usually best if they write them down as soon as they can – daydreams can be easily forgotten and recording the details whilst they are fresh in their minds is usually the best way to ensure that they can be recalled. To this end, it is recommended that clients should carry something to write in all the time. The research articles outlined in the box below suggest giving clients each a 'daydream journal', an exercise book specifically designed for the task, with a definition of work-related daydreams written at the top of each page and directions on how to record daydreams on the first page. This sounds like a great idea but, as long as the notes can be taken as soon as the daydream is noticed, it doesn't matter how they are recorded. Your clients might prefer to make notes on their phones or tablets, or even record themselves talking about their daydreams.

The more daydreams your clients can record, the more data you have to go on in your follow-up session, but, as long as they can manage to identify and describe at least one daydream, that is enough for a useful discussion.

You should encourage your clients to record as much detail as they can. Beyond the basic storyline, they could include visual and emotional details such as what they were wearing and how they felt in the daydream. Their reaction to the daydream afterwards might be interesting too, as this can reveal perceived barriers or limiting beliefs.

*Step 2: interpretation*

At the next session you work collaboratively with your client, encouraging them to re-tell their daydreams and interpreting them in the light of their current career dilemmas. The interpretation can be divided into three parts.

1 **Exploration**. The first part of the process is to encourage your client to re-tell their story as vividly as possible. They might want to start off by reading out to you their diary entry or they might prefer to re-read the entry to themselves and then to describe it to you. You can help them to re-live the daydream by asking questions to elicit a more vibrant account. Focus on the visual and emotional aspects, pushing your client to depict the clothes, the rooms and the other people involved, as well as their feelings about the behaviours and roles that they adopt.
2 **Insight**. Once you feel that you have found out as much as you can about the daydream itself, the next step in the process is to encourage your client to make links between the themes identified in the daydream and their current career dilemma. You could ask your client first, quite simply, what their daydream has to say about their current situation – does it reveal any underlying preoccupations or highlight the things that really matter to them? It might be interesting to explore how the ideas in their daydream, or the version of themselves revealed in the daydream, relate to previous or current roles or identities they have adopted. And it can be interesting to ask them which aspects of the daydream they would like to hold on to for the future.

It is your client's responsibility to make these links. You are not interpreting their thoughts for them and, unless you have undertaken specialist training, it would not be appropriate to claim to offer insights. Having said that, if you notice anything of interest that occurs to you during the conversation, it can be helpful to your client to share your ideas. Delivered cautiously within the context of a collaborative and person-centred relationship, the responses from someone else can serve to stretch clients' thinking, but do make sure that your opinions are not taken as expert advice.

3   **Action.** In the final part of the interpretation discussion your client should consider what they should take away from the exercise and what their next step should be. The daydreams can be an interesting window into your client's hopes and dreams unencumbered by fears, limiting beliefs and barriers. In this part of the discussion you can work with your client to try and find out what is realistic and whether any barriers are insurmountable, or whether there are some strategies to alleviate or circumvent them that might be worth trying.

### *In practice*

The description above assumes a one-to-one context and an ongoing relationship with your clients. Many career coaches will be more likely to work in group contexts or see clients on a one-off basis. If you spend more time working with groups, then you can set the exercise up in a group context and arrange for one-to-one sessions for the interpretation. If you are looking for an activity that doesn't require any one to one work, there is some evidence that the process of just keeping the daydream diary leads to a significantly increased understanding of oneself in relation to career planning. The exercise could be introduced in a group context as a technique that clients can choose to use on their own if they feel that it might be of value.

| | |
|---|---|
| One to one | ✓ |
| Group sessions | ✓ |
| Within the session | ✓ |
| As a self-directed intersessional task | ✓ |
| Initial career choice | ✓ |
| Career changes | ✓ |
| Indicative timing | 15 minutes per daydream |

## Why it works

The power of daydreams lies in their ability to tell stories. Stories are all around us and we develop our understanding of the world through constructing narratives – stories are how we make sense of the world around us. Through constructing a story about ourselves we refine our understanding of ourselves and can isolate particular aspects and then integrate these aspects into our self-concept – the things we tell ourselves about ourselves become part of who we are and how we see ourselves. Within career development there has been a considerable amount of research that suggests that stories can help in career practice. Narrative approaches to career exploration help individuals to identify life themes and make sense of their experiences (Savickas, 2015). But, whilst most approaches to narrative career coaching focus on looking backwards, daydreams are usually set in the future. As such, daydreams can add a new dimension to the more mainstream approach to narrative career coaching and can shed light on hopes, dreams and fears for the future (Pisarik & Currie, 2015).

## What's the evidence base?

There has been considerable focus on narrative approaches to career practice in the career literature over the last decade, and encouraging your clients to tell their career stories in one way or another has been shown to work well both in one to ones and group contexts (Hartung & Santilli, 2017; McMahon, 2016; McMahon & Watson, 2015). Daydream narratives have not had a huge amount of attention paid to them in the research literature, but there are two studies that indicate that the approach has good potential for use in career coaching. Pisarik, Rowell and Currie (2013) conducted a fairly large-scale study (using 46 university students) that demonstrated that the students did have and did remember work-related daydreams. As well as verifying the existence of these daydreams, the authors conducted an analysis of the nature of the daydreams. They found that the participants' work-related daydreams were, for the most part, depicting their careers in a holistic and multidimensional way, with images that focused on the clothes they might be wearing in the future and their future selves in a variety of roles, combining work and family life.

Two years later, Pisarik and Currie (2015) published a follow up randomised control study with a slightly larger cohort, which indicated that the students found that the process of recording and discussing their daydreams had a significant impact on their levels of self-awareness and their understanding of their own values.

## Holland's Hexagon

In this final technique of this chapter I will be looking at a model devised by John Holland in the mid-20th century. It is no exaggeration to say that Holland has been the single most influential figure in career development, and his ideas dominated career theory and practice in the 20th century and continue to underpin many career coaching sessions today.

## 76 What job do I want to do?

In many ways, Holland's ideas are unfashionable these days. Some of the evidence for and against his approach is presented in the box below but, in general, the criticisms levelled at his model tend to focus on the way it is interpreted and applied. The model itself has stood the test of time and, used appropriately, can be a useful addition to your professional repertoire.

Holland's approach focuses on the idea of career interests and proposes a hexagonal model of six areas of career interest that can be used to categorise both jobs and people (Figure 6.1). Holland's basic idea is that people are likely to be both more effective and more fulfilled when their career interests align with the content and requirements of the job. Holland spent considerable time finding out about the people who had chosen to do particular jobs and found that the people working in any particular role tended to have a lot in common. He classified the similarities that he identified into six discrete categories that are known as RIASEC, which stands for: realistic, investigative, artistic, social, enterprising and conventional. The model places the personality types in a hexagon with more similar types adjacent to each other. The least similar types are opposite each other (Realistic and Social, Artistic and Conventional, Investigative and Enterprising) but it is useful to note that the opposites are distinct types with different characteristics and do not represent the two poles of a single dimension.

Holland offered his model as a tool for matching people to jobs. You may have come across online tools that suggest suitable career ideas for people on the basis of their responses to a series of questions, and the chances are that they are underpinned by Holland's framework. Computer programmes such as these provide some possible answers to people's career dilemmas, but give no clues as to why one particular job has been chosen and, as such, they fail to build any understanding. In the approach described below, the model is used differently. The focus of the exercise is to develop self-awareness and the model is used to generate possible answers that can then be scrutinised. It is through this process of analysis that the individuals come to a better understanding of themselves and their relationship with the world of work.

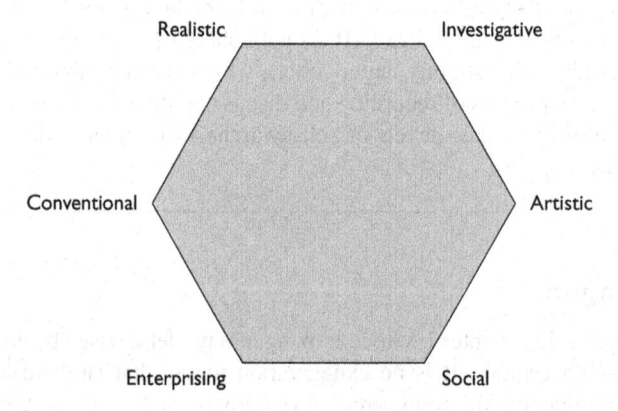

*Figure 6.1* Holland's Hexagon. (Source: the author, based on Holland, 1959.)

## How to use

The aim of the exercise is to raise a client's awareness of their own areas of career interests, and this can be particularly valuable for people whose personal experience of the world of work is limited.

The approach offers a framework that divides the world of work into discrete categories and there are obvious potential problems with this. A taxonomy that attempts to categorise something as vast, amorphous and rapidly changing as the labour market into just six boxes is bound to miss some of the nuance. But, as long as you stress that this is not an exact science, the approach can be useful for clients who don't know where to start.

## Step 1: introduce the framework

The first step is to introduce your client to the six different personality types. It can be helpful for people to see them represented as the hexagon, so you could show them the diagram above, and then you could talk them through each type and give them some written notes to clarify. This is how Holland describes the six types:

**Realistic**: conforming, frank, genuine, hard-headed, materialistic, natural, normal, persistent, practical, self-effacing, inflexible, thrifty. Realistic types usually have mechanical abilities and often enjoy working with things. They will often excel in hands-on roles and tend to be good at fixing things. They can enjoy work that is physically active and that involves using tools.

**Investigative**: intellectual introspective thinkers who are inquisitive, curious and methodical. Investigative types enjoy academic pursuits and like to understand things. They often enjoy working with facts and finding out the truth and can excel in scientific arenas.

**Artistic**: creative, intuitive, expressive with a strong imagination and an enjoyment of abstract thoughts and ideas. Artistic people enjoy using their imagination and can be creative both intellectually and aesthetically.

**Social**: kind, caring, empathic and warm. Social types enjoy being with and analysing people. They like to help people to solve their problems and are interested in how relationships work and how people interact. They are often found in caring professions, such as social work, counselling and teaching, but can excel in any role that relies on strong relationships.

**Enterprising**: energetic, sociable, lively, ambitious risk-takers. Enterprising types like to influence, persuade, lead and direct. They will often have strong leadership skills and enjoy public speaking. Their ability to persuade and influence means that they can enjoy working in highly political environments and can excel in sales roles.

**Conventional**: detail-orientated completer finishers. Conventional types enjoy order and routines and prefer working in a more predictable way, where expectations and standards are clear. They are likely to enjoy work that involves organisation and are often found in work that focuses on things and systems, rather than data and people.

*Step 2: what's your three-letter code?*

Holland's classification assumes that each of us (and each occupation) might touch on three of the six codes. You should encourage your client to identify first the code that most resonates with them and then two others that also strike a chord. It is usual that the three codes that resonate will be adjacent to each other as there tend to be similarities between the codes that are close to each other and fundamental differences between codes that are positioned opposite each other on the hexagon.

*Step 3: matching this with jobs*

In Holland's publications there are hundreds of job titles included and his model also includes a slightly more sophisticated analysis that looks at a match between an individual and a job based on three-letter combinations. There isn't space here to provide the full list but, leaving the constraints of space to one side, there is another reason not to produce the full list here. This reason links to one of the criticisms often levelled at Holland's model, which is that it can risk rendering the client passive. The value of this exercise is in the ways it can stimulate your clients' thinking – it is not intended to provide an answer but to offer some ideas that encourage your client to generate some new thoughts of their own. The process allows people to consider their personality through the lens of these career interests and to think about what this means in terms of jobs. A fully formed list of apparently perfect matches would short circuit this thought process and cut short your client's learning.

So, pragmatically and philosophically then, here is a list of a limited number of job titles that are associated with the six areas of career interest and that should be used to stimulate a conversation about types of jobs and different aspects of various roles:

**Realistic**: accountant, aerospace, architect, carpenter, chef, chemist, computer engineer, dance, dentist, engineer, environmental scientist, firefighter, graphic designer, interior designer, nurse, personal trainer, physiotherapist, driver, surgeon, vet, web developer, zoologist;

**Investigative**: academic, accountant, actuary, archivist, carpenter, chemist, computer engineer, counsellor, dietitian, economist, engineer, financial adviser, lawyer, mathematician, pharmacist, physicist, psychologist, social worker, technical writer, teacher;

**Artistic**: architect, broadcast journalist, chef, counsellor, fashion designer, fine artist, graphic designer, park ranger, psychologist, PR, photographer, teacher, trainer;

**Social**: academic, customer service, dentist, diplomat, doctor, educator, education administration, fitness trainer, HR, lawyer, nurse, pharmacist, social worker, teacher, trainer, vet;

**Enterprising**: accountant, actuary, advertising, business, buyer, diplomat, entrepreneur, estate agent, fashion designer, fundraiser, HR, journalist, lawyer, manager, management consultant, market research analyst, PR, sales;

**Conventional**: accountant, actuary, administration, archivist, carpenter, chemist, computer engineer, economist, engineer, estate agent, financial adviser, HR, nurse, pharmacist, statistician, technical writer, web developer.

You will note that a number of jobs appear more than once in the list above (who knew that accountancy would be suitable for so many of us?). This highlights the idea, mentioned above and useful to share with your client, that both jobs and people are complex and will rarely be a pure version of one of the six types described here. It could also be a useful reminder that one job title could encompass a very wide range of actual jobs. Accountants can work at many different levels, in every type of organisation you could imagine, and the range of skills required to be an accountant will stretch considerably further than just an understanding of tax law and an ability to make sure the books balance. It is also useful to stress the idea that there is not only one type of person who can make a success of a particular job: not every accountant will be a carbon copy of every other one, and different types of people will bring different strengths and craft the job to suit themselves.

*Step 4: the analysis*

Having identified some job titles that, in theory at any rate, match the interest areas of your clients, you should move on to a discussion of both the career interests and the jobs identified. This is the aspect of the exercise that is likely to add most value to your client, so do make sure that you leave enough time to explore the ideas fully. The skill in your discussion is to draw out some analysis from your client. You are not really expecting them to seize on one of these job titles and decide that that is the one for them. This is a starting point.

Have a look together at the jobs that are listed under their preferred career interest area(s). Invite your client to reflect on which of them appeal and why, and which don't and why not. If the jobs look good, but not quite right, perhaps the two of you could have a think together about other job titles that, for example, are on the more artistic side of engineering or the social side of web design. It might also be interesting to have a look at the job titles that are associated with the opposite personality types. If your client has come out as a strong *investigative* type, have a look at the jobs listed under *enterprising* to see whether there are any insights to be gained there: it may be that looking at a series of jobs that don't appeal allows your client to identify exactly what they don't want in a job, and this could be turned on its head to add to a list of attractive attributes.

### In practice

There are many online versions of this approach. They tend to ask participants a series of questions about things that they might find interesting in the workplace (for example, 'would you like to work with children?', 'would you enjoy working outdoors?'). This information is then used to classify their career interests and the computer programme then matches the individual to a list of jobs. For some clients this can be a useful start to a career conversation but, as is so often the case, that kind of shortcut to an answer does not usually reap the rewards that come from a conversation with a career coach that drives a client to stretch their own thinking.

It can be interesting to combine a Holland-based conversation, such as that which is suggested above, with a computer-generated analysis. After you have followed the steps outlined here, you could invite your client to take one of the online tests that is underpinned by Holland's codes. Having explored the theory behind the process, your client will be in a much stronger position to understand and learn from the computer-generated list.

| | |
|---|---|
| One to one | ✓ |
| Group sessions | ✗ |
| Within the session | ✓ |
| As a self-directed intersessional task | ✗ |
| Initial career choice | ✓ |
| Career changes | ✓ |
| Indicative timing | 20–30 minutes |

## Why does it work?

Holland's approach has been enormously influential both in theory and practice. As such there have been myriad publications that explain it, prove it, question it, admire it and challenge it. Holland assumed that a close match between vocational personality and the career chosen would be likely to lead to job satisfaction (Nordvik, 1996), and he went to considerable effort to explain and account for this. His theory was based on his findings that similar people can be found within occupations (Holland, 1959). This does seem to be fairly widely accepted and you are indeed more likely to find common personality characteristics and interests within a single occupational group than across occupations. It also seems to be the case that there is considerable internal validity within Holland's codes: they do seem to be six quite distinct categories and most people find that they resonate with one or two of them.

I said earlier that Holland's approach is not very fashionable at the moment and it might be useful to explore the reasons for its fall from grace. Most of the reasons against it can be traced back to how it is used, although there are some more fundamental concerns that are outlined below.

Many academics complain that the approach assumes both that personalities are fixed and stable and that career decisions are taken once in life (Savickas et al., 2009). They question the value of the technique given that we now acknowledge that career development for many is a lifelong project, that personalities can change and we see that the labour market is characterised by rapid change (International Labour Organisation, 2016). But these criticisms can be mitigated through thoughtful and nuanced practice, with practitioners stressing that the ideas generated are just a snapshot and that both the jobs and their personalities might change during the course of their working lives.

More problematic, perhaps, is the inference that you could draw from the approach that is that there is one personality type that is suitable for one particular occupation. This assumption could be detrimental to individuals and to professions that would benefit from a diverse workforce, and it is for this reason that I think it is important to emphasise that this is primarily a self-awareness tool, and to limit the focus on the aspect that matches individual interest profiles with specific job titles.

## What's the evidence base?

Considerable evidence has been produced since Holland's model was introduced in 1959 that indicates that a good *person–job fit*, which is Holland's term to describe a close match between the individual and the job, is linked to a range of positive work outcomes. One large meta-analysis, which combines the results of 73 separate studies, suggests a clear link between person–job fit and job performance and turnover intentions (Van Iddekinge et al., 2011). The links between person–job congruence and job satisfaction have also been demonstrated quite convincingly (Assouline & Meir, 1987; Tranberg, Slane, & Ekeberg, 1993). The association with job satisfaction, however, is not generally very high – the correlations rarely go higher than 0.3 (which means that a good person–job fit accounts for no more than about

*(continued)*

> *(continued)*
>
> 10% of the variance in job satisfaction). This may not sound like very much but, as identified in Chapter 3, there are a lot of different factors that combine to predict job satisfaction. A good match between interests and jobs can therefore be assumed to make a positive contribution to a good career decision, but should be considered alongside a number of other important factors.

# Chapter 7

# I want to go for it, but I am just not sure I am good enough

This chapter looks at techniques that can help clients who know what they want to do, but are being held back because they aren't sure that they are good enough. Later in the book we look at tools that can help clients who feel generally negative about the world or lack motivation. The clients we are aiming to help in this chapter have issues with their ability to perform in one particular context. This specific lack of confidence is sometimes referred to as a lack of self-efficacy and is *domain specific*, meaning that you might have a client who is generally quite confident about themselves and some aspects of their ability, but has a particular concern about speaking in public, or interview skills, or even may lack confidence in their ability to make a good decision.

This lack of confidence can often be traced back to what is described in the literature as *faulty thinking* or *cognitive distortions*. Faulty thinking describes a range of specific thinking errors in which people's assessment of a situation is not grounded in reality, perhaps overestimating the probability that something negative will happen ('I am bound to forget my train of thought during the presentation') or exaggerating the possible impact of an incident ('if I do not get this job, my career is over'). Cognitive behavioural therapy (CBT) provides a number of techniques that can help to address faulty thinking. The first technique introduced in this chapter is the ABCDE model (Ellis, 1962), which provides a framework for a conversation that elicits new thinking in clients. The second technique (Performance Inhibiting Thoughts to Performance Enhancing Thoughts, or PITS to PETS) is one that can help to reframe or rationalise some of the most common thinking errors. The final approach introduced in this chapter concerns Psychological Capital, a series of interventions that have been shown to increase hope, optimism, resilience and efficacy.

## Cognitive behavioural therapy

The first two techniques proposed in this chapter come from CBT and I will give a brief introduction to this approach before launching in to a description of the two specific techniques. The boxes that describe the theory underpinning CBT and the evidence of its impact in practice are placed immediately below this introductory section as the two CBT techniques draw on the same literature.

As with many of the approaches introduced in this book, CBT has its origins in psychotherapy. It was introduced by Albert Ellis and Aaron Beck in the 20th century as an approach to behavioural change and the evidence for its effectiveness in a range of contexts is fairly robust.

The philosophy underpinning CBT is that it is not events that disturb us but our reactions to those events; whilst we cannot always dictate events, there are some aspects of our reactions to events that are within our control. The disaggregation of events and thoughts is not new. Epictetus, nearly two thousand years ago (55–135AD), pointed out that 'men are disturbed not by the things that happen but by their opinion of the things that happen', highlighting that it is sometimes our response to the world around us that causes us problems, rather than the events that we experience.

The assumptions of CBT centre on the links between behaviour, emotions and thoughts, and the central idea is that, whilst it is difficult to make a deliberate change to one's emotions, it is more feasible to decide to change one's thoughts. If this change in thoughts can be effected, then it will automatically lead to a shift in emotions, and this is likely to have a knock-on impact on behaviour.

An example might be of a person who has been rejected after a job interview. Figure 7.1 provides an example of a negative response to this kind of event.

Cognitive behavioural therapy suggests that, whilst aiming to 'cheer up' is likely to meet with limited success, it may be possible to reframe the thoughts to something more positive and probably more realistic. Instead of thinking 'I am a failure', the individual might think 'I did not manage it this time'. Instead of 'my boss doesn't rate me', they might think 'my boss doesn't think I am quite ready for this job yet'. Instead of 'my colleagues will think that I am useless', they could consider 'I know my colleagues respect me for what I bring to the team. They probably really empathise with what I am going through right now – after all, who hasn't been through this kind of thing?'. The resulting behaviour might then be more productive as they ask their boss which skills they need to further develop and appeal to their colleagues for some emotional support. In the example given

**Activating event:**
*I was rejected after a job interview*

**Thought:**
*I'll never get out of this job*

**Behaviour:**
*I stop applying for other roles*

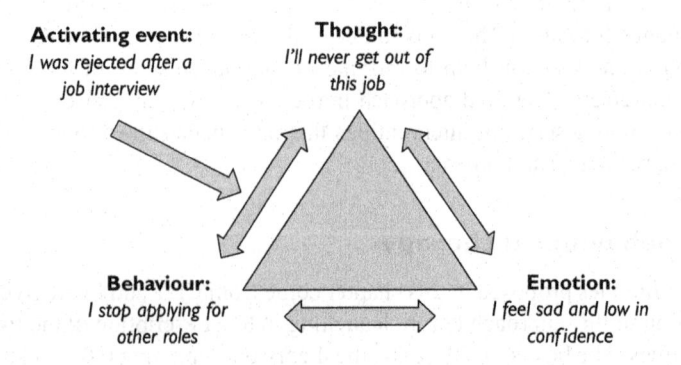

**Emotion:**
*I feel sad and low in confidence*

*Figure 7.1* The negative CBT model. (Source: the author.)

I want to go for it, but am I good enough? 85

**Activating event:**
*I was rejected after a job interview*

**Thought:**
*I didn't make it this time, but I can see where I went wrong*

**Behaviour:**
*I start developing my skills and apply next time round*

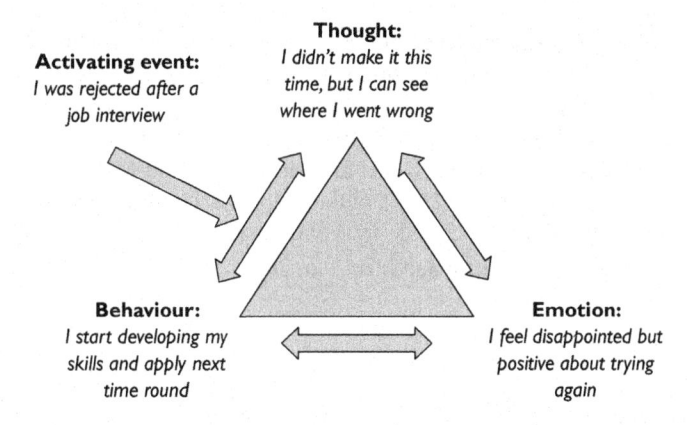

**Emotion:**
*I feel disappointed but positive about trying again*

*Figure 7.2* The positive CBT model. (Source: the author.)

above, the negative thought 'I'll never get out of this job' could be replaced by 'I didn't make it this time but I can see where I went wrong'. This more realistic assessment of the event could be empowering for the individual, as they see that there are practical steps that they could take that might have an impact on their chances in the future. This then makes them feel a little more in control of their own destiny and hopeful that there might be a more positive outcome next time round. This more positive cycle of thoughts is illustrated in Figure 7.2.

## What's the evidence base?

Cognitive behavioural therapy is one of the most widely researched psychological interventions. Not only have a number of meta-analyses been published, but there have also been meta-analyses of meta-analyses conducted, exploring the effects of CBT on a range of different conditions.

There is clear support for the idea that irrational negative beliefs lead to psychological distress and that rational negative beliefs lead to what they call adaptive behaviours, such as problem solving and skill acquisition (Dryden, 2005). The links between beliefs and behaviour have been quite well established (see Szentagotai & Jones, 2010 for a review). The links between irrational beliefs and emotions are a bit more mixed but, in general, the research supports this (David, 2014).

The research supports the effectiveness of CBT for a range of conditions (such as pain management, anxiety and depression), for different client groups (children, adults, both clinical and non-clinical populations) and different formats (one to one, groups) (David, 2014).

*(continued)*

*(continued)*

There has also been some evidence of the value of CBT with non-clinical populations (often described as cognitive behavioural coaching or CBC), and the evidence suggests that CBT has an impact on work-related behaviour. The approach has been shown to reduce perfectionism (Kearns, Forbes, & Gardiner, 2007), procrastination (Karas & Spada, 2009) and work stress (Gardiner, Kearns, & Tiggemann, 2013), and to improve time-management (Kearns, Gardiner, & Marshall, 2008), workplace well-being, goal attainment and resilience (Grant, Curtayne, & Burton, 2009).

## Why it works

The theory that underpins CBT was outlined earlier in the chapter. The secret lies in the links between thoughts, emotions and behaviour. The theory holds that these three things are inextricably linked and each of them has an impact on the other two. Behaviour and emotions can both be difficult to change on their own – it is difficult to simply decide to behave more confidently or decide to feel happier, but thoughts can be easier to manipulate. If it is possible to identify and articulate the specific thought that is causing trouble, it may be possible to make a conscious decision to replace one thought with another. If this happens successfully, then there will be an automatic shift in both emotions and behaviour as they align themselves with the new thought pattern.

The theory may sound straightforward but it is not necessarily easy to put it into practice, and clients need to be committed to the process and be prepared to practise the approach between coaching sessions.

## The ABCDE model

### Introduction

Developed by Ellis (1962), the ABCDE model is the classic framework for CBT interventions and is based on the assumptions behind the two CBT models presented above in Figures 7.1 and 7.2. The acronym ABCDE stands for:

**A: the activating event** – the situation or context that has made the individual feel negative in some way;

**B: the beliefs** – the cognitive thoughts that emanated from the event itself;

**C: the consequences** – the feelings and behaviour that were the result of the beliefs;

# I want to go for it, but am I good enough? 87

**D: the disputing beliefs** – the alternative thoughts that could help to reframe the experience;

**E: the effective new approach** – which the individual could put into practice next time.

The model is particularly useful when working with clients who seem to have been particularly effected by a single event. This event could be an incident at work, negative feedback or a hurtful comment from a colleague or friend, a less than successful internship or job, or an unsuccessful job search. The CBT techniques are often useful for preparing clients for interviews, and this model can be effective if the client reveals that they have had a difficult history with their job interviews.

## How to use

### Step 1: introduce the theory

When using this approach with clients it is useful first to introduce the concepts. The disaggregation of the beliefs and consequences is sometimes challenging to grasp, and it can take the two of you some time to unpick the differences. The particular choice of words used can confound the distinction. It is common to use the language of *feeling* to express *thoughts* ('I felt like a failure' or 'I felt that I'd failed') and it is important to clarify what is a belief and what is an emotion. In this example, you could point out that 'failure' isn't an emotion and offer some alternatives such as sadness, anger, frustration, despair or humiliation – emotions that people commonly associate with the belief that they are a failure. Sharing the underlying principles with your clients in the first instance can allow you to explain why making the distinction between beliefs and emotions is important, and explaining that it is sometimes difficult to separate the two can allow you to approach the exercise as a shared endeavour as you work through the story together.

### Step 2: looking back – Activating events, Beliefs and Consequences

In the next part of the conversation, the focus is on the past. Ask your client to tell you a bit about what happened and where their current negative emotions may have arisen. Then take them through the ABC part of the model, asking them to identify the Activating event and then to unpick the Beliefs and the Consequences. It can be useful to write these down. Committing the ideas to paper serves two purposes. First, the process of writing the ideas down helps to crystalise their thinking, as your clients need to identify their thoughts quite precisely in order to put a name to them. The second benefit that can be conferred by having a written record is that it gives your client a chance to look at their story in black and white. This can allow for additional reflection. The analysis could look something like this:

> **Activating event**: my last presentation went badly wrong.
>
> **Beliefs**: I am just no good at presentations; I can never remember what to say; I am bound to mess up the presentation at the job interview next week.
>
> **Consequences**: I am feeling enormously anxious about the whole event next week; I know I will not do myself justice; I am spending so much time thinking about the presentation I am not preparing for the interview itself; a bit of me wants to call the whole thing off.

### Step 3: looking forwards – Disputing the beliefs and identifying Effective new approaches

In this part of the conversation the focus shifts from what has happened in the past to what might happen in the future, as you **D**ispute the beliefs and discuss the **E**ffective new approaches that your clients might try. As with most good coaching practice, the ideas discussed in this part of the intervention are likely to have more impact if they are generated by the client themselves. But if your client seems to have run out of steam on their own, then some gentle tentative suggestions from you can stimulate further thinking on their part. The analysis might run along these lines:

> **Disputing**: I messed up last time because I did not prepare thoroughly enough. I am not actually bad at presentations, I just did not know the subject. I am actually quite good at interviews, so even if I do not ace the presentation, I may still be able to convince them that I'd be good at the job. Which I would.
>
> **Effective new approach**: first, I am going to prepare differently. I am going to write out every single word I am going to say and learn it off by heart. Second, I am going to put aside an hour each day from now till the interview on Tuesday to focus on interview questions.

### In practice

As noted below, one of the things that makes these techniques so effective is that clients are encouraged to continue their own self-coaching outside the sessions. As such, it is important that they understand the technique and how it works. It is useful to have a discussion about how they can reinforce their new thinking and make sure that they give the new approach a chance.

This approach is suitable for one-to-one work, but is so personal that it is less effective in a group setting. It should be conducted within a session, but its impact will be considerably stronger if your client is encouraged to practise this on their own between sessions. It's almost a style of thinking that needs to become a habit

I want to go for it, but am I good enough? 89

and therefore will have much less impact if it only happens within the coaching sessions themselves.

| | |
|---|---|
| One to one | ✓ |
| Group sessions | x |
| Within the session | ✓ |
| As a self-directed intersessional task | ✓ |
| Initial career choice | ✓ |
| Career changes | ✓ |
| Indicative timing | 30 + minutes |

## Thinking errors: from PITS to PETS

### Introduction

Performance Inhibiting Thoughts are PITS and Performance Enhancing Thoughts are PETS. The idea behind this technique is that clients are encouraged to identify the negative thoughts or ideas that are holding them back or making them feel unconfident (their PITS), and should make a conscious decision to replace them with other thoughts or phrases that are more likely to empower them and make them feel confident enough to do their best (their PETS).

In the introduction to the chapter the idea of faulty thinking was introduced. This is a broad term that includes a range of types of thinking errors. These are specific thoughts or ideas that are not grounded in reality and that can link with both emotions and behaviour, resulting in people who feel more negative about themselves and their ability, and who do not perform as well as they can.

### How to use

#### Step 1: identify the faulty thinking

If you suspect that there may be a negative thought that is holding your client back, the first thing to do is to raise it with them. Reflect their exact words back to them and ask them to explore it in a bit more depth. 'You have said that you are rubbish at interviews. Where does that idea come from?' or 'what did you mean when you said that you were rubbish at interviews?'. A key definition of a thinking error is that it is not grounded in reality, so it is first important to explore whether there is good reason behind your client's negative thought. If it turns out that, yes, in fact they are genuinely rubbish at interviews, then you have a different challenge on your hands, as you work out, together, what is making them perform poorly and what can be done. But if, as is probably more often the case, their beliefs are grounded in an isolated incident or an overly negative interpretation of an event, then this CBT technique may be of use.

## Step 2: articulate the PIT

Once you have ascertained that the negative thought is both unhelpful and untrue, it can be useful to spend some time with your client identifying the emotions and behaviour that may be associated with the thought. This will make sure that your client understands the impact that the thoughts have on their behaviour and the potential implications for their future and, hopefully, this will motivate them to engage with the technique. You could use the ABC model described above or draw the triangle shown in Figure 7.1 at the start of the chapter and encourage them to fill it in for themselves. It is important to get your client to crystalise their negative thought and capture it in a succinct form of words. This is their Performance Inhibiting Thought.

## Step 3: articulate the PET

Your client then needs to identify a more positive Performance Enhancing Thought that can replace their PIT and that will make them feel more confident and positive. It is important that they choose a form of words that works for them, so do resist the temptation to offer your own ideas. 'I am rubbish at interviews' could be swapped to 'I've got the skills needed to do the job' or 'I am great at developing rapport', or 'they'd be lucky to have me'. This PET needs to be grounded in reality, and it can help your client if you spend some time talking through the evidence base for their new thought: it is going to be a much more effective technique if your client genuinely believes themselves, so it is important that this part of the process is not rushed. You could discuss how they know they are good at developing rapport and ask when they last demonstrated this ability and how that might help them at their next interview. As with the PIT, your client needs to be able to articulate their PET in a clear succinct phrase. Your client then needs to train themselves to notice every time their PIT pops into their head, and to consciously and deliberately replace it with their newly identified PET. Saying their PET out loud a few times can help to reinforce its power and help to make sure it sticks.

As you as a coach become more familiar with this approach, you will hone your instinct for picking up on faulty thinking, but there are some types of errors that are quite common and it may be useful to be aware of these.

| Thinking error | What it means | PIT to PET |
| --- | --- | --- |
| All or nothing thinking | This describes the black and white thinking that is often seen in perfectionists. All or nothing thinking can sometimes lead to people who decide not to take action for fear of failing. | PIT: 'There's no point even getting the details of that job – I do not stand a chance.' PET: 'It might be worth a go. I've got a lot of what they are asking for and it will be good experience at any rate.' |

| | | |
|---|---|---|
| Magnification | This kind of thinking exaggerates negative experiences, the chances of something bad happening, or the potential impact of a negative experience. Again, this can discourage an individual from action or can lower their self-confidence as they focus in on the negative parts. | PIT: 'I found a spelling mistake on my application form – I've completely ruined my chances.'<br>PET: 'My personal statement was really well written.' |
| Minimisation | Minimisation occurs when an individual fails to acknowledge the positive contribution that they have made and instead ascribes their success to luck or to others. This kind of thinking can make them feel less positive about themselves than they might, and can make it difficult for them to paint themselves in the best light. | PIT: 'They are just being kind to say that.'<br>PET: 'They wouldn't say it if they did not mean it.' |
| Personalisation | This kind of thinking error sees people conceptualise negative treatment as a personal slight – their focus is on them personally, not on the behaviour. The problem here is that this can lead to a kind of fatalism, where the individual doesn't make any attempt to change their behaviour because they do not see that this could help. | PIT: 'She just doesn't like me.'<br>PET: 'I've got a lot to offer here.' |
| Focusing on the negatives | When getting feedback of any sort it can sometimes be difficult to hear it in a balanced way. Focusing on the negatives refers to the times when the impact of a single negative comment seems to outweigh any number of positives. The risks here are that the individual will lose confidence in their ability. | PIT: 'One of the evaluation sheets said it wasn't useful.'<br>PET: '24 evaluation sheets were very positive.' |

## Psychological capital

The idea of 'capital' has been in mainstream career literature for some time. Originally conceptualised by the French sociologist Pierre Bourdieu as an analysis of the nature of power in society, the concept has been widely applied and its impact can be seen within career development. There are different facets of capital that have been identified. Human capital refers to 'what you know' and, in terms of employability, refers to job-related knowledge or skills. Social capital refers to the useful people in your network who can support your career development and help you to meet your career goals. Career capital then refers to the totality of the learning acquired throughout an individual's entire career, which is defined at the individual level, the organisational level and the industry level. Psychological capital is the subject of this part of the chapter and is described as simply 'who you are'.

The construct is defined as consisting of four elements: *confidence, optimism, hope* and *resilience*. As an overarching construct, psychological capital has been shown to lead to better work performance and job satisfaction, but each individual element has also been shown to be fairly influential in career development, both in terms of making choices and in actually getting jobs. *Confidence* comes up time and again in career development and is the key focus of this chapter. *Optimism* is a general sense that things are likely to turn out well. Fred Luthans, who is perhaps the most influential writer in this field, emphasises the need for 'realistic optimism': it is not about closing your mind to the bad things that could happen, more about seeing the positives and being open and creative about considering solutions. *Hope* is defined a bit differently in the academic literature from the way it is most often used in normal conversation. When used in everyday conversation, the word 'hope' is usually synonymous with a wish: 'I hope I win the lottery this weekend'; 'I hope the weather's fine tomorrow'. In this academic context its meaning is a bit more complex and specifically defined as it refers to a situation where an individual has a goal, can see the path towards the goal and believes that they can reach the goal (described as agency). Finally, *resilience* is the ability to cope when things go wrong – the ability to bounce back. PsyCap (as it is referred to in the literature), then, is a combination of these four aspects and it is described as a higher-order construct, which means that the four aspects have more impact together than the sum of the four constructs. PsyCap is not just a collection of the four aspects but the added value that comes from the combination of the constructs.

### How to use

Luthans et al. (2006) offer what they describe as a micro-intervention, which (see the box below for more details) has been shown to make a difference to levels of PsyCap in just two hours. Their intervention focuses explicitly on enhancing hope and resilience, but they suggest that these two interventions will increase individuals' levels of confidence and optimism by stealth.

### PsyCap 1: increasing hope

This intervention involves three steps, focusing on each of the three aspects of hope described above: goals, plans and agency. The intervention, as described by Luthans and colleagues, was planned for a group context. It can be adapted to one-to-one work, but it is great, for once, to be starting with something that was explicitly designed with groups in mind.

STEP 1: GOALS

Ask participants to identify a goal that they want to work with in this session. The goal can be large or small but your clients need to make sure that it meets the following three criteria: it needs to be concrete and measurable ('I want to be promoted' rather than 'I want to be successful'); it needs to be an approach rather than an avoidance goal ('I want to be promoted' rather than 'I want to make sure I do not lose my job'); there need to be a number of sub-goals identified as steps on the way ('I need to finish my management qualification'; 'I need to get a mentor').

STEP 2: PATHWAYS

Ask your participants to brainstorm as many different pathways to this goal as they can. In keeping with the rules of brainstorming, you should encourage your participants to be uncritical of their ideas at this stage and not to rule anything out because it is not practical. Then, working now within smaller groups, invite the members of the group to help to identify any alternative pathways. In the last part of the session, participants are asked to start thinking about resources, working out what would be needed for each possible option. All options are still on the table at this stage – they should not yet be ruling anything out because the resource demands are too high.

STEP 3: OVERCOMING OBSTACLES

In this final step, participants are asked to consider any potential barriers. They then present their barriers to the other members of their group and, collaboratively, the group should identify routes around the obstacles. Only at the end of this should the participants be invited to make judgements about which options should be rejected and which they plan to pursue.

## *PsyCap 2: building resilience*

Resilient people, those who can cope with setbacks, have been shown to be those who have a) a staunch view of reality, b) a deep and entrenched belief that life is meaningful and c) an ability to adapt to a changing context (Coutu, 2002). This second technique is aimed at developing these qualities. Your overall level of resilience is determined by a combination of asset factors, risk factors and influence processes. Asset factors are those that increase an individual's resilience – they could include having a good education or coming from a secure home. Risk factors are those that can reduce resilience, such as the absence of social support or the lack of clear aims. Influence factors, then, are the processes in place that aim to enhance assets and reduce risks. Assets and risks are often grounded in early life, but they can be changed, added to or reframed later on.

STEP 1: REACTIONS TO SETBACKS

Ask your participants to identify a recent work-related setback. It can be large or small, but should just be one that they are willing to work with during the exercise. They should then write down their immediate reactions to the setback.

STEP 2: A STAUNCH VIEW OF REALITY

The facilitator should spend some time explaining the idea of a staunch view of reality, with pragmatic and realistic expectations, and discussing the idea of control and the importance of identifying what is within their control and what is not. Participants are then invited to reconsider their setback in terms of three questions. What was the impact of the setback? What aspects were within their control? What options are open to them?

Once this is complete, you could try and really fix the process in their minds by asking them to repeat the whole thing with a personal setback they have faced.

## *In practice*

As mentioned above, these interventions were designed for a group setting. They were designed with the workplace in mind and the groups were intended to be fairly small, with perhaps six–ten participants in each. Whilst it may be possible to scale this up and run the exercises with larger groups, the role of the facilitator would become diluted and this may lead to a less valuable session overall.

| | |
|---|---|
| One to one | ✓ |
| Group sessions | ✓ |
| Within the session | ✓ |
| As a self-directed intersessional task | ✗ |
| Initial career choice | ✓ |
| Career changes | ✓ |
| Indicative timing | 45 minutes |

## Why it works

The literature tells us that the four elements of Psychological Capital (self-efficacy, optimism, hope and resilience) all have benefits for those seeking to change career. Self-efficacy is perhaps the most well documented of these, and there is substantial evidence of the impact of self-efficacy on career choice (for example, Lent, Brown, & Hackett, 1994) and career development (Kanfer, Wanberg, & Kantrowitz, 2001) in a wide range of contexts. Positive correlations too have been identified between self-efficacy and job satisfaction (Judge & Bono, 2001). Optimism has been shown to help with resource development (Carver, Scheier, & Segerstrom, 2010) and the development of networks and social support (Brissette, Scheier, & Carver, 2002), and a linear link between optimism and job satisfaction has been identified (Munyon et al., 2010). Hope has been described as a form of positive work engagement (Simmons & Nelson, 2001) and higher levels of hope have been shown to lead to increased job satisfaction (Duggleby, Cooper, & Penz, 2009). Matos, Neushotz, Griffin and Fitzpatrick (2010) found a positive correlation between the resilience and job satisfaction of nurses.

Evidence too suggests links between these elements and successful career changes. Bimrose and Hearne (2012) highlight the value of resilience for career change, and a positive correlation between the goal-setting element of hope and job search outcomes is well documented (Saks & Ashforth, 2000). Positive emotions such as optimism have been shown to enhance creativity and relationships (Fredrickson, 2009), both of which have been shown to improve the chances of making a successful career change (Kanfer, Wanberg, & Kantrowitz, 2001; Van Hoye, Van Hooft, & Lievens, 2009; Wanberg, Kanfer, & Banas, 2000).

## What's the evidence base?

The box above offers plenty of evidence that the four aspects of Psychological Capital have a positive impact on career choice and job search. There is also evidence that the PsyCap interventions described here have an impact on participants' levels of hope, optimism, resilience and self-efficacy (Luthans et al., 2006) and, of particular interest to us, the intervention has been shown to have a positive impact within career coaching contexts. Chen & Lim (2012) applied PsyCap to job search approaches with a large sample of people who had recently been made redundant. They found clear evidence that the PsyCap intervention was positively related to levels of perceived employability and problem-facing approaches. Perceived employability has, in turn, been shown to link with adaptability, a successful job search and a more creative job search.

Chapter 8

# Part of me wants it, but part of me wants something else

## Introduction

Some of the most difficult career conflicts to resolve are those that take place inside your client's own mind. The complexities of people's lives and people's identities mean that it is not uncommon for people to struggle to reconcile what they *want* with what they feel they *should* do, or to balance two conflicting aspects of their identity, for example, being a fulfilled worker and a good parent. A good understanding of the two competing arguments will not automatically lead to a resolution, but, without a certain degree of clarity, a solution is much less likely to be found.

This chapter offers two techniques that may be useful to you when working with clients who are struggling to unpick their inner dilemmas. The first is the Empty Chair technique. This is a tool that is adapted from gestalt therapy and provides a mechanism to help an individual to separate and examine the different arguments going on in their minds. The second technique is Person-centred Dialogue, which is closely based on the humanist approach of Carl Rogers and that has been enormously influential in career practice. It is a powerful technique that allows people the space to unjumble their thoughts and reflect on their own feelings.

## The empty chair

### Introduction

At the heart of this technique is the idea that separating out the different strands of competing arguments within a person's mind is a useful starting point to finding a resolution. Our thoughts are complex and rival options, values and priorities can easily get tangled up in a foggy cloud of confusion in our minds. When they do, it is hard to unravel them and, whilst they are all jumbled up, it is very difficult to know how to respond or to work out the meaning of each one individually and identify how they all fit together. The empty chair technique can help people to isolate each of the competing strands of thought and consider them individually. The technique is particularly valuable for people who are feeling confused or perhaps who have not had the opportunity to explore their feelings about the issues in depth.

## How to use

For this exercise you need to have a third empty chair in your room. Although the chair will stay empty during the exercise, the physical presence of the chair tends to help clients to assume the roles they are playing more convincingly.

### Step 1: the pre-dialogue stage – identify the tension

The first step is to spend some time with your client helping them to identify the nature of their internal dilemmas. It is useful to first ask your client to describe the competing voices and ask them to explain the different messages or to elucidate, as far as they can, the nature of the dilemma. Once you have clarified the two (or more) competing drivers, you could suggest to your client that it can be helpful to think of the different ideas as coming from two different sides of their identity. Ask them to envisage the two sides as different versions of themselves and perhaps give each one a label ('Successful Pete' and 'Worthy Pete'). Then invite your client to imagine one of these embodied versions of themselves sitting in the empty chair.

### Step 2: the opposition stage – the dialogue

Start by asking your client to describe the person (i.e., the personified aspect of themselves) that they are now envisaging in the chair. Ask them to talk about their posture and the meaning this is conveying. Perhaps try to find out something about the voice they are using and the messages that their tone is conveying. Then ask your client to find out as much as they can about this part of themselves. Your client could ask them to explain their point of view, the option that they think your client should pursue and ask them to describe the reasons for their choices. See what your client would like to ask this part of themselves. Is there a particular question to which they would like to know the answer? Your role during this phase is to encourage your client to express themselves fully. You might want to ask your client some questions to clarify their thinking or to explore the issue in more depth. You could invite them to think about the emotions, attitudes, assumptions or actions associated with this version of themselves.

When this dialogue has finished, and your client has explored this part of their identity in as much depth as possible, you should then ask them to invite the other version of themselves, the embodiment of the other point of view or identity, to sit in the empty chair and repeat the process. Again, ask them to imagine this aspect of themselves sitting in the empty chair. Invite them to comment on how this version of themselves looks, what emotions are being conveyed and what kind of voice and tone are being used. At this stage you don't want to interrupt their flow by making comparisons with the earlier version of themselves, but you might choose to note down any striking similarities or differences to follow up later.

A final step could be to invite the two aspects of your client to have a dialogue with each other. What does each version of themselves think of the other version? Is there anything they would like to say to or ask the other?

*Step 3: the integration stage – the debrief*

When the process has finished, it is your turn to have a conversation with your client. The *integration* in the description of this stage refers to the process of integrating the two or more parts of the client's self back into a single whole. During this stage you are aiming to encourage your client to reflect on the exercise, identify any new insights and consider whether there is any change to how they see their future. You could start by asking them how they found the exercise and whether there was anything that surprised them or that was particularly notable about the two conversations. It may be interesting to ascertain whether their opinion of either side of themselves has changed, and which of the voices now sounds louder or more convincing.

## In practice

With this technique, again, it is worth reminding ourselves about the issue of boundaries. Internal dilemmas can have a significant impact on career choices and on people's ability to make good decisions and put their plans into action. It is important that we don't shy away from the difficult topics, and we would be doing our clients, and indeed our profession as a whole, a disservice if we did not acknowledge the full range of issues that are potentially influential. The empty chair technique has been shown to help clients to resolve their inner dilemmas and thus it feels like a good tool to include in this book. But tensions such as these can be deep rooted and complex, and it may be that, as career coaches, the discussions take us out of our comfort zones and perhaps beyond our expertise.

We can mitigate against any possible risks to our clients by being reflective about our own practice and by being open with our clients. Before embarking on this technique it might be useful to have a conversation with your client about the possibility that some deeper issues might surface. You don't want to alarm them unduly, but it could be useful to acknowledge up front that, for some people, the issues can be profound and the exercise can be powerful. You could check with your client that they are comfortable with proceeding, and perhaps touch on how they think they will know that they have gone as far as they want to – how they will know when to stop. You could check in with them during the exercise and make sure that they are still feeling OK to carry on. And, if you do find that the exercise has gone far enough, then you can gently encourage them to close things back down again, and talk with them about whether it might be useful for them to make an appointment with a counsellor of another sort in order to work this issue through.

| | |
|---|---|
| One to one | ✓ |
| Group sessions | ✗ |
| Within the session | ✓ |
| As a self-directed intersessional task | ✗ |
| Initial career choice | ✓ |
| Career changes | ✓ |
| Indicative timing | 30–40 minutes |

## Case study

Anna felt torn. She had worked in the advertising industry for most of her life. This had been great fun in her twenties, and she had loved the fast pace and the vibrant social life. In her thirties, when her children came along, Anna was able to use her creative skills and her excellent network to set herself up as a freelance copywriter, working on a consultancy basis for some of her old clients. This had worked perfectly whilst her children were young as it allowed her to work from home and to fit in her paid writing around her childcare responsibilities. She made a good living and as a family they had a lovely lifestyle that allowed her children to take part in a wide range of activities and experiences that she felt were important for them.

But, a few years down the line, she realised that she wasn't happy. The work was still coming in, but she had found herself a little pigeon-holed and found that she was doing nothing but writing copy for car manufacturers. These were good and lucrative contracts to get, and her clients were happy with the work she did, but the subject matter meant nothing to her and she began to feel trapped. She had some clear ideas about the kinds of things that she wanted to do, but none of the job options that appealed to her would earn the kind of money to which the family had become accustomed.

Anna felt completely trapped. She didn't see any way out of the situation that she had got herself into and didn't feel that there were any options. She had noticed that she had started to blame everyone else, and felt that resentment towards both her children and her husband was beginning to creep in and she didn't understand what was going on.

Her career coach suggested that Anna could try the empty chair technique and first Anna put Anna-The-Mother in the empty chair and explored this aspect of her identity.

*(continued)*

*(continued)*

The coach asked Anna to talk to her Mother Self and find out more about how she felt. The conversation proved revealing and affirming to Anna, as she explored what it meant to her to be a good mother, to identify whose standards she was trying to live up to and to examine what she thought her children wanted and needed.

Anna was then encouraged to put Anna-The-Worker in the empty chair and she had a conversation with her Worker Self. Here she delved into her motivations as a worker and explored what career success meant to her and where this notion came from.

The conversations with the different aspects of her identity helped Anna to understand her own position more clearly. Separating the two competing sets of values allowed her to see each fully, unencumbered by the 'yes but' thoughts that characterised her usual train of thought.

For Anna, the most revealing things about the conversations were the questions about where her notion of a 'good worker' or a 'good mother' came from, and the discussions gave her considerable food for thought. Anna resolved to go home and talk to her children and her husband about which aspects of their current lifestyle were really important to them, and which were not.

## Why it works

The word 'gestalt' is a German one. It doesn't seem to have a direct English equivalent but refers to ideas of a pattern or a meaningful whole. The idea at the heart of gestalt therapy is that people should be encouraged to explore the nature of their authentic, faithful, subjective experience of life and should understand themselves within their personal context. Change, according to gestalt theory, can only take place when people are fully self-aware (Perls, Hefferline, & Goodman, 1951): a sharp focus on the present can result in new understandings about the future. This is described as the *paradoxical theory of change* (Beisser, 1970). The theory holds that our actions will often fail to lead us to fulfilling our goals if they are based on flawed awareness. If we don't really understand our starting point – our present – then we can't possibly map out a route to our goal. The focus of any intervention, then, is to try and enhance self-awareness, encouraging people to engage with the present experience and their authentic selves.

Central to gestalt therapy is the idea of getting *in contact* with oneself. This refers to the idea of representing particular facets of one's mind as different versions of oneself – *the critical me* or *the fearful me*. The gestalt therapist then facilitates a meeting between an individual and one imagined embodied aspect of themselves (Stevenson, 2004). Through this virtual meeting, the individual has the opportunity to learn more about this particular aspect of themselves, and can explore the emotional, cognitive and behavioural meanings associated with this part of themselves.

## What's the evidence base?

The effectiveness of gestalt therapy in general is fairly robust, with a meta-analysis comprising 38 separate studies suggesting that its impact was comparable with a number of other well-respected approaches, including person-centred therapy, discussed in more depth below (Bretz, Heekerens, & Schmitz, 1994). More specifically, evidence suggests that the empty chair exercise can have a significant impact in reducing inner dilemmas or *intrapsychic conflicts*.

The empty chair technique has been shown to enhance self-awareness, increasing the depth of understanding (Greenberg & Dompierre, 1981). It has been shown to help clients challenge maladaptive and self-critical beliefs, and to come to terms with negative beliefs (Kirkpatrick, 2005). It has an impact on people's ability to make a change, reducing indecision and increasing the likelihood that they will meet their goals (Clarke & Greenberg, 1986). Finally, although not specifically aimed at resolving external conflicts, it has been shown that the empty chair technique can have a positive impact on relationships (Johnson & Greenberg, 1985).

The eagle-eyed amongst you will have noticed that these references are not particularly up to date. Most of the large-scale studies took place in the late 20th century and, since then, there has been much less interest in this approach within the academic community. There are exceptions to this. González-Ramírez and colleagues conducted a small-scale study in Mexico in 2017 that showed that gestalt therapy had a positive impact on the symptoms of depression (González-Ramírez et al., 2017). Asadnia, Azar and Torabzadeh (2014) showed that it had an impact on the sleeping patterns of female students with headaches. But it is fair to say that the rate of research has reduced dramatically since its heyday in the 1980s and that the papers published lately are not always mainstream, large scale or published in the major journals.

This lack of recent evidence indicates a lack of interest rather than any concerns about the value or effectiveness of this approach, and illustrates that academic research in psychology is at the mercy of fashion as much as any other arena.

## Person-centred dialogue

### Introduction

Both in terms of underpinning philosophy and in terms of skills, the person-centred approach has had an enormous influence on coaching and career practice. It is introduced here as a technique that can be particularly effective when helping clients to make sense of their internal dilemmas, but it stems from a much broader philosophical position.

The person-centred approach (also known as client-centred, humanistic or non-directive) was introduced by Carl Rogers in the 1950s and constituted a third paradigm in psychology, alongside behaviourism and the psychodynamic ideas of Freud. Person-centred therapy is based on some assumptions about human nature, revolutionary in the mid-20th century and still widely respected today. One core idea is the *self-actualising tendency* that assumes that it is part of the human condition to want to improve and do well and to better ourselves. This is explained as a biological tendency rather than a moral imperative: by this Rogers means that it is something that we are all irrevocably drawn to, rather than something that society has decided we ought to do. Yet Rogers notes that, despite the existence of this tendency, which is present in us all, we don't always act in ways that improve our lives: sometimes we choose not to take advantage of opportunities, we decide not to work hard, or we shout at those we love. According to Rogers, this destructive behaviour is the result of barriers that prevent us from becoming what he describes as a *fully-functioning person*. Rogers suggests that the tendency to self-actualise is always present, but other things can prevent us from working towards a more positive future. These barriers could be internal psychological ones, such as fear or a conflict of values or identities, or could stem from the outside world, presenting more practical challenges such as financial difficulties or a lack of opportunities.

The second key assumption underpinning person-centred approaches is that people are their own best experts. Rogers believed that it is only the individual themselves who will really understand the complexities of their lives and their hopes, fears, dreams and identities. Even with the most empathic of coaches, and the most in depth of coaching relationships, the coach will only have an insight into a very thin slice of the client's world. This thin slice can sometimes lead the coach to offer insightful new ways to look at the world, but it will only ever be based on a fragment of the information that the client themselves can access. As such, the client themselves is in a far better position to solve their own problems and generate their own creative ideas than anyone else.

A person-centred approach, then, assumes that a client wants to improve their lives and assumes that they are best placed to know how to do it. The coach's role is to enable the client to find their own path.

### How to use it

The overriding aim of this kind of dialogue is to get the client to hear their own ideas – their *inner voice* as it is sometimes called – and at the heart of the approach lies the coach's active listening skills. The coach needs to listen and needs to be psychologically present and emotionally engaged as the client unravels their thoughts and unburdens their heart.

This is an approach that relies on skills rather than process. The coach should have no framework that they are working within and no prescribed plan or set of questions. Above all, the coach should try hard not to make any assumptions. The conversation flows where the client takes it, it covers the content that the client feels is relevant, and it ends when the client feels that they have poured their thoughts out.

The coach is not passive. The level of attentive listening required and the empathy that goes along with it can be surprisingly draining; but the coach is likely to be more subdued – quieter, stiller and softer, than in some other approaches to coaching. Your job in a person-centred dialogue is to listen and understand. More than in any other type of coaching, you are trying to get into your client's shoes and have a good walk around in them.

The coach assumes a position of non-directivity, which means that, in terms of both the content and structure of the conversation, the client is in the driving seat. As the coach, you might spot that there is a particular issue that your client is struggling with and you might ask them whether it might be useful to explore it in depth. If they feel that this would be of value, you could start off by asking a very broad open question such as 'tell me a bit more about it', and then wait for them to tell their story. It can be helpful at this stage to sit back, physically, in your chair, to indicate that they should take charge, and being still and attentive is particularly important as any note taking or hand gestures from you may distract your client from their story. Your role is to encourage your client to say everything that is in their minds about the topic, and the skills highlighted below can help you to draw your client out.

When you feel that your client has explored the issue in depth, you could ask them whether they agree, saying something like 'we've talked about this for a while now, and I wonder whether you feel that you have been able to get all of your ideas out?'. If they agree that they have explored this enough, you could change tempo and revert to a more typical coaching style, inviting your client to reflect on what they themselves said during the person-centred exercise, and ask what conclusions they could draw or what action they feel that they should take in the light of this.

## Skills

The skills used within a person-centred dialogue are not very different from those that you might use in any other coaching conversation, but they take centre-stage in this approach and, as there are no frameworks or exercises to rely on, the power of the approach lies exclusively in the execution of the skills. As such, it may be useful to reflect on the skills themselves and how they can best be used within a person-centred dialogue.

### Active listening

The ability not just to listen, but to demonstrate that you are listening, is a skill that you have come across many times before and will use in every career conversation you have. In a person-centred dialogue it becomes even more central to the value of the conversation. It is important to remember that you are not just listening to the words but to the tone and the voice and the expression, and noticing not only what is being said but also what is not being said. One of the most useful things you can do too is to notice the emotions you are feeling in your own body. If you find, as your client tells their tale, that you are feeling a bit confused or exhausted, then it may well be that you are picking up on your client's confusion or exhaustion. This is known as *generative empathic listening* and can be an enormously insightful part of the process. If you notice that you are feeling a sensation that may reflect your client's emotions, it can be valuable to share it with your client. This can help them consider their own feelings and can cement the working alliance as you are illustrating your empathy very clearly. It is important, though, to offer your comment tentatively, both because you might be mis-reading the feeling and to ensure that your comment doesn't turn the attention away from your client and on to you. You might use a form of words such as 'as you talk there, I find that I feel a bit overwhelmed. I wonder if I'm picking up on something you are feeling. Is that something you recognise at all?'

### Pace

During the person-centred dialogue it is important to make sure that you are giving your clients enough space to explore their thoughts thoroughly. If it comes in a little too soon, or is said with a little more enthusiasm than intended, even a supportive nod or a gentle 'mmm' can indicate to your client that you think they have finished talking and therefore cut them off. Make sure that you slow your pace right down and speak softly so that nothing that you say will stop them in their tracks or distract them from their train of thought if they aren't ready to stop.

### Non-judgemental approach

As coaches, being non-judgemental is often one of our most strongly held principles. This principle is important in all of your career conversations, but in person-centred dialogue it is useful to consider whether you are giving away any hints of an opinion in any way and to scrutinise all aspects of your practice to make very sure that you are not leading your client. The idea of leading through listening might sound a bit bizarre, but it's easy to convey assumptions in your responses to a story. If your client tells you that they have got a place at Oxford University, or that they are pregnant, your face might light up on the assumption that they are bound to feel delighted by this news. In fact, they might or might not be pleased by this turn of events, and a more neutral, but always attentive, response, along with a comment such as 'and how do you feel about that?' might allow your client to really think about what they themselves feel.

### Silence

One of the most powerful aspects of a person-centred dialogue is that your client has the opportunity not only to express their inner thoughts but also to hear themselves. To maximise the opportunity for this impact, you need to leave some time after they have finished talking to allow them to reflect on what they have just heard. You could wait until your client has finished speaking and then wait until they meet your eyes again (if they are still thinking, they are likely to be looking elsewhere), and then give them a gentle response (a nod, or a 'mmm') and wait to see whether this sets them talking again. It often will.

Silences can be an effective technique but can make you, as the coach, feel a little uncomfortable. If you are not someone who is naturally at ease during a long pause in a conversation it can be useful to bear in mind that the silence will feel far longer to you than it does to your client. They are busy processing their thoughts and reflecting on how they sounded and what they mean, and experiencing the emotions that accompany their story; you are just sitting in silence. You may want to consider whether to talk about silences as part of your contract with your client. At the start of your first conversation, when you are checking expectations and explaining your approach to coaching, you could explain that silence is a technique that you will be making use of, explaining that silence has been shown to be a useful way to stimulate thoughts. Adding a clause such as this during your first conversation may make you feel a little more comfortable holding the silence a little longer later during your conversation.

### Reflecting

This describes the technique of repeating a word or short phrase that your client has just said. In a person-centred dialogue it can serve two purposes. First, it can be a straightforward aspect of active listening, highlighting to your client that you are taking note of each word they are saying. Second, it can encourage your client to continue with their story, perhaps indicating a particular idea that they might like to explain further or a strong emotion that might be useful to reflect on.

### Non-directivity

Rogers' approach is sometimes referred to as 'non-directive coaching', highlighting how central this particular concept is to this style of intervention. There should be a zero-tolerance approach to anything that could influence your client. Directivity can manifest itself through overt recommendations or advice, through simply giving information, and even through the enthusiasm with which you respond to one or another of your client's ideas. At the end of a person-centred conversation, your client should have no inkling of the course of action that you personally would recommend.

## Questions and comments

Questions are used in person-centred conversations, but not often and with caution. Questions, in this context, are used more to help the client understand themselves better, and less to challenge or move them on. Questions should be supportive and open, and should be used only when the other skills above aren't enough to deepen your client's self-exploration. You may find that you want to comment on your client's story as they tell it. This can be a useful way to deepen the connection between you, and communicate your empathy and your unconditional positive regard, but, again, comments from you should be infrequent and tentative, and not make assumptions – phrases such as 'it sounds as though that was hard for you' or 'if I had been in your shoes I might have found that difficult. How was it for you?' can move the exploration on, whilst keeping the focus on your client. This is not the place for anecdotes, suggestions or amusing asides.

During coaching it is not uncommon for a client to ask their coach a direct question. There are, of course, different ways that you might choose to respond to this, depending on your coaching style, the relationship you have with your client and the nature of the question itself. But during a person-centred dialogue it would rarely be appropriate to respond directly. Rather than giving your own opinion, you need to find a form of words that will allow you to focus the conversation back onto your client, without appearing abrupt or sounding as though you are rejecting them. You could try a non-committal phrase such as 'that's a really hard one, isn't it?' or 'I'm not sure, I wonder where you would start with that?'. Again, this is something that you can contract for at the start of your coaching relationship, which might help you to feel comfortable saying 'I honestly think that you're in a better position to answer that one than I am'.

## In practice

As I mentioned above, this approach forms the basis of most coaching conversations, but takes things one step further and really puts the spotlight on the coaching skills. In some ways, then, it is a fairly easy one to incorporate into your practice – you are doing most of this already and it is great to challenge yourself and try to push yourself to use the skills as well as you can. But, whilst it is similar to standard coaching practice in terms of the skills, it can feel at odds with a more classic approach in terms of the process and tone. In general, coaches embrace the idea that having a structure to your conversations will make them more focused, more effective and will lead to more progress in a limited amount of time; moving the conversation on towards a goal becomes second nature for most of us. In a person-centred dialogue there is no imposed structure, and the conversation flows in the direction and at the pace determined by the client. Career coaching conversations are also, generally, quite positive in tone. We will often encourage and praise and will look for the positives in any story. This bias towards positivity is just the right attitude for many coaching conversations and is particularly valuable in techniques from positive psychology (Chapter 5) and solution-focused therapy (Chapter 12), but it needs to be more muted for an effective person-centred conversation. Person-centred dialogue is, then, a technique that is probably quite easy to incorporate in your practice but could be quite hard to master.

In a way, person-centred dialogue is a very simple technique – for the most part you are just sitting and listening. But doing this well is difficult and, perhaps especially for practitioners who are motivated to help and solve problems and move clients on, this more passive approach can take a bit of practice. Coaches sometimes find it difficult to bite their tongues when they feel that they can genuinely see what their client should do, or when their own personal experience has given them an understanding that they believe might add value to their client. But, with some focused practice, you will soon get used to slowing down and sitting back and allowing your client to lead the conversation, and you may find that it produces some unexpected results.

| | |
|---|---|
| One to one | ✓ |
| Group sessions | ✗ |
| Within the session | ✓ |
| As a self-directed intersessional task | ✗ |
| Initial career choice | ✓ |
| Career changes | ✓ |
| Indicative timing | This is a difficult one to predict. I find it often takes longer than I anticipate and I would be cautious about using it if working to a tight time schedule. |

## Why it works

The theory behind Rogers' approach is summed up by his 'necessary and sufficient core conditions'. Rogers argues that, for a positive therapeutic change to take place, three core conditions need to be met. Rogers suggests that the conditions all need to be present (i.e., are necessary) and that, if they are all there, then nothing else is needed for the change to happen (i.e., they are sufficient). First, there needs to be *empathy*, which is both experienced and communicated by the practitioner. Second, Rogers describes the importance of the practitioner being authentic and developing a genuine connection with the client. Rogers calls this *congruence* but it is akin to the

*(continued)*

*(continued)*

notion of a working alliance, which is a term used widely in the literature to explain a positive client/practitioner relationship. The third core condition is described as *unconditional positive regard*. This is the non-judgemental stance adopted by the practitioner that communicates their belief that the client is basically an OK person (that's the positive regard), and that this belief cannot be shifted and is not dependent (or conditional) on anything they say or any actions they do or have done.

According to Rogers, if these three conditions are met then the practitioner need do nothing else. Simply by being with the client, the practitioner's empathy, unconditional positive regard and authenticity will allow the client to express themselves, hear their own thoughts and reach their own conclusions. The practitioner then needs no frameworks and no specific exercises; the process is just one of a particular kind of listening.

As mentioned above, Rogers' approach is a broad one – akin to a philosophy or a world view. But it is introduced here as a specific technique – a set of skills that can be incorporated into a range of approaches. This dual interpretation of humanism can be explained by what Grant (1990) describes as the difference between *instrumental* and *principled* non-directivity. Principled non-directivity refers to the practice of those whose whole approach is underpinned by this theory. For those practitioners, this is a matter of philosophy or principle. The assumptions described in the introduction above reflect their world view and, as a consequence, they will believe that this is perhaps the only, or certainly the best, approach to practice. In contrast, person-centred dialogue is introduced in this book as an example of *instrumental non-directivity*. In this context, the person-centred dialogue is a set of techniques used alongside and in combination with a range of other techniques, and which is chosen in order to fulfil a particular goal: in this case, to allow clients to explore their conflicting internal views. Those embracing this idea of instrumental non-directivity acknowledge that other approaches may be needed at other times, but can capitalise on the benefits that person-centred dialogue confers when they feel that this will be particularly useful for their clients.

## The evidence base

There is considerable significant evidence that Rogers' three core conditions (empathy, unconditional positive regard (UPR) and congruence) are all critical parts of effective therapy (Kirschenbaum & Jourdan, 2005), but the evidence for their status as 'necessary and sufficient' conditions is less clear.

Research into therapeutic approaches tends to suggest that it doesn't matter what approach a practitioner takes, as long as the core conditions are met a positive change will happen. Orlinsky and Howard (1986) found that clients' perceptions of these qualities was more important than the qualities themselves. This is consistent with Rogers' condition that the UPR must be communicated and, in general, studies that use client ratings of empathy and UPR show more convincing positive outcomes than those that make use of observer ratings.

Sexton and Whiston (1994) highlight the importance of empathy in a meta-analysis that explored career counselling, but argue that empathy is possibly more complex than is usually considered. Bohart, Elliott, Greenberg and Watson (2002), who conducted a large meta-analysis involving over 3,000 participants and 47 different studies, found a medium positive effect between empathy and positive outcomes. Farber and Lane (2002) showed strong positive associations between UPR and therapeutic outcomes. For congruence the evidence is a bit more ambiguous, with some studies showing a positive link but others showing no association or even a negative one (Klein et al., 2002).

So, there is clear evidence that the presence of the core conditions is strongly related to positive improvements in clients. But there is also evidence that calls into question whether they are either necessary or sufficient, with studies showing that some clients demonstrate an improvement even when the core conditions are not in place (suggesting they are not always necessary) and others that show that sometimes, even when the core conditions are clearly demonstrated, clients show no improvements (suggesting they are not sufficient) (Tausch, 1990; Lietaer, 2002).

The conclusions that we can draw are that the core conditions are facilitative: helpful or extremely helpful for almost all clients, but that other factors too play a part.

This suggestion that there are other factors at play is consistent with the research (and indeed with common sense) that indicates that the effectiveness of any therapeutic intervention will be based on a combination of the therapy itself (both the nature of the therapist and the choice of activities), the placebo effect (the positive effect of the client's assumption that the therapy is going to work) and external factors, which might include the opportunities available, the client's health, the economy and a wide range of others (Lambert, 1992).

The research described above focuses almost exclusively on a therapeutic context. The idea of person-centred counselling has been widely adopted and can be seen within a range of professional contexts including social work and education, and forms the basis of many career interventions. Any analysis of the effectiveness of one-to-one guidance therefore provides

*(continued)*

*(continued)*

some empirical evidence for the value of a person-centred approach to career interventions (see Hooley, 2014 for a comprehensive review). But career practice is broader than just a person-centred approach, and makes use of structured frameworks and a range of tools and techniques. The existing evidence therefore provides only an implication that person-centred approaches work in careers rather than a confident assertion. A recent meta-analysis by Whiston and colleagues (Whiston, et al., 2017) tried to unpick the different aspects of career practice to work out what specific approaches or techniques are important. They found that the single most important feature in effective career counselling is the working alliance. The working alliance is a concept that closely maps on to Rogers' core conditions, and Whiston and colleagues' study therefore provides some indirect evidence that Rogers' core conditions are pivotal in effective career conversations.

Chapter 9

# It is what I want, but my family aren't so sure

In the discussion about career decision-making difficulties in Chapter 2, the challenge of dealing with 'external conflicts' was highlighted. These challenges arise when clients themselves believe that one particular course of action would suit them but their families, or significant others, disagree. The 'others' involved will often have your client's best interests at heart and their resistance is usually the result of believing that their loved one's choice of career path is not going to lead them to a fulfilling career or will not reap the rewards promised. Sometimes the career decision made by your client might have a direct impact on their family's lives. The sources of conflict in these situations could be the result of concern about the effect your client's choice might have on their reputation, their financial situation or other aspects of their home life. In many cases these discussions between clients and their families happen naturally and harmoniously, and the conflicts are resolved successfully. In other instances clients find that the conversations are not so easily managed and the resulting tension may cause distress or prevent action. Sometimes clients can bring these issues to a career coach and it is useful for you to have a few suggestions of strategies that your clients could consider.

Two techniques are introduced in this chapter. The first, ego states, is derived from transactional analysis (TA). Transactional analysis is a much broader theory that offers an interesting lens through which to examine human interaction. The section will start with a short introduction to this theory before describing ego states in more depth. The second technique described is perceptual positions, which is drawn from neuro-linguistic programming (NLP).

## Ego states

### Transactional analysis

Transactional analysis examines conversations (transactions) and the theory conceptualises a conversation as an entity in itself, distinct from the people and relationships involved. Thinking about a conversation in this way allows it to be scrutinised from all angles. The analysis allows us to move from a 'she said/he said' description of the conversation to a 'he said, and this is why he said it, and this was probably what he meant, but she thought he meant something else and so she said this, but really what she really wanted to say was . . . ' analysis. It is this depth that leads to greater empathy and understanding, and greater self-awareness. The approach is introduced here as one that may help clients in their relationships, but it can also be useful for us as career coaches as we try to make sense of our own interactions with our clients.

The theory was developed by Eric Berne in San Francisco in the 1950s. Transactional analysis has its origins in psychodynamic theory, but has been used and incorporated into a wide range of contexts. One of Berne's aims in developing TA was to develop a theory that was easy to describe, easy to understand and easy to apply. To this end he has been extremely successful and you may well find that the ideas within TA can become a core part of your career practice quite quickly. But his success in this regard has led to his theory being taken less seriously in some quarters than it perhaps deserves. In many ways Berne was an innovative pioneer, who introduced ideas and approaches that have now become so accepted and entrenched that their origins are not questioned and their originator not acknowledged. One example of this is TA's *Strokes Cluster*. The term 'positive stroke' is widely used and the idea that contact, recognition and a sense of belonging are essential to human development is almost universally accepted; but Berne's role in uncovering, developing and describing this particular idea is largely ignored. Transactional analysis is a sophisticated theory that incorporates personality, motivation and problem solving and, as such, has benefits to confer on educators, counsellors, managers and indeed career coaches.

### *Ego states*

The theory of TA holds that we all have three different versions of ourselves from which we conduct our conversations. We can use each one of them and can switch from one to another within the same conversation. The three ego states are: parent, adult and child (see Figure 9.1). In the parent ego state, our communication style is influenced by past authority figures such as parents and teachers. The parent ego state can be nurturing or controlling. The *nurturing parent* ego state looks to reassure and provide a safe place for a vulnerable conversation partner. The *controlling parent* ego state has strong opinions and seeks to control or manipulate the other in the conversation by administering praise or censure. The second one, the *child* ego state, draws on one's own personal past experience and can manifest itself as the *adapted child*, who is keen to please and feels comfortable and safe doing what they are told, and the *natural child*, who is free to do as they please and can be playful, independent and rebellious. The adult ego state draws on the learning we have gained as adults and is able to make rational decisions, using past experiences to interpret current events.

The adult ego state is considered the best one from which to make good decisions as it is only in the adult state that we can operationalise our rational, strategic, long-term cognitive powers. But it is not always easy to stick firmly to the

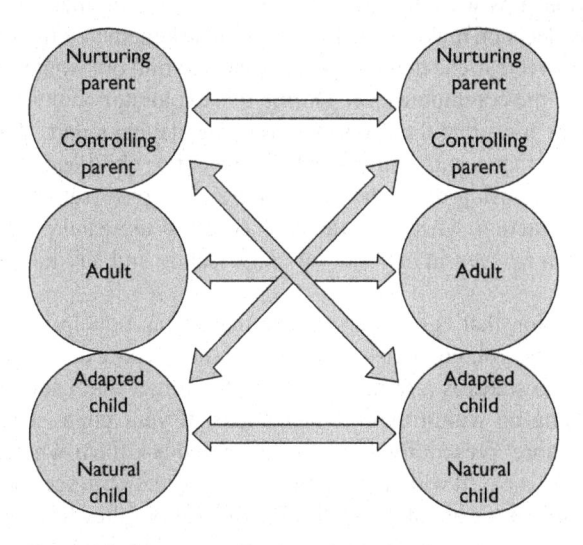

*Figure 9.1* Ego states. (Source: the author.)

adult state, particularly within entrenched family relationships. The ego state from which the other person communicates can serve to push us in particular directions, for example, the parent and child ego states very often end up communicating with each other. A comment from someone's child ego state that reveals some vulnerability, such as 'it is going to be alright, isn't it?', is very likely to elicit a nurturing parent response 'yes of course it is. It'll be fine, I promise', and a controlling parent comment such as 'that's a silly decision' is very likely to push someone into a rebellious natural child response: 'well I do not care what you think, I am going to do it anyway'. These kinds of interactions are commonplace, particularly perhaps within families where the dynamics of relationships are well established, but, given that the most effective communication and the most effective decisions are made from the adult ego state, they are usually unhelpful and often problematic. A client who is struggling to communicate productively with their family about their career plans can find that an understanding of the idea of ego states may shed some light on where their conversation may be taking a wrong turn. If the model does strike a chord, it can then provide a framework to help identify some ideas that could make the conversation more effective another time.

### How to use

Communication can be difficult in many different ways and ego states provides a framework for just one type of transactional challenge. Before launching into a description of this approach with your client it is crucial to work out whether ego states is a technique that could be valuable in a participant context. If a client indicates that their relationships with their loved ones are preventing them from moving on in their career decision making, the first step is to ask them to tell you a little bit more about the conversations that have taken place, to find out what your client thinks is underlying the communication. During this exploratory conversation you may pick up some hints that the ego states could be playing a part. Your client might quote a phrase that seems reminiscent of a parent or child ego state, or might reflect on the relationship or on their response to the conversation that hints at a child/parent interaction. This is particularly common in actual parent/child relationships, but can be seen in any kind of conversation and any kind of relationship.

If you do see a suggestion that ego states may be playing an unhelpful part in your clients' relationships, you could ask whether they have come across TA before and suggest that ego states is a framework that they might find useful in understanding what's going on within their conversations. If your client seems interested in finding out more, present the model to them and ask them whether there is anything that strikes a chord with their conversations. If they can see some links, ask them to talk a little more about the kinds of conversations they have and how the ego states manifest themselves. Then ask them to consider how it might work if they were to respond to a comment from a parent or child ego state from their adult ego state. If it seems as though it might be useful, you could suggest that the two of you practise some possible adult ego state answers and you could discuss strategies for coping if their conversation partner refuses to budge from their parent or child position.

## *In practice*

This approach is introduced as a framework that might help our clients to better understand the difficult career conversations they may be having with their loved ones. But, before leaving this particular technique, it is worth spending a little time thinking about the value that an understanding of these ego states could confer on the coaching relationship. As highlighted above, the best decisions tend to be made from the adult ego state, and it is therefore useful and perhaps important that, for the most part, coaching conversations take place between adult states. At times you may feel that it is appropriate to offer some nurturing parent reassurance, or you may find that child-to-child interactions between you and your client actually allow for more creative discussions and generate more numerous and more interesting ideas and solutions. But, in general, the conversation will lead to more empowered rational action if the client is in the adult ago state during the interaction.

Within a coaching relationship there can be a dynamic that makes sticking to an adult-to-adult interaction particularly challenging, in that there can be something in the nature of the relationship that pushes the coach into *adult* and the client into *child*. It is not uncommon for a client to come along to coaching with the expectation that the coach is the expert and with the assumption that the coach will have the answers and provide some clarity and certainty. Our clients, after all, almost always seek our support because they are feeling unsure about something, and this vulnerability can easily bring out the nurturing parent in us. But it is important to be aware that clients will be more empowered to make good decisions, which they are committed to and able to put into action, if the conversations are mostly adult–adult.

If you notice that the conversation has shifted into a parent/child transaction, the most straightforward response is to consciously and deliberately position yourself firmly in the 'adult' ago state. For example, a comment from your client's child ego state such as this: 'I am hopeless at interviews, I know I'll mess up', might naturally lead a coach to respond as a nurturing parent, saying something like 'no, you'll be great! I am sure you will'. This may be what the client wants to hear, but we know that this kind of response doesn't always constitute great coaching as it is not really addressing the underlying issue and is not necessarily either true (how do you know they'll be great?) or authentic (you may well be saying it because you think it is what they want to hear, rather than because you believe it). This nurturing response also perpetuates the parent/child interaction and provides no encouragement to the client to take responsibility for their own self-belief. Instead, a response from the coach's adult ego-state, such as 'I wonder what is making you think you will mess up?', puts the responsibility for the opinion back on the client and can lead to a more productive discussion.

Sometimes you might notice that, despite your best efforts, the conversation keeps drifting back to parent/child transactions and, in this case, you might decide that it would be useful to discuss this with your client. In this case their comment 'I am hopeless at interviews, I know I'll mess up' might lead you to comment on your own urge to nurture: 'I've noticed that I keep wanting to tell you that everything's going to be alright. I wonder what's driving that? Do you think I am picking up on an idea that you are looking for reassurance?'. This can then lead to an adult to adult ego state conversation that explores this need for reassurance and perhaps identifies some more concrete sources that your client could draw on.

Transactional analysis can be an interesting framework to use with a wide range of clients – it could prove valuable with anyone who is having difficulties with their relationships and interactions. The approach itself can be introduced in a group, but analysing a specific relationship may be best left to a one-to-one context.

| | |
|---|---|
| One to one | ✓ |
| Group sessions | ✗ |
| Within the session | ✓ |
| As a self-directed intersessional task | ✗ |
| Initial career choice | ✓ |
| Career changes | ✓ |
| Indicative timing | 15 minutes |

## Why it works

In a large-scale survey of TA practitioners, ego states were identified as the single most useful aspect of the theory (Steiner, 2005). Research supports the claim that these five ego states (three states plus two extra variants of the child and parent ego states) are indeed distinct forms of thought, feeling and behaviour (Loffredo et al., 2004). There seems to be some support for the idea of different ego states from the neuroscience community. Exploring different 'mind modules', which are particular parts of the brain that serve different evolutionary purposes, the researchers seem to have clearly identified that the adult ego state resides in the prefrontal lobe (Steiner, 2005). Neuroscience is a discipline still very much in its infancy, but it does seem to offer some promise.

What is more difficult to pin down is whether these are the only ego states that exist. It feels fairly unlikely that anyone is ever going to be able to prove that all behaviour always fits into one of the five states and it certainly hasn't happened yet.

## What's the evidence base?

There are hundreds of papers published about TA. It has its own association (The International Transactional Analysis Association) and its own journal (*The Transactional Analysis Journal*), and there is no shortage of articles that describe how it can be used.

As we have seen earlier in this book, finding evidence to prove that any kind of therapeutic intervention works is difficult. Therapy tends to take a long time, often incorporates more than one kind of intervention and, for the duration of the therapeutic intervention, there are a lot of other things going on in people's lives, so it is hard to be confident that any improvement seen is down to the therapy itself. Compounding the challenges associated with these complexities is the highly subjective issue of what constitutes 'success' in a therapeutic sense and how it can be measured. But, acknowledging those caveats, there is plenty of robust evidence to suggest that people who are on the receiving end of TA believe that it has been valuable. Novey (2002) discusses a large-scale long-term research project involving over 900 clients that gives fairly robust evidence that clients who received TA reported better long-term effects than those receiving any other kind of therapeutic treatment including psychotherapy and marriage counselling.

Research that explores the use and value of TA within a career coaching context is limited, but the way in which TA can assist with relationship or

> conversation challenges perhaps means that the context is less relevant. If TA approaches can shed light on relationships they will be able to do this regardless of whether the conversation is about career choices, where to live or how to spend the weekend.

## Perceptual positions

### Introduction

The second technique covered here is known as perceptual positions. This technique is drawn from neuro-linguistic programming (NLP), pioneered by Richard Bandler and John Grinder in California in the 1970s. Neuro-linguistic programming was developed through observing 'what works', rather than starting from a theoretical perspective and developing a practical approach from there. The underpinning principles that guide the approach, such as a focus on building rapport and an outcome orientation, are common to a number of other styles of coaching and, as such, NLP techniques can sit comfortably alongside other coaching approaches.

Perceptual positions is a technique that encourages clients to examine a conversation from three different perspectives. In this it has considerable resonance with transactional analysis. The three perspectives are those of the client themselves (Position 1), the 'other' (i.e., the person the client is imagining talking to) (Position 2) and a neutral observer (Position 3).

This approach can be useful for clients who are struggling to understand why their conversations do not go to plan. It can offer insights to both their own contribution to a conversation and can also encourage empathy and understanding of the contribution of their conversation partner. It can be useful for clients whose own career aspirations are at odds with those that their loved ones have for them, and who are finding it hard to reconcile their different views.

### How to use

For this exercise you need to have three chairs arranged in a triangle. Explain to your client that their chair is in Position 1 and that they should imagine their conversation partner to be in one of the other chairs, in Position 2. Ask them to pick a difficult conversation they have had and to work with this during the exercise.

### Step 1: Position 1

With your client sitting in Position 1, ask them to re-live their side of the conversation, repeating out loud the things that they said. Once your client has represented their comments as faithfully as they can, ask them to reflect on what was going on in their head at the time. What were they thinking? Were their comments a true reflection of their thoughts? Were their emotions communicated effectively?

What were they hoping their conversation partner would say or feel in response? Do they think there might have been a different way to express themselves that might have been clearer or more effective?

Ask them to think about how their partner responded and how they interpreted that response, and how they, themselves, felt about this.

## Step 2: Position 2

When you feel that you have got as much as you can from that, ask your client to move into Position 2. The physical movement helps the client to get into their new role, so do not be tempted just to ask them to switch character – they need to switch seats as well. In their new position, they now need to take on the role of the 'other' in the conversation. Again, ask them to re-live the conversation, but this time saying the words spoken by their conversation partner. Try and get them to remember, as clearly as they can, the actual words uttered. Once they have said the words out loud, ask them to try and identify or imagine the thoughts and feelings held by their conversation partner as they were speaking. Why did they choose to say that? What were they trying to convey? What kind of reaction were they hoping for or expecting?

## Step 3: Position 3

In the final step, your client should move themselves to Position 3, which is the position of the objective observer. Ask your client to reflect on the conversation in its entirety, commenting on the aspects of the relationship that may have revealed themselves during the interaction and reflecting on what was really going on behind the words.

## Step 4: insights and action

Having completed the exercise, it is useful to take a few minutes to make sure that your client can capitalise on the insights from the process. The final stage of the process therefore is a discussion about a possible way forward. Ask your client to reflect on the exercise as a whole and ask whether there was anything about it that surprised them or caused them to consider the interaction in a different light. You could try and get your client to think about what they could do to change the nature of the interaction and, if it helps, you could offer to try to role play some potential conversational gambits with your client to help them to work out and practise a more constructive approach to the conversation.

### *In practice*

The example above suggests that the client should pick a real conversation that they have had. An alternative is to invite your client to think about a difficult conversation they are anticipating, imagining how the conversation might go, what they might say and how their conversation partner might respond. The technique lends itself to a one-to-one context. The principles of the technique can be explained within a group setting, and the participants within a group could be invited to reflect on their relationships in the light of the theory in pairs, for example, but if your client is looking to work on one particular relationship or prepare for one specific conversation, then a one-to-one context is probably more suitable.

Finally, it is worth reiterating my oft-made comment about boundaries. Without specific training our professional expertise does not usually lend itself to in-depth relationship counselling. If you feel that the particular issue with your client's relationship is deep-rooted or far-reaching then it may be more useful for your client to do some work with a relationship counsellor. This is a decision that you can make together so that your client does not feel that they are being rejected by you, but it is important that you raise this if you feel it is appropriate.

## Case study

Jack was in the fortunate position of having a range of options open to him. He was half way through his A levels and came to see his school careers adviser to get some help with his university choices. His A levels were in English, History, Maths and Art and he was on track for good grades in all of them. The sticking point was which subject to choose to study. He had identified three excellent and interesting English degree courses. They were all fairly competitive but he stood a good chance and was now looking for a back-up option to add to his list.

Jack's careers adviser invited him to talk about his A level subjects and, after listening to him for a while, confessed that he was surprised that it was English that Jack had opted for. Jack was clearly enthusiastic about them all, but his demeanour changed when he started talking about his art work and, with no prompting from his adviser, had asked if he could show him his portfolio. The passion and sophistication with which he discussed his work struck his adviser as quite exceptional, and his adviser wondered why art hadn't been mentioned as an option. Jack explained that he felt that art wasn't a very sensible choice and, after a little further probing, Jack's careers adviser uncovered that Jack was convinced that his parents wouldn't let him pursue art. Jack explained that his family were very academic and, whilst they had always admired and encouraged his talent, they were very clear that art wouldn't be considered as a suitable career option.

*(continued)*

*(continued)*

Jack had had one difficult conversation with his parents about the topic, and it had ended with his mum in tears at the idea that he might be throwing his future away and his dad angry that he had upset his mum. Jack had decided that his parents would never change their minds and had resolved to accommodate their wishes.

Using the perceptual positions, Jack re-lived the conversation and reflected on what had happened and why. He concluded that his own attitude hadn't been very helpful. He had assumed that his parents would disagree with him and he had felt resentful and undermined even before he opened his mouth. The careers adviser asked Jack to think about what was behind his parents' views. Jack acknowledged that they had his best interests at heart, but felt that perhaps the problem was that they just couldn't imagine what you could do with a degree in an art-related subject.

Jack and his careers adviser had a look at some destination statistics to explore the range of jobs that arts graduates went into, and found some information about graphic design and a range of other more commercial roles that art-related graduates could pursue. They also alighted on a statistic that showed that most graduate jobs were open to graduates from any discipline. In fact, having researched the area a little, it looked as though a degree in art would be just as versatile as a degree in English. Jack thought that this kind of information could be really useful to share with his parents.

Jack and his adviser then talked through some strategies for the conversation itself. Jack thought about when might be a good time to bring the topic up and identified a form of words that he thought might start the conversation off on a more productive footing.

Armed with information, strategies and a bit more understanding of his parents' motivation, Jack felt more positive about the possibility of having a more amicable and fruitful conversation.

| | |
|---|---|
| One to one | ✓ |
| Group sessions | ✗ |
| Within the session | ✓ |
| As a self-directed intersessional task | ✗ |
| Initial career choice | ✓ |
| Career changes | ✓ |
| Indicative timing | Up to 45 minutes |

## Why it works

This technique draws on the theories behind drama therapy and role play. Drama therapy is thought to work in two particular ways. First, drama exercises allow people to play with identities. They enable people to get into the minds of other characters, creating stories, images and emotions (Rousseau et al., 2007). The second thing that drama techniques do is to create a distance between the reality and the exercise. This separation of both time and space offers your client the freedom to be a bit more creative, taking risks and playing with possible solutions in a way that they might not in reality (Myerhoff, 1990). The process of trying out new strategies makes people feel empowered as they realise that there are options that they can try (Brockett, 1977) and increases confidence as they give the participants a chance to reduce the uncertainties and decrease the risks associated with a new approach (Chen, Muthitacharoen, & Frolick, 2003; Jones, 2012).

The ideas behind drama therapy are influenced by the director Konstantin Stanislavski (1863–1938), who highlights the power of pretending to be someone as a way to understand them better. He talks about unleashing the inner truth of a character, which he suggests can be done through focusing on action and intention. Another, and quite different, director whose work has influenced drama therapy is Bertolt Brecht (1898–1956), who, rather than focusing on almost becoming the character, aims instead to enhance the role of the observing self. You can see that both of these approaches are important in perceptual positions, as the participants are invited to both assume identities and reflect on the scenes being played out.

The theory behind role play is very similar to that which underpins drama therapy, but it tends to be described in a slightly less theoretical way. Role plays work by simulating a conversation that is real enough to give the individual some practice, which will then stand them in good stead when it comes to the real conversations. Although the evidence base for role plays is fairly robust, it is not without its theoretical sceptics. There are debates about whether it is actually possible to recreate a situation that is real enough to be meaningful (Van Hasselt, Romano, & Vecchi, 2008), and there are those who suggest that, whilst we might think that we can second guess how a conversation will go, conversation is rarely predictable (Stokoe, 2011).

## What's the evidence base?

Despite the eye-rolling and heart-sinking that is so often associated with the words 'it is time for a role play', role plays do work and there is a robust list

*(continued)*

*(continued)*

of research to support this claim. Role plays are described as an 'accelerated learning technique' and have been shown to improve communication skills in a wide range of contexts, including with computer science professionals (Chen, Muthitacharoen, & Frolick, 2003) and doctors (Nestel & Tierney, 2007), to enhance learning in Higher Education (DeNeve & Heppner, 1997) and in schools (Duveen & Solomon, 1994), and to help people to clarify their thinking (Simonneaux, 2001). It has also been shown to have a longer-lasting impact than many other forms of training.

Drama therapy too has been shown to be an effective approach to practice. The evidence around drama therapy tends to focus more on emotional and psychological well-being, and drama therapy practice can lead to habits forming and more honest behaviour (Slade, 1955). It can help with managing stress and difficult emotions (Positive Futures, 2005), and with relationships and empowerment (Daykin et al., 2008).

# Chapter 10

# What's the point in trying? I am never going to make anything of myself

In Chapter 7 I looked at some techniques that help to increase clients' confidence in specific areas. In this chapter I will introduce three techniques that have been shown to make a difference to people who are lacking in confidence more generally.

Low self-esteem presents a major challenge to the career development process. It lowers aspirations and significantly reduces the chances of success. People with low levels of confidence find it harder to make a career decision (Lent, Brown, & Hackett, 1994), are less able to network effectively, and are considerably less likely to get the jobs they apply for (Kanfer, Wanberg, & Kantrowitz, 2001).

Low confidence, however, is something that is seen a lot in career practice. If things are going well at work, and people are feeling good about themselves, they are much less likely to seek out professional support, less likely to want to leave their jobs, and perhaps more likely to feel that they can make the next move under their own steam. It is those who do not feel that they are succeeding or who are not feeling fulfilled in their current role who are likely to seek out the help of a professional. Given how important and how rare high self-esteem seems to be, it is useful for career coaches to have a few techniques at their disposal that may help to boost the mood of their clients.

I touched on the importance of clear boundaries earlier in the book. Career coaches are well versed in considering their boundaries, and the skills associated with identifying and managing boundaries are particularly vital when dealing with clients with low confidence. The techniques below can boost self-esteem a little, but are not going to make enough of a difference to those who are really struggling. It may be helpful to talk to your clients about how they are feeling about themselves and to discuss whether they might need a specialist service that is more tailored to their needs.

The three techniques presented in this chapter have all been shown to boost self-esteem. The first one, mindfulness, is a form of secular meditation that has become enormously popular in recent years. The second is a series of evidence-based suggestions from the New Economics Foundation that have been shown to boost well-being. The final technique is a relatively new approach called acceptance and commitment therapy that seems to show some promise as a tool to help with career interventions.

## Mindfulness

### Introduction

Interest in mindfulness has grown exponentially over the last decade or so. Its origins are not new and stretch back to the ancient Eastern tradition of meditation, but mindfulness is a secular adaptation that is easier to incorporate into our hectic 21st-century lives. At its heart is a focus on the present moment. The technique involves not thinking or worrying about the past, nor planning or anticipating the future, but just being fully present and fully engaged with the here and now.

One feature of mindfulness that may make it practical for some of our clients is that it can be done in short bursts. Where the Eastern tradition involves devoting many hours each day to meditation, we are encouraged to incorporate mindfulness into our daily routines. We can brush our teeth, or eat our breakfast, or walk to the station mindfully, and mindfulness writers urge us to take just three minutes out of each day to spend in one mindful activity or another.

Bishop et al. (2004) describes mindfulness as 'a form of awareness that arises from attending to the present moment in a non-judgmental, and accepting manner' and describes four key elements. First, mindfulness is about *awareness*. When being mindful, we aim to notice any stimuli that demand our attention both inside our bodies or minds and outside in the environment around us. The stimuli might be aches and pains, concerns and plans, or sounds, noises and smells from outside: anything that can entrap our thoughts. Alongside this awareness, mindfulness should incorporate *attention*. The goal during mindfulness is to focus attention on one aspect of our present situation – whether that is our breathing, the piece of toast we're eating or the colours we see on our way to the station, and to try and direct attention solely towards that one particular thing. The third key element is *time*, and this is a reminder that mindfulness is focused on the present moment, on the here and now, and ruminations about the past and concerns about the future should be put to one side during mindfulness practice. The final aspect is *acceptance*, which highlights the non-judgemental approach that reminds us not to be too harsh with ourselves. Mindfulness is a skill that needs to be learnt and it is inevitable that other thoughts will intrude occasionally, or even frequently, particularly when we are fairly new to the practice. When they do, we should simply notice that our mind has wandered and, without stopping to wonder why or to rebuke ourselves for not being more focused, we should just gently bring our mind back. With practice, the ability to focus for periods of time increases and the urge to berate ourselves when our minds wander diminishes.

Mindfulness makes a key distinction between doing and being, and aims to get people to make a conscious choice to notice, experience and accept the present moment, rather than functioning on automatic pilot, analysing thoughts and striving to change things.

In career terms, it can be a useful exercise to suggest to clients who seem to be feeling gloomy about their situation or their future. Negative emotions are a common part of all our lives and the challenges associated with making career choices and looking for jobs can often lead people to feel a little dispirited. But, whilst they may be both common and natural, these negative feelings can be damaging to the whole job search process. They can prevent an individual from seeing the options that are available to them, can stop them from pursuing opportunities that present themselves, and can really hinder interview performance. If you are working with a client whose low self-esteem or negative thoughts seem to be limiting their horizons or their success, this could be a valuable exercise to share with them.

## How to use

This technique is introduced here as a way to boost self-esteem. Before you introduce mindfulness to your client, it may be useful to have a conversation with your client about their current levels of confidence. This is not necessarily an easy topic, either from the perspective of the career coach or the client. It can be painful for a client to admit or face the idea that they are feeling down about their current situation and low self-esteem can feel like an admission of a failing, so this needs to be handled with care.

Once it is established that your client might benefit from a psychological boost, you could introduce the concept of mindfulness. Your client may well have come across it before – it has been widely discussed over the last decade – so it can be useful to find out what their understanding of it is and whether they are well-disposed towards it.

In terms of the nuts and bolts of the mindfulness exercises themselves, there are numerous apps, books and online tools that your clients could use. People who are engaging with mindfulness for the first time often find it helpful to have a guided session in which a recorded voice talks them through the steps they need to take. In the 'Further reading' section at the back of the book there are some suggestions, but it might be worth having a look at a few yourself to find ones that you feel most comfortable recommending.

One that is often used is a simple breathing exercise in which an individual focuses on their breathing and counts each breath. You could devise a script for yourself that runs along these lines:

> Take a moment to get yourself comfortable in your chair. Put your feet flat on the floor and keep your hands lying gently in your lap. Close your eyes. Now take a moment just to think about how your body is feeling right now. Notice the floor beneath your feet and feel the weight of your arms in your lap. Notice whether there are parts of your body that feel particularly good

or bad. Are there any aches or pains, or sensations of comfort or discomfort? Now take a minute to become aware of the sensations outside your body. Are there any noises you can hear, or any strong smells? What about the temperature of the room? Are you feeling warm or cool? Do different parts of your body feel different? If your mind starts to wander, that is no problem, but as soon as you notice that your mind has begun to think about something else, just bring it back to your body and to the sensations in the room around you.

Now turn your attention to your breathing. Start to notice each breath, as the air comes in to your body and goes out again. Notice the sensations in your body. What happens to your stomach, diaphragm and chest each time you breathe in and each time you breathe out. What can you feel? Now, start to count your breaths. Count one as you take a breath in and two as you breathe out. When you reach ten, go back and start over at one again. If you notice your mind start to wander, that is no problem at all, just bring your attention back to your breathing.

You can read this text out to your client, slowly and gently, with lengthy pauses in between each part of it, and suggest that they try this within your session. You could then print this off and give it to them so that they could try this at home.

One of the common challenges that people trying to engage with mindfulness face is carving out enough time each day. It may be useful to share this common sticking problem with your client and having a conversation about how they might find the time to prioritise their mindfulness practice.

## *In practice*

The technique is introduced here as one that can help clients to boost self-esteem, but it can also be used to help make career coaching conversations more effective.

We know that the power of a one-to-one intervention lies predominately in the quality of the relationship between the practitioner and the client (Whiston et al., 2017), but slotting clients into busy lives, amidst the daily pressures that can preoccupy us, can make it hard to give our clients our full and undivided attention. Two minutes of mindfulness before meeting with a client can help us to put any intrusive ruminations about the past or anticipations of the future to one side and help us to feel more fully present in the session and focused on our clients.

A two-minute mindful breathing exercise can also be used together with your client at the start of a career discussion. This can fulfill the same function for both of you, allowing coach and client to put other thoughts and preoccupations to one side for the duration of your time together. If you think this could make the session more productive, then you could suggest to your client that the two of you could try a short mindfulness exercise together before the coaching starts. One of the most straightforward exercises is *mindful breathing*, in which the two of you sit silently for two minutes and focus on your breathing. You don't need to control your breathing in any way, just notice it as you breathe in and breathe out.

You can help to focus your attention by counting the breaths. Count up to ten breaths and then start over at one again. Set your phone or watch to alert you after two minutes so that you can relax into the exercise. This short exercise at the start of the coaching session can help to make sure that both you and your client are focused on the topic at hand and are psychologically present in the room.

The introduction above assumes a one-to-one context for mindfulness practice, but this can be introduced and practiced within group contexts as well. The box below offers some of the evidence for the value of mindfulness in learning, and it can be used at the start of a group session to help ensure that your clients' minds are focused on the session.

| | |
|---|---|
| One to one | ✓ |
| Group sessions | ✓ |
| Within the session | ✓ |
| As a self-directed intersessional task | ✓ |
| Initial career choice | ✓ |
| Career changes | ✓ |
| Indicative timing | 5 minutes |

## Why it works

Mindfulness is a way of training the mind to have more cognitive and behavioural control. The idea is that if you can learn to focus attention here, and withdraw it there, then you are in a stronger position to be able to control your mind and emotions. This means that you are more likely to be able to tolerate uncertainty and be more flexible. One of the key features of mindfulness is the way it encourages more openness to ideas. Because mindfulness encourages people to notice what is going on around them it ensures that they cannot be on automatic pilot. In automatic pilot, people end up being fixed in their thinking – trapped in assumptions. When they start to be more aware of things around them then they are required to develop new patterns of thinking as they respond to their immediate environment (Langer, 1989). This openness to new thinking invokes a range of other cognitive processes that help people to be more creative, such as curiosity, insight, analogical reasoning, remote associations, ideational productivity, divergent and convergent thinking, flexibility and critical thinking (Carson & Langer, 2006). Its ability to address depression lies in the way it replaces self-evaluation with acceptance. Part of the practice of mindfulness includes replacing self-criticism with the ability to notice what is going on within oneself but not to self-criticise.

## What's the evidence base?

The evidence base for mindfulness is all fairly recent and this means that it is still a bit too soon for us to be entirely confident that we actually know what is happening. But even the most cynical can't deny that it looks promising. Hart, Ivtzan and Hart (2013) conducted a review of the literature and found a remarkable array of evidence of the impact of mindfulness. They identified that mindfulness can help with a range of outcomes that can be linked with happiness and higher levels of self-esteem: positive emotions, life satisfaction, vitality, sense of autonomy, optimism, self-regulation, and several aspects of cognitive performance. In terms of work-related evidence, it has been shown that mindfulness has a positive impact on job strain, job satisfaction, self-compassion, emotional intelligence, learning, thinking faster and more effectively, creativity and conflict resolution. Collard and Walsh (2008) showed links with a decrease in stress through coaching in the work place and Spence, Cavanagh and Grant (2008) showed it led to an increase in goal attainment.

It is encouraging to see so many studies of the positive impact of mindfulness in so many different contexts, but nothing as yet has demonstrated a direct positive impact on career choice or job search. Nevertheless, there are strong reasons to believe that mindfulness would show significant benefit to those making career choices and looking for jobs as there are so many clear indirect links. Globally, mindfulness has been shown to boost self-esteem and those with high levels of self-esteem are likely to make better career choices and get the jobs they apply for (Kanfer, Wanberg, & Kantrowitz, 2001). More specifically, mindfulness enhances optimism, which has been shown to help people develop the resources and networks to help with their job search (Brissette, Scheier, & Carver, 2002; Scheier & Carver, 2003), and if it has been shown to help people to achieve their goals in a work setting, it is likely that it might have a positive impact on people's career goal attainment too.

The studies for the most part are fairly robust, with large sample sizes and some rigorous designs, but one thing to note is that many of the studies ask participants to undertake an eight-week course learning about mindfulness, which is not something to which we would all commit. More recently there has been some evidence about the impact of short mindfulness sessions (Beng et al., 2016; Shimizu et al., 2017) but the evidence base for this type of mindfulness session still needs to catch up.

## Five ways to well-being

### Introduction

In 2008 the government asked the New Economics Foundation (NEF) to conduct a review of the latest evidence around well-being and to identify some guidelines for behaviour that can make a difference to our lives. A study had found that only 14% of the population reported that they were *flourishing* (i.e., had high levels of well-being) and, influenced by the positive psychology movement (which was introduced in some depth in Chapter 5 as part of the Strengths Coaching technique), the government was keen to make use of the research that showed that relatively small changes in behaviour could make significant changes to overall well-being. The NEF examined hundreds of studies and looked for a range of changes that individuals could make in their lives that could improve their overall levels of happiness and that were backed up by robust empirical evidence.

They found five themes:

- Connect
- Be active
- Take notice
- Keep learning
- Give.

This approach might feel a bit incongruous in this book. In themselves, these five themes have no obvious links to career development and so might feel a little unexpected within a book on career coaching. But, as identified in the box below, positive well-being has a clear and significant link with good career outcomes and so an understanding of these approaches, which have been robustly shown to enhance well-being, makes these seem like a very appropriate addition to the career coach's toolkit.

### How to use

Issues about self-esteem are, of course, personal and sensitive. It is, therefore, important first to establish that your client needs and wants a bit of an increase in self-esteem. If your client feels that they might benefit from a psychological boost, then you could explain to them that these are five themes that have been shown to have an impact. You could suggest that they might want to consider these for themselves, in between their career conversations with you. It might be useful to have these themes written on a handout that your client can then take away and consider at their own time.

## 1  Connect

This first theme is all about connections and conversations. Building and nurturing our relationships on a daily basis has been shown to have a significant impact on well-being. This extends to finding people in our communities and people with shared interests, as well as spending time with established friends and family. For a regular boost to self-esteem, we should be making sure that we prioritise seeking out and developing these relationships.

## 2  Be active

We are encouraged to get off our sofas and start taking some exercise. The NEF is not on a mission to get the nation fit: the recommendations here are about psychological well-being rather than physical health and, to achieve this, the NEF proposes a bit of gentle exercise and fresh air. They suggest that we can all find something that we enjoy and then it will not be such a hardship to do it a few times each week.

## 3  Take notice

The NEF's third theme is about taking notice and overlaps considerably with mindfulness, as introduced earlier in the chapter. The NEF suggests that we should take notice of the here and now, and notice the passing of the seasons, the colours and smells around us and the feeling of the wind in our hair.

## 4  Keep learning

Developing a new interest or reviving a new hobby can boost our confidence as we start to master a new subject or skill, and often provides an opportunity to meet new people and play a more active part in our communities.

## 5  Give

Doing something nice for someone has been shown to do a power of good. The NEF's suggestions are not about money but focus on giving time and kindness – helping a neighbour, smiling at a stranger, joining a voluntary organisation.

### *In practice*

This one differs from the other tools presented in the book as it is not really suitable as an exercise as part of your interventions. Instead, it is offered as a bit of evidence-based advice that can help to make clients more ready for careers support and better equipped to put their ideas into action. It can be introduced within one-to-one sessions or in group contexts, and can be appropriate for any client whom you feel could do with a little psychological lift.

| | |
|---|---|
| One to one | ✗ |
| Group sessions | ✗ |
| Within the session | ✗ |
| As a self-directed intersessional task | ✓ |
| Initial career choice | ✓ |
| Career changes | ✓ |
| Indicative timing | 10 minutes |

## Why it works

As mentioned in the introduction to this section, the ideas suggested do not have a direct bearing on career choice but they are included here because they have been shown to boost self-esteem, and self-esteem has been shown to have an impact on various aspects of career development (Kanfer, Wanberg, & Kantrowitz, 2001). Those with a positive sense of themselves are more likely to make positive choices and get positive outcomes at every stage. Their aspirations are higher and they believe that there are a wider range of options open to them. They are more likely to take the steps needed to make them employable, such as learning new skills, networking and taking advantage of opportunities that come their way. Finally, their job hunts tend to be more successful as they are better able to sell themselves convincingly both on paper and in person, and better able to cope and bounce back after set-backs.

## What's the evidence base?

### 1   Connect

The NEF review of research showed conclusively that social relationships are critical for promoting well-being and protecting against mental ill-health. The 2005 British Attitudes Survey suggests that, as a nation, we are becoming more interested in our work-life balance and reducing working hours in order to spend time with our friends and family.

On top of the evidence identified by the NEF to show that relationships enhance well-being, there is considerable evidence to show that they play a part in a successful job hunt. We know that a high proportion of jobs are found though existing relationships and networks can be a valuable source of intelligence

*(continued)*

*(continued)*

about the job market. Social support can also help people to be more resilient throughout their job hunt and evidence shows that higher levels of social support are linked to finding a job more quickly (Kanfer, Wanberg, & Kantrowitz, 2001).

2  **Be active**

The NEF report shows that taking regular exercise is associated with higher levels of well-being and lower levels of depression for all age groups. Exercise is thought to promote well-being because it increases mastery and perceptions of one's ability to cope. Mood can be enhanced through very short bursts of exercise. Ten minutes may not be enough to keep your heart in tip top working order, but has been shown to be enough to lift your spirits (Acevedo & Ekkekakis, 2006).

3  **Take notice**

The evidence for the benefits of mindfulness are outlined above. The NEF report additionally highlights a piece of research in the US that indicates that the positive effects of an eight-week training programme of mindfulness can last for some years (Huppert, 2008).

4  **Keep learning**

Lifelong learning keeps the brain active and is likely to lead to more social interaction and physical activity too. It has been shown to reduce the chance of depression and it is thought that it works because it increases self-esteem, self-efficacy, hope, a sense of purpose and social integration (Hammond, 2004).

5  **Give**

Getting involved to help the people around you and in your community seems to bring significant rewards. It seems to stimulate a bit of the brain that indicates that it is intrinsically rewarding (Rilling et al., 2007) and volunteering has been associated with positive emotions, meaning in life (Greenfield & Marks, 2004) and even reduced mortality rates (Huppert, 2008).

## Acceptance and commitment therapy

### Introduction

Acceptance and commitment therapy (ACT – pronounced as a single word) is a psychotherapeutic approach that aims to enhance psychological flexibility.

Acceptance and commitment therapy emerged as part of the acceptance-and mindfulness-based developments within the wider field of CBT (Hayes et al., 1999; 2012). Where more traditional forms of CBT are focused on helping people modify the *content* of self-limiting thoughts, ACT focuses on altering the *function* (or impact) of such inner experiences. Cognitive behavioural therapy aims to help individuals to identify their self-limiting thoughts and change them, but ACT acknowledges that these thoughts are very difficult to change – sometimes too difficult. Instead, then, ACT proposes that rather than aiming to change the thoughts, we should aim to change the impact of the thoughts. As a behaviour therapy, ACT particularly seeks to reduce the extent to which difficult or unhelpful thoughts and feelings can make you less likely to be able to live the life you want to live – one that is congruent with your values. The focus on personal values clarification in ACT can be powerful in career development contexts, and the focus on enhancing psychological flexibility may be particularly useful for clients who are negotiating the complexities and insecurities in the current labour market.

### How to use

The ACT interventions target six interrelated processes that together help to increase psychological flexibility (see ACT's model of psychological flexibility shown in Figure 10.1). The six processes are: acceptance, cognitive defusion, contact with

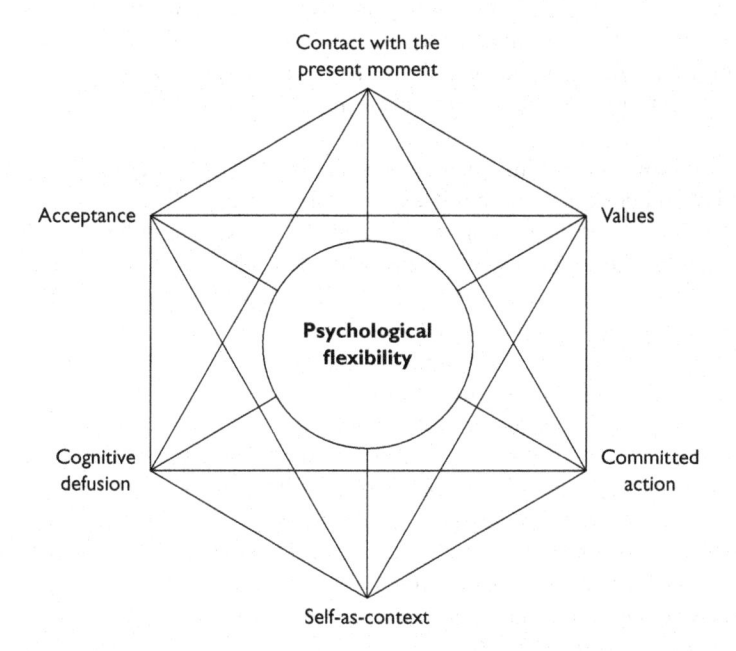

*Figure 10.1* The ACT model of psychological flexibility. (Source: the author.)

the present moment, self-as-context, values and committed action (Hayes, 2004). These processes can be viewed as positive psychological and behavioural skills that can be strengthened to cultivate greater levels of flexibility. The broader construct of psychological flexibility is technically defined as the ability to contact the present moment fully as a conscious human being, and to persist or change behaviour in the service of chosen values (Hayes et al., 2004). Enhancing this ability involves helping people to pursue and expand personally valued patterns of behaviour, even while they are experiencing difficult or unhelpful thoughts, feelings, sensations and urges. As a mindfulness-based approach, ACT does not look to change the form or frequency of people's 'negative' internal states. Instead, ACT focuses on helping people to change their *relationship to* inner experiences so that they do not have an excessive or unhelpful influence over behaviour. In the sections below I offer a brief definition of each ACT process and provide a few examples of how each process can be targeted in ACT-based interventions. Each can be used independently if you feel that just one would be of particular benefit to your clients, or they can be used in conjunction with each other for a more powerful impact.

## Acceptance

In the ACT model, acceptance refers to an increased willingness to experience a range of difficult or unhelpful thoughts, feelings, urges and bodily sensations. Acceptance involves learning to let go of the need to control inner experiences and coming to view even unpleasant inner experiences as a normal and natural part of life. This type of experiential acceptance is not cultivated just for its own sake but rather to increase people's ability to engage in personally meaningful patterns of action (highlighting the close relationship between ACT's processes).

Imagine, for example, a coaching client expresses that she deeply cares about career progression and development, but is experiencing strong feelings of anxiety about stepping into a more senior role and feels that this anxiety is holding her back from agreeing to take an opportunity being offered by her current employer. Instead of trying to reduce the anxiety, an ACT intervention would help the client to 'turn towards' the anxiety (for example by noticing the texture of sensations unfolding in the body), and practise 'sitting with' the anxious feelings that show up as she thinks about this next step in her career.

This acceptance-based process might at first seem counterintuitive to clients, especially because internal control strategies are often subtly endorsed by the surrounding culture. Thus, the cultivation of acceptance skills might at first take the form of affect tolerance exercises, helping the client to sit with discomfort to learn that such discomfort does not have to be changed or avoided to move in a valued life direction. This skill can be developed through brief mindfulness practices and can also be cultivated during the natural flow of a coaching session. For example, as the client in our example begins speaking about her career progression situation, the coach might pause and ask with gentle curiosity: 'what is showing up inside of you right now as we speak about this?' The coach can then (for example) orient the client's attention toward direct sensations in the body (e.g., 'are those sensations sharp or dull?' 'whereabouts in your body do you experience them?'). The stance of the coach has a subtle but important part to play in this process: by adopting a genuine stance of non-judgemental curiosity toward the client's inner experience, the coach is modelling acceptance and communicating that such feelings do not have to be feared, acted upon, or removed before one is able to take steps in a personally meaningful direction.

Just to reiterate, the aim of such acceptance strategies is not to change the form or frequency of difficult inner experiences such as anxiety. Rather, ACT focuses on altering the function of such experiences, to reduce the extent to which they have an unhelpful control over a client's personally chosen behaviour. The cultivation of acceptance skills, in conjunction with personal values work, can often feel empowering to clients as they come to realise that fluctuating internal states do not have to be significant barriers to the pursuit of personally valued actions and life goals.

### Cognitive defusion

The term *fusion* is used in ACT to describe a process of 'entanglement' between an individual and his or her thought content. It is important to note that fusion refers to what is often a normal and familiar human process. For instance, consider those enjoyable moments when you have become deeply engrossed in the story unfolding in a book or film. In such moments you typically would have little sense of the fact that you are conscious person here and now observing these experiences as they are unfolding; instead, you are in some sense 'fused' with the content of the drama or storyline.

Fusion, however, can also create difficulties when we become overly entangled in particular thoughts, self-descriptions or self-judgements and 'stories' about ourselves that – when fusion is present – have the potential to exert an unhelpful influence over our behaviour. When an individual becomes fused with a thought, he or she would take that thought to be literally 'true', with the thought responded to as if it were a fact rather than a symbolic representation.

Acceptance and commitment therapy interventions draw upon a wide range of strategies that can help people defuse from cognitive content whenever they find it helpful to do so. The defusion process might begin with the coach or therapist 'normalising' negative thought content. This could involve discussing why the human mind evolved the way it has – presumably to keep us alive and out of danger, and to ensure we are not rejected by our social group(s). From this evolutionary perspective, it is not so surprising that a large proportion of thought content is negative in nature, with the human mind being very good at worrying about the future, dwelling on difficulties that have happened in the past, comparing ourselves (often unfavourably) with others, generating reasons why we shouldn't do something and predicting all the things that might go wrong (Harris, 2009). There is nothing wrong with the mind for producing such output – it is simply doing what it was designed to do.

The cultivation of self-awareness is an important part of building defusion skills. During daily life, clients can be encouraged to begin noticing the types of thoughts that show up and 'hijack' behaviour in unhelpful ways – particularly beginning to notice the thoughts that seem to interfere with the ability to engage in personally valued patterns of behaviour.

Targeted defusion strategies include 'objectifying' thought content. For example, in one of the most well-known ACT metaphors, thoughts are portrayed as 'passengers' on the bus of life, while the person having those thoughts is portrayed as the driver (Flaxman et al., 2013; Hayes et al., 1999). Other defusion strategies make use of certain language conventions that help cultivate some healthy psychological 'distance' between thinker and thought. For example, when sharing thoughts during coaching sessions, a client might be invited to get into the habit of adding the prefix 'I'm having the thought that . . . '. Also, throughout ACT interventions, 'the mind' is routinely referred to as if it were a separate entity (again helping to cultivate distance between the person *having* the thoughts and thoughts themselves).

Other techniques encourage clients to practice taking unhelpful thoughts a bit less seriously. For example, clients can be encouraged to place unhelpful thought content in an unusual or playful context: a client might be invited to say a thought out loud extremely slowly (like a slowed-down record) in a rather comical voice, or to repeat the essence of a thought over and over again rapidly until its literal meaning drifts into the background and its more direct properties (e.g., the cluster of strange sounds, the feel of the word on the lips) are revealed. It is important that such techniques are presented skilfully by the coach to ensure that clients do not feel ridiculed by the playful nature of this process. It can be helpful for the coach to disclose some of her own unhelpful thoughts and practise such techniques along with the client.

As with all ACT interventions, such exercises are typically not introduced in isolation. Instead they are presented as ways of relating to thoughts in a more skilful way so that our own thoughts do not interfere with our ability to engage in patterns of behaviour that are consistent with personal goals and values. The aim with defusion is not to alter the form or the frequency of unwanted thoughts, but rather to raise awareness of our own mind chatter and to reduce the extent to which certain thoughts can (often subtly) interfere with life-enhancing behavioural choices.

## Self-as-context (or the observing self)

The notion of the 'self' has been studied endlessly in a range of philosophical and psychological contexts. The self is a complex entity and, in 'the observing self', people are encouraged to identify and distinguish between the *conceptualised* self and the *observing* self. The conceptualised self is an expression of who we think we are – our concept of ourselves (I am kind person; I am a terrible parent). The observing or contextualised self is the temporary and fluid self that we notice ourselves to be in a particular moment or context (I notice that I have done a kind deed; I observed that I lost my temper with my children). Problems can come when we become too attached to our conceptual self – too fused with it – and start believing that everything we do or feel is an integral part of who we are: losing your temper once with your children instantly defines you as a terrible parent.

The *observer exercise* can help people to distinguish the concept of the self from the context and accept thoughts and feelings for what they are: just thoughts and feelings rather than defining characteristics. In this exercise people are asked to notice something and then notice who is doing the noticing. Ask your clients to recall an event and describe to you the feelings and sensations associated. Then ask them to notice who did the noticing and who is remembering and telling the story. You can, explicitly, point out that it is the same 'you' who experienced the event as the 'you' who is, here and now, telling the story. This process can help people to reflect on the fluid and changing nature of the self, and they then may be in a position to change a thought such as 'I am terrible at job interviews' to 'last time I did a job interview, I did not perform well'.

## Contact with the present moment

This takes us back to the technique of mindfulness that was described earlier in the chapter. The ACT model is particularly interested in the links between psychological discomfort and the past and the future. Anxiety is often sparked off by worries about future events and depressive thoughts can be rooted in rumination about the past. Mindfulness, with its focus on the present moment, allows people to break away from the focus that can be causing their discomfort.

One mindfulness exercise that is suggested in the ACT literature focuses specifically on noticing. People are asked to notice five things that they can hear, five things they can see and five things they can feel. This kind of specific task can help people to keep their minds from wandering as they focus on experiencing the present moment.

## Values

Values within ACT are described as distinct from but related to goals. In an ACT context, values are described as the direction of travel where goals constitute the end point. Values are therefore likely to be broader and tend to focus on ways to achieve a more meaningful and satisfied life. Hoare, McIlveen and Hamilton (2012) give an example to illustrate the difference, saying that where being a good parent could be a value (a broad construct that could lead to a more fulfilled life), putting aside an hour each day to play with your child is a goal – a more tangible proposition that can be more easily measured. In a more career-oriented context, an ACT value could be to make a meaningful contribution to society through work and the goal could be to re-train as a teacher.

Within an ACT intervention, clients are encouraged to think about their career-related values and then identify goals that might emanate from these values. The discussion could encourage clients to think about what job they would do in an ideal world, what appeals to them about this, what kinds of colleagues or clients they might work with, and how they would like to be remembered after they leave the organisation. The *retirement speech* is an exercise in which individuals are asked to identify what they hope their colleagues might say about them in a retirement speech. This can then form the basis for a discussion about the values that the exercise may have revealed.

## Committed action

The final process identified within the ACT approach is described as *committed action*. This process is similar to the action planning phase that is common to many coaching and career intervention models, and enables clients to capitalise on the motivation and energy generated by the other steps. This goal-setting phase might cover long-term goals, the short-term steps the individual needs to take to get there, and a discussion about any obstacles or barriers that they can anticipate may present them with challenges on the way. The values identified through the processes outlined above should be at the heart of the committed-action part of the conversation. Clients could be encouraged to think about different roles that would allow them to live a life that is more congruent with their values, and use these values as a starting point to assess how well things are going and where changes could be made. Once the big-picture goals are established, the next part of the conversation focuses on the small steps. What can your client do today or tomorrow to start them moving down this path and towards a more values-driven life? Once the first couple of steps are clear, it can be useful to steer the conversation towards any possible challenges. A conversation that allows them to anticipate the obstacles that might come up can help them to be more prepared in terms of their emotions and to have a few creative solutions up their sleeves.

## What's the point in trying? 139

### *In practice*

This is a relatively new therapeutic approach. It is only just beginning to reach career writers and practitioners, but its relevance to our work and the strength of the emerging evidence base convinces me that it will become increasingly mainstream within career practice in the decades to come. The nature of the technique could suggest that it could provide a range of improvements within career development. The approach uses techniques that help with goal setting and identifying values, and which have been shown to boost confidence. These are important aspects of career development and this indicates that the approach is highly likely to be of value to career practitioners. Whilst this could be seen as an exciting new development for career practice, ACT's relatively brief history does mean that there is not a wealth of advice in the literature about how to apply the approach in a career context. Outlined above are some suggestions of exercises that you could use that fit within the ACT approach, but the details of how exactly these should be incorporated within career practice are left to you to experiment with.

### Case study

Sanjeev came to see a careers adviser three years after graduation. He had completed a degree in Business Management but, since leaving university, hadn't really managed to find his feet. He had done a variety of short-term jobs, then done a bit of travelling; he had tried his hand at recruitment, which he didn't really enjoy, and spent some time working in the family business, which didn't seem to suit him either. By this stage, Sanjeev was feeling quite dispirited by the whole affair, wondering whether his decision to go to university had been the right one and feeling at a loss as to what to do next.

In exploring his story in more depth, Sanjeev's career coach wondered if one of the bits missing was Sanjeev's understanding of his own work values. He didn't seem to have a very clear idea of what mattered to him in a job or a career and Sanjeev agreed that gaining some clarity on this might help him focus his mind on a more tangible future.

The career coach invited Sanjeev to fast forward his career right through to his retirement and asked him to think about his last ever day at work, at the end of a successful and fulfilling 40-year career. Sanjeev pictured the scene at his farewell party and observed that, not only was he surrounded by colleagues from his last organisation, but he had also been joined by colleagues, friends

*(continued)*

*(continued)*

and clients stretching right back throughout his career. This felt important to Sanjeev and it struck him as he described the scene in his mind's eye that these kinds of close working relationships mattered to him.

As Sanjeev's boss started to talk about Sanjeev's career history, Sanjeev listened with interest. He had worked in a number of different organisations but had stuck within the same sector, gradually building up expertise along the way, and he had stayed in most places for long enough to make a difference and to build up some strong relationships. As Sanjeev's boss talked, the themes of the speech seemed to be of relationships and expertise. People had enjoyed working with him, valued his integrity and personal loyalty, and had appreciated his in-depth knowledge and his specialist expertise.

Reflecting on this scene with his career coach, Sanjeev felt that those two elements of relationships and expertise mattered to him. He liked the idea of being known for his particular knowledge base and liked the idea that he could use this to make a contribution to a range of different kinds of team. The exercise in itself had made Sanjeev feel more positive about his own future, making him feel that there was a positive future out there for him. It also gave him a starting point for the next stage in his career research as he started to consider what kinds of expertise interested him and what kinds of roles would allow him to carve out a niche of this sort.

| | |
|---|---|
| One to one | ✓ |
| Group sessions | ✗ |
| Within the session | ✓ |
| As a self-directed intersessional task | ✓ |
| Initial career choice | ✓ |
| Career changes | ✓ |
| Indicative timing | 10–15 minutes per exercise |

## Why it works

The potential contribution that ACT can make to career coaching lies in its ability to address emotions (Kidd, 2008), values (Brown, 1996) and relationships (Schultheiss et al., 2001), all of which have been shown to have an impact on career development and to add value to clients when addressed in career interventions. The importance of values in careers work has been well established. In Chapter 5 an exercise that helps clients to explore their implicit values was presented and Brown (1996) has written extensively on the importance of values in career choice.

The ACT is grounded in *Relational Frame Theory* (Hayes, Barnes-Holmes, & Roche, 2001), which is a form of behaviourism that highlights the impact of language on cognition, emotion and behaviour. This theory is very influenced by the ideas underpinning cognitive behavioural therapy (CBT) outlined in Chapter 7 but, where CBT aims to solve the problems caused by unhelpful thoughts by challenging and re-structuring them, relational frame theory (RFT) aims to address the relationships between an individual and their thoughts and feelings. The authors of RFT are concerned with the way that humans relate events or objects to each other and, in particular, the nature and processes associated with the links created between language and objects, feelings or events (Hayes, Barnes-Holmes, & Roche, 2001). They suggest that if we can learn to associate a random set of letters and sounds with a particular idea (e.g., the way we associate the sounds and shapes of the word 'book' with the physical object that we read), then we can also unlearn these associations. If we have learned to associate the word 'presentation' with a stomach-churning sense of inadequacy, then the word itself is going to trouble us every time we think about it or say it. But, if we can learn to dissociate the word from the negative feelings, then it loses its power. The ACT focuses on the idea that trying to control language leads to limited values-driven action. Instead, altering the symbolic meaning or the context of language allows for more values-driven action (Arch & Craske, 2008).

## What's the evidence base?

The evidence base for the efficacy of ACT is growing and is really promising, but it should be pointed out that this approach has not been tested empirically in career practice. A meta-analysis in 2014 (Öst, 2014), which looked at the data from 60 randomised controlled trials incorporating over 4,000 participants, showed that ACT seemed to provide good outcomes for the treatment of stress and depression. In an earlier meta-analysis, Powers, Vörding & Emmelkamp (2009) indicated that ACT was also effective in reducing anxiety and in dealing with physical health conditions.

In non-clinical populations ACT has been shown to be effective. Moran (2011) used ACT when working with leaders and his study suggested that the process led to improved performance and innovation, and reduced work stress and work errors. In other work settings ACT has been shown to

*(continued)*

*(continued)*

increase performance (Bond & Flaxman, 2006), reducing work stress and increasing job satisfaction (Bond & Bunce, 2003; Flaxman & Bond, 2010), increasing innovation (Bond & Bunce, 2000), reducing work errors (Bond & Bunce, 2003) and improving the acceptance of new training at work (Luoma, Hayes, & Walser, 2007; Varra, Hayes, Roget & Fisher, 2008).

The research therefore suggests that ACT can be a powerful tool for increasing well-being, both within clinical populations and in the workplace.

# Chapter 11

# I just can't decide between these options

## Introduction

We have spent some time in the book so far looking at techniques that can help individuals to generate possible career options. Sometimes, however, identifying the options are isn't enough. Even if you have managed to narrow it down to two or three alternatives that all seem to fit the bill, taking that last step and making a final choice can be tough. The literature on decision making gives us some clues as to why career decisions are so hard. Researchers have identified the kinds of factors that make one kind of decision harder than another, and career choices seem to tick pretty much every box.

First, there is the issue of the number of options. Research indicates that having about six options to choose from is ideal (Iyengar & Lepper, 2000). With this degree of choice, people feel that they have some control and they are able to research each option thoroughly and can make thoughtful comparisons. People choosing between just a handful of options find the decision-making process satisfactory and report higher levels of satisfaction with their final choices. In the UK, the government (ONS, 2010) recognises around 36,000 different job titles, and that number of alternative career options increases once you consider the different training routes and different types of industries and organisations. For most people the full range of 36,000 job titles are not all going to be in the frame: astrophysicist and army fitness trainer, for example, have never been on my personal list of possible options. But that still leaves quite a few left over. So career decisions are hard because there are so many options.

The second factor that is known to make decisions harder concerns information. Decision-making literature tells us that choices are harder when we do not have complete or comparable information. When researching careers, it is nigh on impossible to gather all the possible relevant data. You can research a career option thoroughly on the internet, talk to people currently in the field and pour over data about market trends that claim to predict future developments; but no amount of scrutinising will tell you how well you are likely to get on with your new colleagues or how the organisation's culture might change following a surprise takeover.

Finally, we know that decisions are rendered more difficult if we see great potential for loss should we make the wrong choice. With career decisions there are two avenues for loss that could stem from a poor choice. The first is the opportunity cost. It can take months or even years and cost tens of thousands of pounds to pursue some career paths; if the career choice disappoints, that means an enormous wasted investment. The second, potentially greater, source of loss concerns identity. As we have discussed earlier in the book, decisions about careers are decisions about our identity; we are not just making a choice about what we want to do, but who we want to be. As such, a false career choice might say something about ourselves that we do not like or that damages our self-esteem in some way.

So, a career choice involves the Herculean task of researching unpredictable information about innumerable options and getting it wrong can be both psychologically and materially costly. No wonder then that clients sometimes find it difficult.

In this chapter two techniques are described that can help clients to take the plunge. The first, Head and Heart, explains the two decision-making systems we use and shows how they can be combined to help with decisions. The second, Imaginary Conversations, is a technique that can help clients to see their current dilemmas from a different, and more distant, angle.

## Head and heart

For decades it had been thought that good decisions should be made independently and rationally. This advice has been reflected in the career development literature, and scholars and practitioners have suggested that clients should make their career decisions consciously, deliberately and on their own. But, some years ago, the decision-making literature began to explore the cognitive processes that underpin decisions and uncovered some information that has turned the traditional advice on its head. Kahneman (2011) describes two different cognitive information-processing systems. System 1 is what we more commonly think of as the gut instinct. These instincts have evolved over millennia to be able to absorb vast quantities of information and to make reasonably sensible decisions in an instant. The gut instinct has been shown to outperform conscious rational logic in situations where there is too much information to process easily, and where the decision involves weighing up probabilities and there is no one right answer. System 2 is the conscious rational part of our brains. It is slower and can't cope with as much information at once but, because it is within our conscious awareness, it has two great advantages over the gut instinct. First, it is not as susceptible to the enormous number of errors and biases that are associated with gut instinct. The flawed thinking associated with our unconscious instincts has been well documented and Kahneman's book contains numerous shocking and entertaining examples of the errors that are linked to gut instinct. Second, because System 2 is conscious, the thinking processes can be scrutinised. If it is possible to see the train of thought that has led to a particular viewpoint, it is easier to identify the sources of information, make rational decisions about their value and decide whether it is a good idea to heed this advice.

Neither approach to decision making is without its flaws, but in this head and heart technique clients are encouraged to identify the thoughts and ideas that emanate from each system, compare them and then make conscious decisions about which to trust. There are three good reasons to try this approach. First, because (as highlighted in the box below) there is some empirical evidence that suggests that combining the two approaches is a good strategy for decision making and can lead to better career decisions. Second, because, even if your client swears against it, the chances are that their decisions will be influenced by their System 1 logic and, as such, may be subject to bias and flaws. Being consciously aware of this System 1 information can give individuals the chance to scrutinise this data, work out where it comes from and decide whether they value it. The third good reason is that the approach might just bring something new. People are often more likely to use one of these decision-making systems over the other. Clients come to see career coaches when they are stuck and it may be that their usual approach, for whatever reason, isn't working in this context. If you can explain the two approaches to your client then they may be able to identify their usual approach and see whether using the other sheds any new light on their situation.

## How to use

In this technique, clients are invited to identify the advice from each of the two systems, and then to spend some time thinking about which of the two approaches is making more sense.

It is useful at the start to explain and describe the two systems. You may find that your clients have come across them before but, if not, you can use the descriptions above or find your own form of words that you feel explains the two approaches more clearly. The language used in the literature tends to refer to conscious and nonconscious processing, or Systems 1 and 2, as mentioned above. I have used the term gut instinct because I think this is fairly easy to identify, but the terms I use in describing this technique below are that of the head and the heart. This works for me as it is a well-known phrase that sets the two systems in opposition to each other, but do, of course, use whatever language you feel works best.

### Step 1: what are the messages?

Once you feel that your client is convinced that there are two different systems, and has some understanding of the nature of each, your next step is to ask them what advice each system is giving them. I find that a direct question, such as 'what is your head telling you?' and 'what is your heart telling you?', often elicits a response (sometimes to the surprise of the client themselves) and, once the answer has been stated out loud, the two of you can work together to examine the reasons behind the answers. If your client finds it difficult to answer straightaway, it may be worth pressing them a little more. Their initial reaction might well be 'I don't know' but, with some encouragement, they may find themselves able to come up with an answer. Sometimes softening the language can help – moving from 'what does your gut instinct say?' to something such as 'where do you think your gut instinct is leaning?' can help your client feel more inclined to commit themselves.

Identifying the preferences of the gut instinct can sometimes be achieved through techniques that involve chance. If there are two options under consideration, you could take a coin and assign one option to 'heads' and the other to 'tails'. Then toss the coin, but, before you unveil it, ask your client whether they are hoping it is going to be heads or tails. A variation that can be used if there are more than two options is to write each on a small piece of paper, crumple the pieces of paper up and put them in a container of some sort, and then invite your client to pick one piece of paper out. Before they smooth out the paper, ask them what they are hoping it will say, or wait until they have read it out and then ask them how they feel about having made that choice.

Most often, there is some difference in the advice coming from the two sources – it is usually this distinction that has led to the indecision but, once in a while, your client may report that their head and heart are in complete harmony. In this case, it would be interesting to try to identify the source of their indecision – if everything is pointing in one direction, then what is stopping them from committing? It may be that the techniques described in Chapters 8 and 9, that explore internal conflicts (part of me wants one option, part of me wants something else) and external tensions (it is what I want but my family want something else), may be of more value.

*Step 2: what are the influences?*

Taking the two approaches in turn, spend some time encouraging your client to identify the reasons for the advice. Ask them to identify the underpinning information or assumptions, and have a discussion about the sources of information and whether they think that the information is accurate and relevant. It is important here to maintain your non-judgemental stance. Our unconscious thoughts are sometimes a bit off the wall, but this doesn't mean that they are not relevant. If your client's gut instinct is warning them off being a librarian because it doesn't seem very glamorous, then this is an important area to explore, even if neither you nor your client believe that this is a good basis for a career decision.

If your client really hasn't been able to say what advice their head and heart are giving, then you might need to start from another angle. Rather than asking for the advice itself, you could suggest that they try to tell you a bit about what the head and heart are saying. For the conscious processes, you could suggest writing a pros and cons list, or trying to identify which factors are the most important and filling in a table in which each possible option is given a score out of ten for each factor. If your client is struggling to articulate the System 1 perspective, you could try a visualisation. The information in System 1 is thought to be stored in the form of images, so inviting your client to close their eyes and tell you what scene is depicted when you mention each of the options under consideration ('picture yourself as a police officer. What do you see?') may help to uncover some of the ideas buried a little deeper.

*Step 3: which system is giving better advice?*

When your client has identified the advice and the reasons behind the advice from each decision-making system, the final step involves a bit of analysis. Which system do they feel is giving better advice? Which is shouting louder? Which system have they trusted in the past – has it let them down before? Why do they think the two systems are at odds with each other? This may uncover a clear front runner or may highlight that more information is need in order to reach a conclusion. And, ultimately, if no one option is coming to the fore, it is appropriate to lay down a gentle challenge to your client, 'well, how are you going to make a decision?'.

## In practice

The description of the two cognitive systems can be delivered in either a group setting or one to one, but the conversation that allows the individual to examine and scrutinise their own thought processes is often more effective if it is conducted with a professional career coach. As such, I think clients might well get more value from this technique in a one-to-one context.

| | |
|---|---|
| One to one | ✓ |
| Group sessions | ✗ |
| Within the session | ✓ |
| As a self-directed intersessional task | ✗ |
| Initial career choice | ✓ |
| Career changes | ✓ |
| Indicative timing | 15 minutes |

## Why it works

The whole idea of trying to work out what the unconscious is telling you is problematic: if it is unconscious, then it is going to be impossible to find out. But there is a store that is described as the 'preconscious', and it is the information stored here that we are trying to uncover with this technique. It is described as below the level of consciousness, but not buried very deep (Freud, 1915). The information stored there is fairly easily accessible, but only with the addition of attention and words (Zepf, 2011). This is the information you are trying to unearth in this approach, and you do this by asking your client to focus their attention on the information and to articulate it. The link between language and thought is fairly well established in the literature (Roth, 2009; Vygotsky, 1986).

## What's the evidence base?

In decision-making literature this approach is fairly mainstream now and well evidenced. Kahneman won a Nobel prize for the research and they do not give those out lightly. As mentioned in the box above, it is quite difficult to evidence what is going on below the level of consciousness, but dozens of experiments and observations seem to support the existence of this dual processing system, its prevalence and the value it can bring (Dijksterhuis, Aarts, & Smith, 2005; Hastie & Dawes, 2010; Phillips, 1997). Within the career literature there isn't a vast evidence base, but there have been a number of studies over the years that demonstrate that the biases and flaws that have been identified in other spheres can also be seen in career decisions. In particular, a number of studies (for example, Blustein & Strohmer, 1987; Soelberg, 1967) have shown that, whilst we think that we are making conscious rational choices, our career decisions are inevitably influenced by our gut instinct. The studies also suggest that we even construct rational reasons to justify our instinctive career choices.

The evidence then is compelling that the two systems of thinking do exist and that System 1 thinking is probably stronger and more pervasive than System 2. The systems seem to work best when they are in harmony. One study, which explored the career decision-making mechanisms of 361 adult career changers, concluded that decisions made through a combination of head and heart were more likely to lead to more suitable job choices (Singh & Greenhaus, 2004).

## Imaginary conversations

### Introduction

The second technique for helping an individual to make a choice again encourages them to uncover and make use of information they may not know that they have. This approach allows your client to observe and analyse their current dilemma from an external perspective and this can admit a more objective analysis. With a big decision, it can be easy to get lost in the moment and bogged down in the detail. Because your client is inevitably at the heart of the process, it can be difficult for them to get any perspective and, whilst others are often happy to share their views and advice, no-one else can quite grasp the situation in the way that they themselves do, and no-one else will quite be able to understand their values system and their personal hopes and fears. Their own brain usually has the solution, but it is not always easy to access it. This technique provides a way for clients to access their own views, filtered through an imagined conversation with someone else.

## How to use

### Step 1: who to choose?

This technique invites the client to imagine a conversation about their current career dilemma with another person and to imagine the advice that they would be given. For this they could choose anyone whom they admire and whom they feel would give them good advice – a role model. It could be someone they know, a real person they haven't met, or even a fictional character.

An alternative option is for the person to think about themselves in the future. You could suggest looking five or ten years' hence – it needs to be a version of them that is close enough for them to relate to but far enough away to have moved beyond this current dilemma and into a different era of life.

To set the task up and to get their imagination going, you might suggest that they close their eyes and picture the scene. You do not want to get distracted by irrelevant details, but it can be useful to ask some specific questions to stimulate your client's thoughts. You could, for example, ask them to think about the location of the conversation and to describe the room and the context.

### Step 2: what advice would they give?

Your client should start by explaining their current career dilemma to their imagined conversation partner. This process of setting out their problem can be useful to help them to crystalise their thoughts and feelings at this point. Once they have told their story, your client might be able to formulate a specific question for their partner or role model, and the next part of the process is to find out what response this person would give them. Encourage your client to be as detailed and comprehensive as they can be. You can prompt them to give further details and encourage them to get into a dialogue with their role model, perhaps suggesting 'how would you respond to that?' and 'what answer would your role model give to that?'.

### Step 3: what does this mean?

In the final part of the discussion you should ask your client to come out of role and invite them to reflect on the advice given. It is sometimes worthwhile to remind your clients at this stage that the advice that they came up with actually came from their own minds – it was imagined through the character of their role model, but the ideas were generated entirely by them. Your discussion can go in whatever direction you and your client feel is fruitful, but here are a few questions that might spark you off.

- Does this seem like good advice?
- What do you like about it?
- What bits do you think are particularly valuable?

- Are there any aspects that you do not think are useful?
- What was behind your role model's advice?
- In what ways do you agree with this advice?
- Do you think you should or could act on this advice?
- If you do not think you can act on it, why is that?
- What would need to change to enable you to act on the advice?
- What is the first step you need to take?

The way the technique is presented above assumes that it is carried out within a one-to-one session. An alternative that works well can to be suggest that clients write down the advice in the form of a letter. This can then become an exercise that your clients can do either at home, between sessions, or within a group context.

### *In practice*

In Chapter 6 the technique of possible selves was introduced as an approach to help clients generate ideas about future jobs. As part of that technique clients are asked to imagine their future selves, and this detailed image that they invoke as part of the possible selves exercise can be harnessed for their imaginary conversation. Once you feel that you have got as much as you can from the possible selves exercise, you could suggest that your clients do one last thing and, whilst they still have their future self clear in their minds, you could invite them to imagine a conversation between their current self and their future self and then launch into the imaginary conversation.

| | |
|---|---|
| One to one | ✓ |
| Group sessions | ✓ |
| Within the session | ✓ |
| As a self-directed intersessional task | ✓ |
| Initial career choice | ✓ |
| Career changes | ✓ |
| Indicative timing | 20 minutes |

## Why it works

The process works through the power of the imagination. Imagination takes reality and presents it from a different angle, considering different possibilities. It does this by filling in the gaps. When we are asked a question to which we do not know the answer, we fill in the gaps (Pelaprat & Cole, 2011). Our brains are not comfortable with the uncertainty that comes with an unknown answer, so they do what they can. They draw on the personal experience, cultural stories and knowledge we have amassed and they try their best to come up with a plausible answer, one that fits in with what we already know but reconfigures existing information to fill the gap (Zittoun & Gillespie, 2015). In these imaginary conversations, clients will take what they know about this particular role model or future version of themselves and, prompted by an unanticipated question, will seek out any information they can source to devise a story line that seems plausible – generating advice that seems to be consistent with that kind of person.

## What's the evidence base?

There is a robust evidence base that demonstrates the power than role models can have on career development. They influence aspirations, attitudes, behaviour and career choices (Quimby & DeSantis, 2006).

The idea of 'imagined interactions' has been studied in depth in the literature (Honeycutt, 2002, 2008). These imagined conversations help people to anticipate, prepare for and make sense of events and are shown to have a positive impact on planning and preparing. They provide a different view of people's reality and make use of symbols and visual images to provide an alternative perspective.

# Chapter 12

# I am not feeling very motivated

Lack of motivation is all too common a phenomenon. Each of us has, at one point or other, felt sluggish and unenthusiastic about putting our plans into action, perhaps looking for every excuse under the sun (isn't it about time I hoovered behind the sofa or rearranged my sock drawer?) to postpone any action. Sometimes, too, we can find ourselves in a situation where a change is inevitable, yet we ourselves are not quite ready for it. Students finishing their college or university courses can find that, whilst they know that a new chapter in their lives will start soon, they drag their heels, half pretending that it is not going to happen.

Reasons for a lack of motivation are many, varied and often quite individual. In this chapter, three specific techniques are introduced that have been shown to enhance motivation. In addition to tools such as these, there is a substantial body of work that explores motivation more generally and that may be useful to touch on here. One theory that seems to have considerable support is from Ryan and Deci (pronounced DeeCee) and is known as 'self-determination theory' (2000). This theory suggests that there are three essential ingredients to motivation: *autonomy*, *relatedness* and *competence*. The theory holds that if any one of these is missing, then full commitment to a course of action is not possible. Applying this theory to career development, then, an individual needs to feel that they genuinely have some control over their own future; that they are not alone in facing such challenges; and that they have the skills or qualities that are required to choose a career, secure a job and perform well in their future position. If any of these three aspects are lacking it will be much more difficult for anyone to put their heart and soul into their job search. This self-determination theory can be a useful framework to have in the back of your mind when working with your clients, and can help you and your client to make links between their current levels of motivation and other aspects of their story. Techniques for addressing some of these challenges to motivation have been introduced in earlier chapters. In particular Chapter 9 (It is what I want but my family aren't so sure) offers some ideas for clients whose relationships seem to be constraining their choices, and Chapters 10 (What's the point? I am never going to make anything of myself) and 7 (I want to go for it but I am just not sure I am good enough) offer ideas for those whose belief in their own ability may be holding them back.

Perhaps the clients who really need a bit of help with their motivation are those who do not come and see us – those who haven't even managed to summon up the will to make an appointment. For career practitioners working in some contexts this may be an insurmountable problem – if you work with private clients who seek you out and choose to use your services, then it may be difficult to work out how to access those who have no interest in asking for your help. But, for career coaches who work within the public sector – for example, within schools, colleges and universities – there might be opportunities, within compulsory classes for example, to introduce an exercise or two from one of the techniques below.

The first approach in this chapter deals with the notion of 'career time perspective'. This concept is not widely used within career practice but there is a wealth of research that attests to its importance in motivating people to act. The second is 'the miracle question'. This is a tool adapted from solution-focused therapy. This approach to therapy has been adopted in mainstream coaching and there is some robust empirical evidence that it seems to work. The final approach introduced in this chapter is Change Talk. This too is a tool that was originally introduced within a broader approach, this time from motivational interviewing, which is a therapeutic approach that originated in health care. As both solution-focused therapy and motivational interviewing are interesting as approaches in their own right, an introduction to each is given before the specific tool is described.

## Career time perspective

### Introduction

The ability to reflect on the past and imagine the future is thought to be a uniquely human quality (Suddendorf & Corballis, 1997). This mental time travel has been called *time perspective* and it has an impact on our decisions, behaviour and actions (Zimbardo & Boyd, 1999). Time perspective is described as a measure of psychological distance – it is our own personal understanding of the relative distance between yesterday, today and tomorrow and it will vary both from one person to another, and within an individual, from one time and another. It is developed during childhood, as parents teach children about the world and provide role models for behaviour, and young people from higher socioeconomic groups have been shown to be more likely to develop a stronger sense of future time perspective or *futurity*. A strong future time perspective allows people to make clear links in their own minds between the present and the future, and enables them to feel that their current choices will have a direct impact on their future lives. From the perspective of those making career choices, this futurity will enable people to see that time spent, for example, networking, applying for work experience, or engaging in extra-curricular activities whilst at university will all have a positive impact on their chances of getting the job they want when they graduate.

## How to use

The approach outlined below was developed by Mark Savickas (1991), whose name you may recognise from the career construction interview that was introduced in Chapter 3 as an approach to allow people to make sense of their career stories. This time perspective modification intervention (TPMI) is divided into three stages: orientation, differentiation and integration.

### Step 1: orientation

In this first phase, clients are encouraged to increase their futurity and helped to feel more optimistic about the future. The intervention starts by using something called the 'circles test' (Cottle, 1967) in which clients are asked to try and think about their past, present and future as being in the shape of circles. They are asked to draw three circles, one to represent their past, one their present and one their future, and to arrange them on the page in such a way as to show their relationship with each other. The circles can be of any size and arranged in any way that is meaningful to them. Clients are then asked to think about their choices using the following six prompts.

- What were you thinking about as you drew the circles?
- What do their relative sizes mean to you?
- Describe a recent choice you have made and identify the time zone you focused on while making that decision.
- Use three words to describe how you feel about your past, your present and your future.
- Define work and play. Compare and contrast them.
- How will your future adult life be different from that of your parents? How will the world be different than it is now?

### Step 2: differentiation

During this step, clients are encouraged to develop what Savickas describes as a 'differentiated future'. This means an idea of a future that is clear and elaborate and full of events that extend far into the future. This process tends to make people feel more optimistic about the future and provides them with a meaningful context for decision making. With a differentiated future, they are making a career decision that fits into a realistic and holistic future. The decision then becomes less abstract and, as such, it can be easier to work out what might be the best fit.

Invite your clients to draw their lifelines into the future – right up until their death. Ask them to draw a line on a piece of paper that starts at the present day and stretches right through past retirement. Suggest that they identify ten (or more) events that are likely to happen in their future lives and mark them on their lifelines. Invite them to identify those over which they will have some control. For each event, encourage them to consider and articulate 'who will you be?' and 'what will you do?'.

# I am not feeling very motivated 155

The key during this stage is to get them to think about their future in some breadth and depth, and to make links to career and life planning.

### Step 3: integration

In this final step, clients are encouraged to make the links between the present and the future explicit. Clients are asked to think about their career goals in the light of their lifelines and then to think about what this means for their career planning. They might want to add some suggested actions to their lifelines as they work out their own career plans, and you could encourage them at this stage to identify a number of specific short-term goals that they can start to implement and that will help towards their longer-term plans.

### In practice

Career time perspective has been introduced here as a tool that can help clients become more motivated to put their plans into action. The technique can also be useful for both career planning and goal setting. The process of thinking about the future and imagining oneself ten years or so from now can help people to crystalise their hopes or expectations for the future, and this process can facilitate setting both long-term plans and immediate actions that need to be taken.

The approach can be conducted either in group settings or in one to ones, and is possibly most effective with younger clients who are still in education and for whom the actual job search process is a little way off, although there is, of course, no reason not to try the approach with other clients if you feel that they could benefit.

| | |
|---|---|
| One to one | ✓ |
| Group sessions | ✓ |
| Within the session | ✓ |
| As a self-directed intersessional task | ✗ |
| Initial career choice | ✓ |
| Career changes | ✓ |
| Indicative timing | 45 minutes |

## Why it works

A high level of futurity is associated with people who have a clear sense of themselves, clear career goals and plans, and who work harder to put these plans into action. So any intervention that can focus on developing and enhancing futurity is likely to be of value.

*(continued)*

*(continued)*

Future time perspective has been shown to have strong links with a range of positive career learning outcomes. A strong sense of futurity has been shown to be related to career maturity (Savickas, Silling & Schwartz, 1984), better career planning (Janeiro, 2010), harder work (Ferrari, Nota & Soresi, 2012), vocational identity (Taber & Blankemeyer, 2015) and career decidedness (Ferrari, Nota & Soresi, 2012; Savickas, Silling & Schwartz, 1984). One interesting study that examined this was from Greenbank and Hepworth (2008) who explored the decision-making processes of students at Edge Hill University. They identified a clear distinction between the time perspective of the students from middle-class and working-class backgrounds, finding that the students from lower socioeconomic groups approached their studies and career as a linear sequence: first I'll get my degree and then I'll think about jobs. In contrast, those from higher socioeconomic groups felt that the two groups should be approached contemporaneously, thinking about developing the skills and experience needed for their future employability alongside their degree studies.

## What's the evidence base?

Given how useful this idea of future time perspective appears to be, there has been a surprisingly limited focus on providing the profession with a strong evidence base of the effectiveness of interventions, but there are some studies that show that FTP interventions work. Anuszkiewicz (1983) offers a convincing study that shows the impact of a future time perspective intervention on 40 young offenders. It showed that the intervention increased participants' levels of hope and optimism, but that study used a longer and more complex design than many of us have the scope for. Another study (Ferrari, Nota & Soresi, 2012) demonstrated that a group of 50 adolescents benefitted from a FTP intervention but, again, this was a somewhat unrealistic ten-week course of workshops. More usefully, Marko and Savickas (1998) used the approach described in this chapter with groups of young people at senior school. They found that the intervention did increase their futurity, had an impact on their attitudes towards career planning and on their sense of hope and optimism about the future. More recently, Schuitema, Peetsma and van der Veen (2014) found that university students developed clearer goals and worked harder following a one-off 45-minute future time perspective intervention, and they found that the effects were still noticeable a year after the intervention itself.

## The miracle question

### Introduction

The miracle question is one of the most popular and accessible tools that has emerged from solution-focused therapy. Solution-focused therapy (SFT) was developed in the context of family therapy at the Milwaukee Brief Family Therapy Center in the American state of Wisconsin. Solution-focused therapy offers an interesting approach that could be of value to career practitioners and I will introduce it as a whole approach first before honing in on the miracle question itself.

The development of the approach was practice-driven rather than theory-driven, in that it emerged as the team at the Family Therapy Center observed the techniques that seemed to work in practice and developed a framework on that basis. They noticed that even clients who brought multiple and profound problems to their counselling sessions were able to identify and describe times when the problems were much reduced or gone altogether. They also noticed that when clients were invited to focus on those times and to reflect on how they themselves behaved differently, the clients often ended up making positive changes in their lives.

At the heart of SFT lies the assumption that solutions are not found in problems and that, whilst an in-depth discussion of what has gone wrong can be interesting and even cathartic, it is not usually the best route to working out what to do next. The focus instead should be on exceptions: 'tell me about a time when things **did** go well' and resources: 'what was it about you that made that work so well?'. The general principles of the SFT intervention are to find out what works and then do more of it, and find out what doesn't work and do something different.

One of the key principles underpinning SFT is that the intervention should focus just on what is going to help and not waste any time discussing any details that do not prove productive. It is this narrow focus that has led to SFT being described as a 'brief therapy'. In practice, this means that career coaches should spend little time exploring or interpreting past events, or discussing where things have gone wrong for the client, and instead should devote their energy to finding out what the client's preferred future could look like and on the resources that the client has used in the past and that could be useful in working towards their goals. Miller (2006) suggests that career practitioners should adopt an attitude of curiosity, and ask positive questions that assume and communicate the assumption that the client has the resources and the capability to achieve their goals.

The role of the solution-focused coach is to keep the conversation focused on the future and on possibilities, rather than trying to unpick and understand the past.

### How to use

One commonly used technique from SFT is the miracle question, which is an effective approach to focusing clients' minds on exceptions and possibilities. The miracle question invites people to imagine what their lives would be like if their current dilemma was resolved. The idea is that this kind of visualisation will both increase motivation and help the individual to identify the steps they need to take to start them on the path towards this new future. It can be used to help clients to identify their own strengths and goals, to increase motivation and hope, and to encourage them to be open to possibilities and solutions. The question runs along these lines:

> Imagine that tonight you go for a long sleep and, whilst you are asleep, a miracle happens and your career dilemma is entirely resolved. You wake up six months in a future in which you have a secure and fulfilling job. The problem has entirely gone away but, because you were asleep whilst the miracle happened, when you first wake up you do not realise that anything has changed. What is the first thing that happens in the morning that lets you know that things are different? What's next?

The detail and wording of the question can be altered to suit your client's particular situation, but there need to be four key elements:

- a miracle happens;
- the problem is resolved;
- you do not know when you wake up that anything has changed;
- the future is gradually revealed, step by step.

A client might start their response in this way:

> I hear the alarm go off and normally, these days, I want to just sink under the duvet and make it all go away, but in this scenario, I don't. I just feel OK. I feel a bit dopey and sluggish, but not at all unhappy. And I would just get up quietly – no groaning or moaning, or complaining that it's too early. I would just get up and go and have a shower. I think even my shower would be different. I can see myself standing taller and doing everything faster. And I'd be thinking different things. I'd be planning the day, and thinking about the things I would need to get done at work, the meetings, the people, the projects. I'd be looking forward to it. I could see myself thinking back to the previous day or the previous week and going over a conversation, maybe laughing at a joke in the office. Then over breakfast, I can imagine that I'm more focused on everyone else than I normally am. I'm asking my kids what they've got on at school today, and offering to make everyone more toast. I think I'm dressed differently too. I seem to have bought myself a new suit, and I just look a bit better groomed – a bit sharper.

Once the miracle question has been answered broadly, you should follow up with questions that encourage your client to elaborate their visualisation, providing details of their lives, routines, emotions and relationships. You could use all kinds of questioning techniques to elicit a detailed description, focusing on the client inside ('how are you feeling?') and out ('what do you look like?'), asking about things from their own perspective and the perspective of others ('how can your partner tell that things are different?'), and asking about behaviour ('what do you do that's different?), emotions ('how optimistic are you feeling?') and thoughts ('what are you thinking about on the way to work?'). You could start the visualisation by asking them about how they feel in the morning and encourage them to think through their journey to work and the start of their day, finding out details of the behaviour they might demonstrate in the workplace and the feelings that accompany it.

One important role for the coach is to help the client to articulate feelings in terms of behaviour. If a client, describing their preferred future, says 'I am feeling so much better', you should follow up with 'what looks different, as a result of this change?' or 'how could your colleagues tell that you are feeling better?'. This translation of inner states to outer ones is a key aspect of SFT.

## *In practice*

One important assumption within the approach, and one that must be embraced by the coach for the interventions to be most useful, is that the clients already have the resources they need and that they have it in themselves to solve their own problems (Miller, 2006). Here we see resonance with a number of other approaches and theories that have been discussed in this book, such as positive psychology (introduced in the context of strengths coaching in Chapter 5) and the client-centred philosophy of Rogers (1957) that underpins so much of traditional career practice.

The miracle question has been used here as a technique for enhancing motivation and the box below highlights the supporting evidence for its ability to fulfil this function. It can also be used as a technique that can help with goal setting. From this perspective it has some resonance with the possible selves technique that was introduced in Chapter 6, in that it allows people to start imagining their future in anyway they want and to build up a fuller picture, gradually leading to specific goals.

| | |
|---|---|
| One to one | ✓ |
| Group sessions | ✗ |
| Within the session | ✓ |
| As a self-directed intersessional task | ✓ |
| Initial career choice | ✓ |
| Career changes | ✓ |
| Indicative timing | 15 minutes |

## Why it works

Solution-focused therapy was developed through observing practice (de Shazer et al., 1986). Steve de Shazer was a psychotherapist who founded the Brief Family Therapy Centre in Milwaukee, and who pioneered this approach. He observed that his wife's approach to family therapy seemed to be effective and to work fast, and he decided to watch her work and try to identify what she did that was different and what seemed to make the difference to her clients. The approach is the result of hours of observation and analysis.

Solution-focused therapy is a constructivist approach that supports the idea that people create their own realities through their own perceptions and interpretations of their experiences (Brown & Brooks, 1996). This explains the focus in the conversations on the client's perceptions of reality and the assumptions that it is only the clients who have the solutions: given that it is the clients' reality you are dealing with, then it can only be the client who can identify which solutions will work within their reality.

The miracle question (also described as the magic wand question and linked to Milton Erickson's 'crystal ball' (Haley, 1967)) seems to work because it encourages the client to consider their problem within a multifaceted context. Specifically, this works because it allows them to see that their problem isn't or doesn't need to be present all the time. It awakens the possibility that the problem can go away. This then allows the person to envisage a preferred future and with this image comes goals, hope and optimism.

One reason the miracle question works so well is that it removes from the client any pressure to think about how they might make this happen. They are freed from being constrained by the practicalities, the barriers and the lack of confidence that can make the first step so challenging and, instead, can just allow their imagination free rein to take them wherever it wants to take them.

## What's the evidence base?

The evidence base for SFT is not as comprehensive as that which can be seen for some of the more medicalised therapies such as CBT (Franklin et al., 2015), but there is nevertheless growing support for the approach and there have been a number of papers that support the potential value of SFT in career practice (Burwell & Chen, 2006; Miller, 2017).

Much of the evidence examines the impact of SFT as a broad approach, but there are some studies that explore the specific impact of the miracle question. It seems that the miracle question is popular, both with practitioners, who described it as easily integrated with other approaches (Miller, 2017) and with clients (Gingerich & Peterson, 2013). It has been shown to be effective with a range of types of clients including young people in secondary schools (Greene & Lee, 2011) and adolescents in Scotland (Wells & McCaig, 2016).

One note of caution comes from Mulawarman (2014) who suggests that the miracle question is not suitable for clients who feel that they have no hope and who simply cannot envisage a positive future. In general, people who are feeling this way may not be ready for career conversations but, in thinking about our professional boundaries, it is useful to have this reminder that referring on to a more specialist service, where appropriate, is important.

## Change talk

### Introduction

Change talk is a key tenet of motivational interviewing and, as with the miracle question described above, the approach as a whole has some interesting insights that can make a useful contribution to career coaching.

Motivational interviewing is an approach that was developed within a medical context by Miller and Rollnick (1991). It was created as an approach to help patients deal with substance abuse, smoking cessation and weight loss, but since then has been applied successfully in a range of contexts. The approach draws from Rogers' person-centred philosophy and aims to increase intrinsic motivation. The distinction between intrinsic and extrinsic motivation is a useful one to unpick. People motivated *extrinsically* engage in particular behaviour because they believe that the behaviour will lead to something that they consider desirable. Those motivated *intrinsically* act in a particular way simply because they like it – they get something out of the activity itself and enjoy it for its own sake. Intrinsic motivation tends to be more powerful and longer lasting than extrinsic motivation (Deci & Ryan, 1992).

A key assumption of a motivational interview is that there is usually some ambivalence associated with a change, and that people in general find it difficult to motivate themselves because the change involves giving something up. A summer internship might mean sacrificing a holiday with friends; a new job might come with a lower salary; my efforts to lose weight involve eating less cake. It is this ambivalence that is at the heart of the motivational interview. When the scales are equally weighted on each side, change is not likely to happen. The goal of the practitioner is to try to get the client to shift the balance in favour of the positive reasons for change. Until the reasons for change outweigh the advantages of inaction the client is highly unlikely to make any changes; once the balance has shifted so that the change looks more appealing than the status quo, the individual may be able and willing to take action.

A motivational interview is an intervention that acknowledges the ambivalence of change and that aims to increase the intrinsic motivation of the client. Within a motivational interview the practitioner listens to the client, encourages them to explore their feelings about the change, asking about the pros and cons of the current status quo and the pros and cons of making the change. The practitioner then gently keeps the focus of the conversation on the positive aspects of the change, and it is this focus that is known as change talk.

### How to use

Change talk is the term used to describe any of the client's conversation that focuses on the positives of the change or the action needed to make it happen. Change talk might include a description of the positive aspects of your client's future should they choose to make a change, and a discussion of the steps they would need to take in order to achieve this goal. The specific content of the conversation is less important than the overall amount of time spent. The key is to get your client to spend as long as possible talking positively about their change.

There are three specific techniques that can be used to encourage your clients to use change talk.

### 1   Describing two futures

Ask your client to imagine themselves perhaps two years in the future. First, ask them to think about what that future would be like if they made the decision not to put their current plans into action; if they, for example, decided not to apply for that new job or chose not to spend their summer doing an internship. Ask them to imagine what they might be doing and how they might be feeling in this scenario. Once that image seems fairly clear in your client's mind, ask them then to imagine an alternative future, one in which they made the decision to act – applying for that job or taking the internship. Again, invite them to imagine this future in some detail. Then suggest that they compare the two images in their mind. Ask them to highlight the differences between the two futures and encourage them to focus on the aspects of their second future, which might be better. These aspects could be discussed in some detail and your client should be encouraged to describe them fully.

### 2   Scaling

Scaling is a versatile technique that can be used in a variety of ways within career coaching conversations. Within motivational interviewing it is applied in quite a specific way and can be a useful approach to encourage your client to think more positively about the possible change. First, ask your client on a scale of one to ten to state where they would rate their current enthusiasm for the change in question: how keen are they to apply for a new job or spend the summer interning? It doesn't matter where they place their current level of motivation as long as it is something above 1. Even if they say it is just 1.5 then this is enough – it gives you something to work with. The next thing is to ask them why they decided on that number rather than a lower one: even if it is only 1.5 there must be something that made it a 1.5 rather than a 1. Whatever that thing is, it can be a useful starting point for some positive change talk. Perhaps the new job might be a little closer to home or they wouldn't be sad to see the back of their micro-managing boss. Perhaps the internship would at least mean that they wouldn't be stuck at home with their parents all summer or that they would have something to report to their tutor at the start of the next year.

Once you have established the reasons why their choice of number is not lower, invite your client to consider what it would take to raise the number a little. It is important not to be over-ambitious here. Asking someone who is currently on a 1.5 to imagine what it would take to reach a 10 may well seem unrealistic to your client, and the discussion would probably add limited value and might even be demotivating. Inviting a client on 1.5 to imagine how it would feel to be at 3 might be more realistic. Ask your client to identify what they would need to do to raise their motivation levels just one or two points. What can they think of that would change how enthusiastic they feel about the plan in question? If they can identify one or two practical ideas you could then suggest that they translate their ideas into tangible goals.

3   **Last two minutes of the session**

The final key aspect of change talk lies in the timing. Any change talk that takes place at any point during the whole intervention is a good thing: the more your client says out loud about the positives associated with the change in question, the more they will believe themselves and the more likely they are to put their plans into action. But this effect has been found to be particularly valuable in the last two minutes of the intervention. So, just before you part company, ask your client to say out loud what would be good about making a change and what action they plan to take.

*In practice*

It may be that this technique does not sound terribly different to your current practice. The idea of empathising with and listening to clients lies at the heart of career coaching. As such, this approach may well be fairly easy to incorporate within your practice. With just a little bit of practice the focus on the positives of a change can become second nature and using a scaling technique in this way can become a mainstream aspect of your practice. But it is worth just a moment to reflect on the possible ethical implications of this technique.

For most career practitioners, the core values of a person-centred, impartial and non-judgemental approach are an important part of our professionalism. By using motivational interviewing techniques, the career coach is deliberately shifting the emphasis of the conversation away from an accurate reflection of the client's story towards a more positive analysis. The coach is deliberately re-framing their analysis in order to persuade them to a particular course of action and, even if this is done with the very best of intentions and with the good of the client at heart, it would be difficult to reconcile this with a non-judgemental person-centred approach.

One response to this hint of manipulation is to discuss this approach with your client before you put it into use. If your client appears to lack motivation, you can share with them that you have noticed this and you can ask whether they want to feel more positive or enthusiastic about their plans. If they do, then you can be quite explicit with them about the techniques that you are using. There is no mystery about them and no evidence that they are more effective if the client is unaware of the process. I think it is entirely appropriate, and might actually add to your professional credibility, if you share with your client that research has shown that if they say words out loud in the last two minutes of the conversation they end up more committed and more likely to put their plans into action.

| | |
|---|---|
| One to one | ✓ |
| Group sessions | ✗ |
| Within the session | ✓ |
| As a self-directed intersessional task | ✗ |
| Initial career choice | ✓ |
| Career changes | ✓ |
| Indicative timing | 15 minutes for two futures, 10 minutes for scaling |

## Why it works

The key to this technique lies in Festinger's (1962) theory of cognitive dissonance. This theory holds that we are not comfortable having two conflicting messages within our minds and will do what we can to reconcile them. Festinger suggests that recognising the presence of conflicting thoughts and ideas within our minds generates cognitive discomfort. This discomfort can lead to a change in behaviour, bringing thoughts and actions into alignment and thus resolving the dissonance. Change talk raises the possibility of a conflict between what an individual says and what they do. An individual, for example, might say that they are committed to applying for a new job, but their lack of action towards this indicates that they are not committed to this plan. If you encourage your client to spend considerable time saying out loud why a particular future looks rosy and explaining the actions that they are planning to take, then a subsequent inaction will lead to a conflict: they are saying one thing and doing another. An easy way for the individual to resolve this cognitive dissonance is simply to put the plans into action and, in this way, the words and actions will be in harmony.

One other theory that seems to have some bearing on the power of change talk is Bem's theory of self-instruction (1967). This theory suggests that we believe what we hear ourselves say. Evidence supports the idea that if we use persuasive language and if we believe that we are generally trustworthy, then we end up convincing ourselves by our language. This effect can be quite powerful. Bem even demonstrated that, in certain conditions, individuals can be persuaded to believe their own, overtly false, statements. This phenomenon is harnessed in change talk as if people hear themselves saying 'I will apply for that job', they are likely to believe that they are telling the truth and this then increases their motivation to act accordingly.

## What's the evidence base?

Motivational interviewing has been found to add value to coaching in a range of contexts including educational settings (Hettema, Steele, & Miller, 2005; Lundahl et al., 2010), and Miller and Rose (2009) suggest that the approach could be appropriate for clients in any context facing ambivalence to change.

In a careers guidance context, this technique has the potential to be what Muscat (2005, p. 182) describes as 'an underused model that can provide career counsellors with strategies to create change', and which Stoltz and Young (2013, p. 332) depict as an 'untapped resource for career counselors', but, whilst support for its use in career practice is becoming more widespread (for example Beven, 2009; Yates, 2013), motivational interviewing as an approach for career support remains a relatively new concept. Stoltz and Young (2013) provide a useful theoretical argument for the use of MI in career practice and offer some practical approaches for MI interventions. Empirical support for the value of MI in a career context has been reported recently, with research showing that MI reduces client ambivalence and increases clients' readiness to make career choices (Klonek et al. 2016; Rochat & Rossier, 2016).

# Chapter 13

# Multi-purpose tools

The chapters that have gone before have identified tools that are specifically designed to address some of the career coaches' most common client dilemmas, but there are other effective coaching tools that coaches can apply in a wide range of contexts. In this chapter I will present seven of the most well-evidenced techniques in brief: Kolb's Learning Cycle, metaphors, mind-maps, post-its, scaling, Socratic questioning, and the wheel of life. Each is described only briefly, but these are simple ideas that are fairly easy to adopt and are well-established in coaching practice.

## Kolb's Learning Cycle

The idea of learning is central to coaching. We are expecting our clients to learn about themselves, learn about researching jobs and learn new skills. An understanding of how people learn is clearly relevant to our work. One theoretical framework that offers a step-by-step account of the process of learning is Kolb's Learning Cycle (Kolb, 2014). This can be a useful model to keep in your mind during your one-to-one work and to help you structure your group sessions. Kolb conceptualises learning as the process of developing an abstract idea that can then be applied in different concrete contexts. And, continuing this interplay between the abstract and the concrete, Kolb suggests that a concept can only be learned through engaging with it in a concrete context and reflecting on this experience. His model is circular and has four stages.

1. **Concrete experience.** This stage is all about actually doing something. Examples of this could include writing a CV or going for a job interview.
2. **Reflective observation.** In this stage, the individual reflects on their experience. How good do they think their CV is? What happened in the job interview? How well did they perform and what was good and not so good about it?
3. **Abstract conceptualisation.** This is when the individual starts to develop their own analysis, one stage removed from the situation itself. Here the individual might conclude that a specific personal profile is a good thing on a CV and that interview answers should be fairly in depth.
4. **Active experimentation.** Here the individual tests their newly developed hypotheses, re-writing their personal profile on their CV and preparing more in-depth interview answers for their next attempt.

Kolb suggests that all four of these stages need to take place for learning to happen, but that the learner can start at any point in the cycle. A CV session, for example, could start with the concrete experience of creating a CV or could start with the abstract conceptualisation, as you encourage your client to consider what they believe makes a good CV, before inviting them to put this into practice.

## Metaphors

A metaphor is a linguistic expression that describes one thing in terms of another. By a strict definition, we use metaphorical language all the time (*I'm feeling a bit down, I'm swamped with work, I was gutted, I'm stuck*, etc.). Many of these kind of metaphors have become so much part of normal conversation that they barely count as a metaphorical use of the language – it is more just an alternative meaning. But some clients will make use of more unusual metaphors as they tell their stories and these can be a great starting point for a conversation. The first step is to ask your client to explain their choice of metaphor in a bit more depth. If, for example, your client comments that their days at the office just seem really 'grey', you could ask them to explain what a grey day looks like; what makes it grey and why they chose that particular word? Were there, perhaps, any other words they could have chosen? The next step is to ask them to restructure the metaphor, asking them to use a metaphor to describe a better day. They might choose to stick with the colours – perhaps a better day is a deep purple, or a sunshine yellow – or they might choose another kind of metaphor altogether – perhaps a good day is like a gentle breeze, or a clifftop view, or a fabulous handbag. Again, invite them to explain this image – what does a deep purple day, or a day like a clifftop view look like?

The value of a metaphor is that it can capture complexity and emotions in a single construct, and often a very visual one. It can be easier for an individual to unpick and make sense of a metaphor than to try and explain the complexities of the real story – the metaphor simplifies things and makes it more manageable.

## Mind maps

Mind maps are a way of organising ideas visually. There were popularised by Tony Buzan in the 1970s but, as a concept, they have been around since the ancient Greeks.

The use of a tangible tool such as a mind map can help to shift ownership to the client. If you feel that the balance of responsibility in the coaching session has shifted towards you, perhaps you feel that you have been talking a little more than your client, or that your client seems to be expecting you to come up with all the answers, then a tool such as a mind map can help to refocus the session. You could draw a circle in the middle of a blank sheet of paper, put your client's name in it and pass it over to them. The physical act of handing them the pen and the more or less blank sheet of paper puts them back in the driving seat. You might be directing the process, but it is the client who gets to decide what words go on the page. It can also be a nice tangible thing that your client can take away with them at the end of the session to remind them of the ideas discussed.

Mind maps can also be useful as a tool to help brainstorm ideas. Our brains find it easier to make sense of a single image (even when it is made up of a number of different elements) than a list of items, and the diagram is flexible – you can add bits as you go along and join things up as links become clear.

## Post-it notes

These little sticky squares are enormously versatile and can be used in numerous different ways in coaching conversations. One value of any kind of physical prop is that it can take the pressure off the relationship between the coach and the client. Sometimes the one-to-one conversation, and the idea of having someone listen so attentively, can feel a bit intense or intimidating for clients. This may particularly be the case with younger clients, who perhaps are not so used to one-to-one professional conversations with adults, but can be discerned with clients of all ages and from all walks of life. If you sense that your client is feeling a bit daunted by the conversation then moving the focus from them to a series of sticky notes on the table may take the pressure off for a little while, as you both concentrate on the notes rather than on each other.

One valuable use of the notes is when a client is feeling a bit overwhelmed by the magnitude or complexity of the tasks ahead of them. In this context, you could ask your client to write down all the different things that they need to do on post-it notes. They should break their tasks down into a series of very manageable tasks and put each one on a single post-it note. Your client should then have a think about which of the tasks they will address first and then develop a timeline of planned activities. The post-its should then be stuck together in a single pile with the first, single, manageable task at the top. The broad overwhelming complex mountain that they face has now been reduced to a small pile with just one task visible. Your client will take the pile of notes away with them and just peel the top task off when they have completed it. This approach breaks the overwhelming task into small manageable chunks and this can make the whole process seem more achievable.

## Scaling

Using scales is introduced in Chapter 13 in the context of change talk, but it is such a useful, simple and versatile tool that I thought it was worth including here. In essence, this tool is a mechanism for making something abstract more concrete. A typical approach would be to ask your client to rate a particular aspect of their current situation on a scale of 1–10. It could be their current job satisfaction, their level of career decidedness, their degree of enthusiasm for a particular future opportunity, their confidence levels – really, whatever the topic is that is under discussion. When your client has stated, for example, that their current levels of confidence about their interview skills are at a 4, you could start finding out why they picked a '4'. In particular, why was it not a 2 or a 3? What do they already feel confident about? This might lead to a positive and affirming conversation about their skills and successes, and, in itself, this might push them gently up to a 5. The next step is to ask them where they would like to be. They might suggest that a 7 would be a more appealing place to find themselves, and this would then lead to a conversation about why a 7 would be good – what would be different in terms of how they would feel about themselves and how this might be communicated to others. Finally, and perhaps most crucially, you should generate a discussion about what your client can do to get to a 7. What is useful about this approach is that, in ascribing a number to a feeling, it becomes something less abstract and more tangible, and this facilitates a more concrete discussion about what the number means and what can be done to increase it.

## Socratic questioning

Named after the Greek philosopher Socrates, this approach allows clients to reality-check their assumptions or fears. The technique involves simply asking your clients 'What if?'-type questions over and over again. This allows your client to follow their thought processes through to the end, and then they are in a better position to judge whether their initial response was an appropriate one.

For example, if a client is feeling anxious about the idea of giving up their job and working freelance, you could ask them to explain what it is that is making them anxious:

*Client:* Well what if I give up my job, my regular income, and no work comes in?
*Coach:* And what if that were to happen?
*Client:* I've got a couple of jobs lined up already, so I would have a bit of a buffer, and I've saved a bit of money to tide me over. But I've got nothing else in the pipeline.
*Coach:* So, what if no other work comes in?
*Client:* I guess I would have to make some efforts to let people know that I am available to work. I've amassed quite a large network over the years, so there would be a lot of potential clients. But what if there aren't?
*Coach:* What would happen then?
*Client:* Well I guess I would set myself a target. I could do the sums and see how much money I need each month, and then work out how long I could manage without work.
*Coach:* And then what?
*Client:* Well I suppose, ultimately, if it didn't work out, I could always go back to work here. They are always looking for people with my skills. In fact, they would probably take me on as a freelancer, which might work out quite well.
*Coach:* And what if you did end up having to go back to work?
*Client:* It would be disappointing. Really quite disappointing. I've always wanted to be my own boss.

*Coach:* And then?
*Client:* But I would have tried it. I'd have given it a go, and I think that would be better than always wondering if I could have done it.

The scenario above illustrates how the Socratic questioning can lead clients to reflect on whether their generalised fears ('*What if it all goes wrong?*') can be broken down and can then sometimes feel much less daunting. This conversation too could have led to a discussion about the client's chances of being successful – it is sometimes the case that people overestimate the chances of things going wrong and underestimate their chances of success, and this is useful to unpick to see whether or not your client's fears are grounded in reality. Finally, it can be a useful starting point for a conversation about what steps your client could take to increase their chances of success.

## The wheel of life

This is a well-loved staple of many coaching diets, popularised by Paul Meyer in the mid-1990s. It is an approach that allows people to develop their own visual representation of how things are going for them. A large circle is drawn on a piece of paper and the spokes of the wheel are added to divide the circle into a number of different segments. Each segment represents one aspect of your client's life. In a typical life coaching context, these elements could be health, career, leisure, friendships and such like. In a career coaching session they could be different important aspects of an individual's career, such as autonomy, work conditions, colleagues and opportunities for learning. Your client is then asked to colour in each segment of the wheel according to how fulfilled they feel in that particular part of their lives or careers. If they would score ten, on a scale of one (not at all fulfilled) to ten (total fulfilment), they should colour in the whole segment. If they score five, then the first half of the segment, from the centre and half way up, would be coloured in. The client then ends up with a clear visual analysis of their current situation.

Your client could choose which features should be represented within the wheel. If it is a career-focused wheel, then you might start with a conversation about what matters to them in a job and then ask them to label the segments of the wheel according to their personal requirements. They can then use this to examine their current situation and reflect on the aspects that are working well or not so well for them.

In a group setting it would be possible to use this tool too, either in just the way described here or using pre-determined categories.

# Chapter 14

# Conclusion

In this final chapter I want to take some time to focus on you. The book has concentrated (rightly so) on your clients and the issues that they are going through, and how you can work on your practice to make sure that they are gaining the most value possible from their interactions with you. But it is vital to look after your own professional practice, both to ensure that you continue to give great career support to your clients and because you are important too. In the final pages of the book I will offer a few thoughts about how to choose and master these techniques, how to make sure you maintain an ethical approach to your practice and, finally, how you can keep your knowledge up to date.

## Getting going

The chances are that you won't take to all 35 different tools and techniques introduced here and I am quite sure that you won't end up using them all. But I hope that you have found a handful that you are drawn to and that seem to have a positive impact on your clients. It is important that you choose tools that you like. One of the key factors that makes a coaching session successful is the degree to which the coach believes in the approach they are using (McKenna & Davis, 2009). If you like it, your client is more likely to benefit from it, so don't feel that it is self-indulgent to select only tools that suit you.

Once you have alighted on a tool that you are keen to try, it can seem a bit daunting to put your learning into practice. The information offered in this book is an introduction and not a comprehensive how-to guide. Before you get going, you might want to have a look online to see if you can get further information, or get hold of some of the further reading suggested in the appendices. But you may feel that you don't need any extra input and, in truth, it is only by trying a technique out in practice that you are really going to master it. This process of mastery may include a period of trial and error before you work out exactly the right way for you to use the tool with your clients but, through practice and reflection, you will hone your skills. If you are working with a team of other career practitioners, then you could first try the tool out on each other; family and friends too might be happy to be your guinea pigs. This can be a great way to start, but you will still, at some point, just need to bite the bullet and try one of the techniques with a client. It is perfectly professional to acknowledge to your client that this is a technique that is new to you. You could explain why you are interested in trying it and (more importantly) tell them why you believe that this tool might be particularly suitable for them. If your client doesn't want to proceed on these terms that is completely fine and you can offer an alternative approach that they might be more comfortable with. But it might surprise you how often your clients relish the idea of trying something new.

One affirming finding from Whiston, Sexton and Lasoff (1998) suggests that it is trainee career practitioners who have the best outcomes for their clients. Practitioners who are learning new theories and ideas and who are actively developing their practice are shown to be more effective even than experienced career coaches, as practitioners trying something new are likely to put more thought and effort into their practice and this will have a positive impact for clients. This could suggest that you might even find that your new techniques are more effective for your clients than those from your staple toolkit.

## Ethical practice

Many of the tools described in the book are drawn from a therapeutic tradition. Both coaching and career guidance owe a considerable amount to the process and skills identified and refined by counsellors. But, although they are distinct approaches, the links between counselling and career coaching are evident. Our understanding of how people make choices has come on leaps and bounds over the last decades and we have a greater understanding that a career decision is holistic and will touch on many aspects of life. As such, practitioners need a wider range of tools at their disposal to increase the likelihood of being able to find an effective way to support each and every client. We need tools that will uncover unconscious knowledge, that will help resolve inner dilemmas and that will provide frameworks to explore personal relationships. These kinds of issues are relevant to career development and career decision making and may be important to address. But these topics can touch on quite personal, deep-rooted and difficult areas for our clients. Most of us are not trained counsellors and so we need to be very mindful of our boundaries, and very aware of where a conversation seems to be going, and how our clients are responding and how we ourselves are feeling. However much we would like to help our clients resolve their difficulties and move on towards a fulfilling goal, this may not always be appropriate or possible, and it is important that we recognise this and act accordingly.

There are things that we can do before, during and after our coaching conversations to manage the risks and ensure that our conversations are safe, ethical and valuable. Before the career conversation starts in earnest, it is important to contract clearly. This, no doubt, is something that you do anyway. It is during this part of the conversation that you clarify expectations and talk about issues of confidentiality. You could, at this stage, have an explicit conversation about boundaries, explaining that you want to make sure that the discussion can go wherever it needs to and that career choices can relate to a wide range of aspects of life, but that you are not a trained counsellor and it may be that issues come up that are better dealt with by somebody who has a more appropriate skillset or background. This kind of 'clause' in your contract may help your client to be more aware of their emotions during the conversation, which could be valuable in itself, but it may also make you feel more comfortable discussing the issue later on. If you do become aware that you are nearing or crossing the boundary of your professional expertise, it is important to raise this with your client without sounding as though you are rejecting them. Being able to refer back to the contract helps to ensure that your client does not feel that your concerns are personal.

If you notice, during the course of the conversation, that you are feeling uncomfortable or that your client is straying into territory that you don't feel professionally able to deal with, it is important that you talk to your client about it. This conversation can often be a negotiation. Your client will have a better idea than you do of how deep and difficult the issue is and of how much more there is to uncover. It may be that the issue unearthed needs to be resolved before a career decision is made – it may be getting in the way and until it is sorted out the career conversation cannot move on. In these instances it is likely that you may need to pause your coaching relationship until their issue is resolved. It is important I think to express it as a 'pause' rather than an ending – this helps to ensure that your client doesn't feel that they are being rejected. Alternatively, the issue identified may be one that, whilst important to your client, is actually quite separate from the career dilemma. In these contexts you could ask your client what they think would be the best course of action. It could be that they would like to put the issue to one side and carry on with their coaching relationship with you. If you both feel comfortable continuing with the coaching relationship and working towards identifying or achieving their career goal then there is no reason not to carry on. You can always raise the discussion again if you continue to feel that the issue is dominating or getting in the way.

Finally, it is important to think about how you yourself deal with this kind of issue afterwards. It is good practice to keep a reflective professional journal. In this you can jot down thoughts or ideas about your own performance, identifying the kinds of skills, questions or tools that seemed to work well and those that appeared to be less effective. You can use this as an opportunity to reflect on why you made the choices that you did and what made it all go so well, and to consider what you could do next time, or between sessions, to give you more confidence or improve your skills for another time. This is good practice for any coach at any time but, when it comes to issues relating to boundaries, it is particularly important to reflect. It may be that you might find it useful to have a conversation with someone about this too. I mentioned the value of supervision in the introductory chapter. During supervision you have the opportunity to reflect on your practice with a disinterested observer – it is a bit like having a coaching conversation about your own coaching practice. You can talk through your behaviour during your interaction with your client and you can reflect on your feelings. As well as making sure that you are feeling positive and being the best coach you can be, these conversations will also provide the opportunity to reflect on whether there are any issues going on inside you that are having an impact on your coaching performance and on your client. Our clients' stories can strike a chord or touch a nerve when we least expect it, and it is important that we have a chance to explore the impact their stories have on us to ensure that we can offer them the most non-judgemental person-centred approach we can.

## Keeping up to date

A final word here should perhaps be devoted to keeping up to date with the latest research in our field. Research papers are published every week that introduce new techniques, evaluate existing approaches or that enhance our understanding of our clients' experiences. It should be a source of shame to the system and to the academic community that these papers, all too often, are both difficult to access and difficult to understand. But, whilst you might find it hard to get hold of some articles, there will be others that you can access and that make some sense to you. Google Scholar can be a good starting point and will provide a link directly to the paper where possible. Otherwise, you might be able to find research summaries or journals linking research and practice, which are provided by professional bodies or other organisations with an interest in supporting professional practice. Books are often an excellent source of accessible and relevant syntheses of research but you do need to remember that it is often two years between the time the author starts writing and the time the book is published, so the information may well be a little behind.

An even better way to engage with the latest research is to conduct some yourself. There is a need for practitioner-led research as it is the practitioner community that best knows the topics that need to be examined and that has access to clients to whom it can talk. You could just run an evaluation project of your own or why not get in touch with an academic or an organisation who works on a topic that you find interesting and see if there might be opportunities to collaborate?

The very fact that you are reading a book like this, which explores the links between theory, research and practice, suggests that you are engaged in some quite thoughtful reflection about your clients, their stories, and about your own practice. This is fantastic and no doubt makes your professional experience richer and adds considerable value to your clients. I hope that the ideas in this book have added to your professional portfolio and given you some food for thought. I wish you all the best with your future career conversations.

# Further reading

This section isn't as comprehensive as I would like. Ideally, I would have included one or two sources of further reading for each idea or approach described in the book but, all too often, there just isn't much to choose from. The academic papers that are referenced in each chapter are all included in the list of References at the back of the book and, for many of the tools and techniques, these papers are the main sources of further information. Topics such as job satisfaction or the career genogram, for example, are not the subject of books, so the academic papers remain your best resource. The books listed here are either introductory guides or books written specifically for practitioners. Some of the books and readings suggested below are more theoretical and some are more practical, but each one will provide a different and broader perspective.

## General introductions to coaching and career coaching

Bird, J., & Gornall, S. (2016). *The Art of Coaching*. Abingdon: Routledge.
Highmore Sims, N. (2006). *How to Run a Great Workshop*. Harlow: Pearson Education Limited.
McMahon, M. (2016). *Career Counselling*. Abingdon: Routledge.
Reid, H. (2015). *Introduction to Career Counselling and Coaching*. London: Sage.
Van Niewerburgh, C. (2017). *An Introduction to Coaching Skills*. London: Sage.
Yates, J. (2013). *The Career Coaching Handbook*. Abingdon: Routledge.

## Chapter 3

### *Personality and careers*

Briggs Myers, I., & Myers, P. (1995). *Gifts Differing: Understanding Personality Types*. Palo Alto, CA: Davies-Black.
Tieger, P. D., & Barron-Tieger, B. (2014). *Do What You Are*. Boston, MA: Little Brown and Company.

### *Career construction interview*

Savickas, M. L. (2015). *Life Design Counseling Manual*. Ohio: Mark L. Savickas.

## Chapter 4

### Art tools

Malchiodi, C. (2007). *Art Therapy Sourcebook*. New York, NY: McGraw-Hill.

### Personal construct theory

Fransella, F., & Thomas, L. F. (1988). *Experimenting with Personal Construct Psychology*. Abingdon: Routledge.

## Chapter 5

### Positive psychology

Boniwell, I. (2008). *Positive Psychology in a Nutshell: A Balanced Introduction to the Science of Optimal Functioning*. London: Personal Well-Being Centre.
Rath, T., & Harter, J. (2010). *Wellbeing: The Five Essential Elements*. New York, NY: Gallup Press.

### Career values

Brown, D. (2002). The role of work values and cultural values in occupational choice, satisfaction and success: a theoretical statement. In D. Brown (Ed.), *Career Choice and Development*. San Francisco, CA: Jossey-Bass.

### Career anchors

Schein, E. H. (2006). *Career Anchors*. San Francisco, CA: Pfeiffer.
Schein, E. H., & van Maanen, J. (2013). *Career Anchors: The Changing Nature of Work and Careers*. San Francisco, CA: Pfeiffer.

## Chapter 6

### Possible selves

Ibarra, H. (2004). *Working Identity: Unconventional Strategies for Reinventing Your Career*. Boston, MA: Harvard Business Review Press.

### Holland's hexagon

Holland, J. L. (1997). *Making Vocational Choices*. Lutz, FL: Psychological Assessment Resources.

# Chapter 7

### Cognitive behavioural therapy

Sheward, S., & Branch, R. (2012). *Motivational Career Counselling and Coaching: Cognitive and Behavioural Approaches*. London: Sage.

Whitten, H. (2009). *Cognitive Behavioural Coaching Techniques for Dummies*. Chichester: Wiley.

### Psychological capital

Luthans, F., Youssef, C. M., & Avolio, B. J. (2007). *Psychological Capital: Developing the Human Competitive Edge*. Oxford: Oxford University Press.

# Chapter 8

### Gestalt therapy

Perls, F., Hefferline, R. F., & Goodman, P. (1994). *Gestalt Therapy: Excitement and Growth in the Human Personality*. London: Souvenir Press Ltd.

### Person-centred dialogue

Egan, G. (2017). *The Skilled Helper*. Andover: Cengage Learning EMEA.
Maslow, A. H. (1954). *Motivation and Personality*. New York, NY: Harper.
Rogers, K. (1962). *On Becoming a Person*. London: Constable & Co. Ltd.

# Chapter 9

### Transactional analysis

Berne, E. (1964). *Games People Play: The Psychology of Human Relationships*. London: Penguin.

Harris, T. (1969). *I'm OK You're OK: A Practical Guide to Transactional Analysis*. New York, NY: Harper & Row.

### Neuro-linguistic programming

Bandler, R., & Grinder, J. (1975/1976). *The Structure of Magic: A Book About Language and Therapy* (Vols 1 and 2). Palo Alto, CA: Science & Behavior Books.
Linder-Pelz, S. (2010). *NLP Coaching*. London: Kogan Page.

## Chapter 10

### Mindfulness

Williams. M., & Penman, D. (2011). *Mindfulness*. London: Piatkus.

### ACT

Flaxman, P. E., Bond, F. W., & Livheim, F. (2013). *The Mindful and Effective Employee: An Acceptance and Commitment Therapy Training Manual for Improving Well-Being and Performance*. Oakland, CA: New Harbinger.

Harris, R. (2009). *ACT Made Simple*. Oakland, CA: Harbinger Publications Inc.

## Chapter 11

### Decision making

Gigerenzer, G. (2008). *Gut Feelings*. New York, NY: Penguin Books.

Kahneman, D. (2011). *Thinking Fast and Slow*. London: Penguin Books.

## Chapter 12

### Miracle question

Iveson, C., George, E., & Ratner, H. (2012). *Brief Coaching: A Solution Focused Approach*. Abingdon: Routledge.

Szabo, P., Meier, D., & Dierolf, K. (2009). *Coaching Plain and Simple: Solution Focused Brief Coaching Essentials*. New York, NY: W.W. Norton & Company.

### Change talk

Miller, W. R., & Rollnick, S. (2012). *Motivational Interviewing: Helping People Change*. New York, NY: Guilford Press.

## Chapter 13

### Kolb's Learning Cycle

Kolb, D. (1984). *Experiential Learning: Experience as the Source of Learning and Development*. Upper Saddle River, NJ: Prentice Hall.

### Metaphors

Inkson, K., Dries, N., & Arnold, J. (2014). *Understanding Careers: The Metaphors of Working Lives*. London: Sage.

### Mind maps

Buzan, T. (1974). *Use Your Head*. London: Ariel Books.

# References

Abdallah, S., Steuer, N., Marks, N., & Page, N. (2008). *Well-being Evaluation Tools: A Research and Development Project for the Big Lottery Fund*. London: New Economics Foundation.

Acevedo, E. O. & Ekkekakis, P. (2006). *Psycho-Biology of Physical Activity*. Champaign, IL: Human Kinetics.

Anuszkiewicz, T. M. (1983). The psychology of career consciousness: modifying temporal experience. Doctoral dissertation: Kent State University.

Arch, J. J., & Craske, M. G. (2008). Acceptance and commitment therapy and cognitive behavioral therapy for anxiety disorders: different treatments, similar mechanisms? *Clinical Psychology: Science and Practice, 15*(4), 263–279.

Asadnia, S., Azar, F. S., & Torabzadeh, N. (2014). EHMTI-0366. Efficacy of cognitive behavior therapy and gestalt therapy on poor sleep quality among college female students with headache. *The Journal of Headache and Pain, 15*(S1), J13.

Assouline, M., & Meir, E. I. (1987). Meta-analysis of the relationship between congruence and well-being measures. *Journal of Vocational Behavior, 31*(3), 319–332.

Bandler, R., & Grinder, J. (1976). *The Structure of Magic* (Vol. 2). Palo Alto, CA: Science and Behavior Books.

Bar-Haim, Y. (2010). Research review: attention bias modification (ABM): a novel treatment for anxiety disorders. *Journal of Child Psychology and Psychiatry, 51*(8), 859–870.

Beail, N. (Ed.) (1985). *Repertory Grid Technique and Personal Constructs: Applications in Clinical & Educational Settings*. Abingdon: Routledge.

Beal, S. J., & Crockett, L. J. (2010). Adolescents' occupational and educational aspirations and expectations: links to high school activities and adult educational attainment. *Developmental Psychology, 46*(1), 258.

Beisser, A. (1970). The paradoxical theory of change. In J. Fagan & I. L. Shepard (Eds), *Gestalt Therapy Now* (pp. 77–80). Palo Alto, CA: Science and Behavior Books.

Bem, S. L. (1967). Verbal self-control: the establishment of effective self-instruction. *Journal of Experimental Psychology, 74*(4), 485.

Bem, D. J. (1967). Self-perception: an alternative interpretation of cognitive dissonance phenomena. *Psychological Review, 74*(3), 183.

Beng, T. S., Ahmad, F., Loong, L. C., Chin, L. E., Zainal, N. Z., Guan, N. C., . . . & Meng, C. B. C. (2016). Distress reduction for palliative care patients and families with 5-minute mindful breathing: a pilot study. *American Journal of Hospice and Palliative Medicine®, 33*(6), 555–560.

Berg, I. K., & De Jong, P. (1996). Solution-building conversations: co-constructing a sense of competence with clients. *Families in Society: The Journal of Contemporary Social Services, 77*(6), 376–391.

Berne, E. (1958). Transactional analysis: a new and effective method of group therapy. *American Journal of Psychotherapy, 12*(4), 735–743.

Beven, P. (2009). Client narratives, language and motivation. In: *Constructing the Future: Career Coaching for Changing Contexts, 1* (pp. 12–20). Stourbridge: Institute of Career Guidance.

Bimrose, J., & Hearne, L. (2012). Resilience and career adaptability: qualitative studies of adult career counseling. *Journal of Vocational Behavior, 81*(3), 338–344.

Bishop, S. R., Lau, M., Shapiro, S., Carlson, L., Anderson, N. D., Carmody, J., . . . & Devins, G. (2004). Mindfulness: a proposed operational definition. *Clinical Psychology: Science and Practice, 11*(3), 230–241.

Blustein, D. L., & Strohmer, D. C. (1987). Vocational hypothesis testing in career decision making. *Journal of Vocational Behavior, 31*(1), 45–62.

Bohart, A. C., Elliott, R., Greenberg, L. S., & Watson, J. C. (2002). Empathy. In J. C. Norcross (Ed.), *Psychotherapy Relationships That Work: Therapist Contributions and Responsiveness to Patients* (pp. 89–108). New York, NY: Oxford University Press.

Bond, F. W., & Bunce, D. (2000). Mediators of change in emotion-focused and problem-focused worksite stress management interventions. *Journal of Occupational Health Psychology, 5*(1), 156–163.

Bond, F. W., & Bunce, D. (2003). The role of acceptance and job control in mental health, job satisfaction, and work performance. *Journal of Applied Psychology, 88*(6), 1057.

Bond, F. W., & Flaxman, P. E. (2006). The ability of psychological flexibility and job control to predict learning, job performance, and mental health. *Journal of Organizational Behavior Management, 26*(1–2), 113–130.

Bretz, H. J., Heekerens, H. P., & Schmitz, B. (1994). A meta-analysis of the effectiveness of gestalt therapy. *Zeitschrift fur Klinische Psychologie, Psychopathologie und Psychotherapie, 42*(3), 241–260.

Brissette, I., Scheier, M. F., & Carver, C. S. (2002). The role of optimism in social network development, coping, and psychological adjustment during a life transition. *Journal of Personality and Social Psychology, 82*(1), 102.

Brockett, O. (1977). *History of Theater*. Boston, MA: Allyn and Bacon.

Brown, D. (1996). Brown's values-based, holistic model of career and life-role choices and satisfaction. In D. Brown & L. Brooks (Eds), *Career Choice and Development*, 3rd Edition (pp. 327–338). San Francisco, CA: Jossey-Bass.

Brown, D., & Brooks, L. (1996). *Career Choice and Development* (3rd Ed.). San Francisco, CA: Jossey Bass.

Burwell, R., & Chen, C. P. (2006). Applying the principles and techniques of solution-focused therapy to career counselling. *Counselling Psychology Quarterly, 19*(2), 189–203.

Cardoso, P., Gonçalves, M. M., Duarte, M. E., Silva, J. R., & Alves, D. (2016). Life Design Counseling outcome and process: a case study with an adolescent. *Journal of Vocational Behavior, 97*(1), 58–66.

Carson, S. H., & Langer, E. J. (2006). Mindfulness and self-acceptance. *Journal of Rational-Emotive and Cognitive-Behavior Therapy, 24*(1), 29–43.

Carver, C. S., Scheier, M. F., & Segerstrom, S. C. (2010). Optimism. *Clinical Psychology Review, 30*(7), 879–889.

Chartrand, J. M., & Robbins, S. B. (1997). *Career Factors Inventory: Applications and Technical Guide*. Palo Alto, CA: Consulting Psychologists Press.

Chen, D. J., & Lim, V. K. (2012). Strength in adversity: the influence of psychological capital on job search. *Journal of Organizational Behavior, 33*(6), 811–839.

Chen, L. D., Muthitacharoen, A., & Frolick, M. N. (2003). Investigating the use of role play training to improve the communication skills of IS professionals: some empirical evidence. *Journal of Computer Information Systems, 43*(3), 67–74.

Chope, R. C. (2002). *Family Matters: Influences of the Family in Career Decision Making.* Available online at: https://files.eric.ed.gov/fulltext/ED470005.pdf.

Chusid, H., & Cochran, L. (1989). Meaning of career change from the perspective of family roles and dramas. *Journal of Counseling Psychology, 36*(1), 34.

Clarke, K. M., & Greenberg, L. S. (1986). Differential effects of the Gestalt two-chair intervention and problem solving in resolving decisional conflict. *Journal of Counseling Psychology, 33*(1), 11.

Coiner, J., & Kim, K. H. (2011). *Art Therapy, Research, and Evidence-Based Practice.* Thousand Oaks, CA: Sage.

Collard, P., & Walsh, J. (2008). Sensory awareness mindfulness training in coaching: accepting life's challenges. *Journal of Rational-Emotive & Cognitive-Behavior Therapy, 26*(1), 30–37.

Colozzi, E. A. (2003). Depth-oriented values extraction. *The Career Development Quarterly, 52*(2), 180–189.

Cooperrider, D. L., & Srivastva, S. (1987). Appreciative inquiry in organizational life. *Research in Organizational Change and Development, 1*(1), 129–169.

Costa, P. T., & McCrae, R. R. (1992). Four ways five factors are basic. *Personality and Individual Differences, 13*(6), 653–665.

Cottle, T. J. (1967). The circles test: an investigation of perceptions of temporal relatedness and dominance. *Journal of Projective Techniques and Personality Assessment, 31*(5), 58–71.

Coutu, D. L. (2002). How resilience works. *Harvard Business Review, 80*(5), 46–56.

David, D. (2014). Rational emotive behavior therapy. In R. L. Cautin & S. O. Lilienfeld (Editors-in-Chief), *Encyclopedia of Clinical Psychology* (pp. 175–221). Hoboken, NJ: Wiley-Blackwell.

Daykin, N., Orme, J., Evans, D., Salmon, D., McEachran, M., & Brain, S. (2008). The impact of participation in performing arts on adolescent health and behaviour: a systematic review of the literature. *Journal of Health Psychology, 13*(2), 251–264.

Deci, E. L., & Ryan, R. M. (1992). The initiation and regulation of intrinsically motivated learning and achievement. In A. K. Boggiano & T. S. Pittman (Eds), *Achievement and Motivation: A Social-Developmental Perspective* (pp. 9–36). Cambridge: Cambridge University Press.

Deci, E. L., & Ryan, R. M. (2008). Self-determination theory: a macrotheory of human motivation, development, and health. *Canadian Psychology/Psychologie Canadienne, 49*(3), 182.

De Haan, E. (2008). *Relational Coaching. Journeys Towards Mastering One-to-One Learning.* Chichester: Wiley & Sons.

DeNeve, K. M., & Heppner, M. J. (1997). Role play simulations: the assessment of an active learning technique and comparisons with traditional lectures. *Innovative Higher Education, 21*(3), 231–246.

DeRoma, V. M., Martin, K. M., & Kessler, M. L. (2003). The relationship between tolerance for ambiguity and need for course structure. *Journal of Instructional Psychology, 30*(2), 104.

De Shazer, S., Berg, I. K., Lipchik, E. V. E., Nunnally, E., Molnar, A., Gingerich, W., & Weiner-Davis, M. (1986). Brief therapy: focused solution development. *Family Process, 25*(2), 207–221.

Destin, M., & Oyserman, D. (2010). Incentivizing education: seeing schoolwork as an investment, not a chore. *Journal of Experimental Social Psychology*, *46*(5), 846–849.

Di Fabio, A., & Maree, J. G. (2012). Group-based life design counseling in an Italian context. *Journal of Vocational Behavior*, *80*(1), 100–107.

Dijksterhuis, A., Aarts, H., & Smith, P. K (2005). The power of the subliminal: perception and possible applications. In R. Hassin, J. Uleman and J. A. Bargh (Eds), *The New Unconscious*. New York, NY: Oxford University Press.

Dijksterhuis, A., Bos, M. W., Nordgren, L. F., & van Baaren, R. B. (2006). On making the right choice: the deliberation-without-attention effect. *Science*, *311*(5763), 1005–1007.

Dik, B. J., Strife, S. R., & Hansen, J. I. C. (2010). The flip side of Holland type congruence: incongruence and job satisfaction. *The Career Development Quarterly*, *58*(4), 352–358.

Donnellan, M. B., Oswald, F. L., Baird, B. M., & Lucas, R. E. (2006). The mini-IPIP scales: tiny-yet-effective measures of the Big Five factors of personality. *Psychological Assessment*, *18*(2), 192.

Dryden, W. (2002). *Fundamentals of Rational Emotive Behavior Therapy*. London: Whurr Publishers Ltd.

Dryden, W. (2005). Rational emotive behavior therapy. In A. Freeman, S. H. Felgoise, C. M. Nezu, A. M. Nezu & M. A. Reinecke (Eds), *Encyclopedia of Cognitive Behavior Therapy* (pp. 321–324). Boston, MA: Springer.

Duggleby, W., Cooper, D., & Penz, K. (2009). Hope, self-efficacy, spiritual well-being and job satisfaction. *Journal of Advanced Nursing*, *65*(11), 2376–2385.

Duveen, J., & Solomon, J. (1994). The great evolution trial: use of role-play in the classroom. *Journal of Research in Science Teaching*, *31*(5), 575–582.

Edwards, J. R., & Cable, D. M. (2009). The value of value congruence. *Journal of Applied Psychology*, *94*(3), 654.

Ellis, A. (1962). *Reason and Emotion in Psychotherapy*. New York, NY: Lyle Stuart.

Epting, F. R., & Nazario, A. (1987). Designing a fixed role therapy: issues, techniques and modifications. In R. A. Neimeyer & G. J. Neimeyer (Eds), *Personal Construct Therapy Casebook* (pp. 277–289). New York, NY: Springer.

Erdogan, B., Kraimer, M. L., & Liden, R. C. (2004). Work value congruence and intrinsic career success: the compensatory roles of leader–member exchange and perceived organizational support. *Personnel Psychology*, *57*(2), 305–332.

Farber, B. A., & Lane, J. S. (2002). Positive regard. In: J. Norcross (Ed.) *Psychotherapy Relationships That Work*, 2nd Edition (pp. 175–194). New York, NY: Oxford University Press.

Ferrari, L., Nota, L., & Soresi, S. (2012). Evaluation of an intervention to foster time perspective and career decidedness in a group of Italian adolescents. *The Career Development Quarterly*, *60*(1), 82–96.

Festinger, L. (1962). Cognitive dissonance. *Scientific American*, *207*(4), 93–106.

Fiebert, M. S. (1990). *Stages in Gestalt Therapy Session and An Examination of Counselors Interventions*. Retrieved on 2 July 2002 from California State University: www.csulb.edu/~mfiebert/gestalt.htm.

Fiske, S. T. (1980). Attention and weight in person perception: the impact of negative and extreme information. *Journal of Personality and Social Psychology*, *38*(6), 889–906.

Flaxman, P. E., & Bond, F. W. (2010). Worksite stress management training: moderated effects and clinical significance. *Journal of Occupational Health Psychology*, *15*(4), 347.

Flaxman, P. E., Bond, F. W., & Livheim, F. (2013). *The Mindful and Effective Employee: An Acceptance and Commitment Therapy Training Manual for Improving Well-Being and Performance*. Oakland CA: New Harbinger Publications.

Ford, K. M., & Bradshaw, J. M. (1993). Introduction: knowledge acquisition as modeling. *International Journal of Intelligent Systems, 8*(1), 1–7.

Franklin, M. E., Kratz, H. E., Freeman, J. B., Ivarsson, T., Heyman, I., Sookman, D., ... & March, J. (2015). Cognitive-behavioral therapy for pediatric obsessive-compulsive disorder: empirical review and clinical recommendations. *Psychiatry Research, 227*(1), 78–92.

Fredrickson, B. (2009). *Positivity: Groundbreaking Research Reveals how to Embrace the Hidden Strength of Positive Emotions, Overcome Negativity, and Thrive*. New York, NY: Crown Publishing Group.

Freud, S. (1915). *The Unconscious*. Standard edition, 14, 159–204. Available at: http://dravni.co.il/wp-content/uploads/2014/01/Freud-S.-1915.-The-Unconscious.-.pdf.

Gardiner, M., Kearns, H., & Tiggemann, M. (2013). Effectiveness of cognitive behavioural coaching in improving the well-being and retention of rural general practitioners. *Australian Journal of Rural Health, 21*(3), 183–189.

Gati, I., Krausz, M., & Osipow, S. H. (1996). A taxonomy of difficulties in career decision making. *Journal of Counseling Psychology, 43*(4), 510.

Gibson, D. E. (2005). Role models in career development: new directions for theory and research. *Journal of Vocational Behavior, 65*(1), 134–156.

Gingerich, W. J., & Peterson, L. T. (2013). Effectiveness of solution-focused brief therapy: a systematic qualitative review of controlled outcome studies. *Research on Social Work Practice, 23*(3), 266–283.

González-Ramírez, E., Carrillo-Montoya, T., García-Vega, M. L., Hart, C. E., Zavala-Norzagaray, A. A., & Ley-Quiñónez, C. P. (2017). Effectiveness of hypnosis therapy and Gestalt therapy as depression treatments. *Clínica y Salud, 28*(1), 33–37.

Grant, A. M., Curtayne, L., & Burton, G. (2009). Executive coaching enhances goal attainment, resilience and workplace well-being: a randomised controlled study. *The Journal of Positive Psychology, 4*(5), 396–407.

Grant, B. (1990). Principled and instrumental nondirectiveness in person-centred and client-centred therapy. *Person-Centred Review, 5*(1), 77–88.

Greenbank, P., & Hepworth, S. (2008). Improving the career decision-making behaviour of working class students: do economic barriers stand in the way? *Journal of European Industrial Training, 32*(7), 492–509.

Greenberg, L. S., & Dompierre, L. M. (1981). Specific effects of Gestalt two-chair dialogue on intrapsychic conflict in counseling. *Journal of Counseling Psychology, 28*(4), 288.

Greene, G. J., & Lee, M. Y. (2011). *Solution-Oriented Social Work Practice: An Integrative Approach to Working with Client Strengths*. Oxford: Oxford University Press.

Greenfield, E. A., & Marks, N. F. (2004). Formal volunteering as a protective factor for older adult's psychological well-being. *Journals of Gerontology, Series B: Psychological Sciences and Social Sciences, 59*(5), 258–264.

Haley, J. (Ed.). (1967). *Advanced Techniques of Hypnosis and Therapy: Selected Papers of Milton H. Erickson*. New York, NY: Grune & Stratton.

Hall, D. T., & Mirvis, P. H. (1996). The new protean career: psychological success and the path with a heart. In D. T. Hall (Ed.), *The Career is Dead: Long Live the Career. A Relational Approach to Careers* (pp. 15–45), The Jossey-Bass Business & Management Series. San Francisco, CA: Jossey-Bass.

Hammond, C. (2004). Impacts of lifelong learning upon emotional resilience, psychological and mental health: fieldwork evidence. *Oxford Review of Education, 30*(4), 551–568.

Harris, R. (2009). *ACT Made Simple: An Easy-to-Read Primer on Acceptance and Commitment Therapy.* Oakland, CA: New Harbinger Publications.

Hart, R., Ivtzan, I., & Hart, D. (2013). Mind the gap in mindfulness research: a comparative account of the leading schools of thought. *Review of General Psychology, 17*(4), 453–466.

Hartung, P. J., & Santilli, S. (2017). My career story: description and initial validity evidence. *Journal of Career Assessment,* doi:1069072717692980.

Hastie, R., & Dawes, R. M. (2010). *Rational Choice in an Uncertain World: The Psychology of Judgment and Decision Making.* London: Sage.

Hayes, S. C. (2004). Acceptance and commitment therapy and the new behavior therapies: mindfulness, acceptance, and relationship. In S. C. Hayes, V. M. Follette, & M. M. Linehan (Eds), *Mindfulness and Acceptance: Expanding the Cognitive-Behavioral Tradition* (pp. 1–29). New York, NY: Guilford Press.

Hayes, S. C., Barnes-Holmes, D., & Roche, B. (Eds) (2001). *Relational Frame Theory: A Post-Skinnerian Account of Human Language and Cognition.* New York, NY: Springer Science & Business Media.

Hayes, S. C., Strosahl, K. D., Bunting, K., Twohig, M., & Wilson, K. G. (2004). What is acceptance and commitment therapy? In S. Hayes & K. Strosahl (Eds), *A Practical Guide to Acceptance and Commitment Therapy* (pp. 1–30). New York, NY: Springer.

Hayes, S. C., Strosahl, K., & Wilson, K. G. (1999). *Acceptance and Commitment Therapy: A Contextual Approach to Cognition and Emotion in Psychotherapy.* New York, NY: Guilford.

Hayes, S. C., Strosahl, K. D., & Wilson, K. G. (2012). *Acceptance and Commitment Therapy.* New York, NY: Guilford Press.

Haynie, J. M., & Shepherd, D. (2011). Toward a theory of discontinuous career transition: investigating career transitions necessitated by traumatic life events. *Journal of Applied Psychology, 96*(3), 501.

Hettema, J., Steele, J., & Miller, W. R. (2005). Motivational interviewing. *Annual Review of Clinical Psychology, 1,* 91–111.

Hoare, P. N., McIlveen, P., & Hamilton, N. (2012). Acceptance and commitment therapy (ACT) as a career counselling strategy. *International Journal for Educational and Vocational Guidance, 12*(3), 171–187.

Hock, M. F., Deshler, D. D., & Schumaker, J. B. (2007). Enhancing student motivation through the pursuit of possible selves. In: C. Dunkel, and C. J. Kerpelman (Eds), *Possible Selves: Theory Research and Applications* (pp. 205–221). New York, NY: Nova Science Publishers.

Holland, J. L. (1959). A theory of vocational choice. *Journal of Counseling Psychology, 6*(1), 35.

Honeycutt, J. M. (2002). *Imagined Interactions: Daydreaming about Communication.* Cresskill, NJ: Hampton Pr.

Honeycutt, J. M. (2008). Imagined interaction theory. In L. A. Baxter & D. O. Braithwaite (Eds), *Engaging Theories in Interpersonal Communication: Multiple Perspectives* (pp. 77–87). London: Sage.

Hooley, T. (2014). *The Evidence Base on Lifelong Guidance: A Guide to Key Findings for Effective Policy and Practice.* University of Derby, UK: ELGPN.

Hooley, T., & Sultana, R. G. (2016). Career guidance for social justice. *Journal of the National Institute for Career Education and Counselling, 36,* 2–11.

Huppert, F. (2008). *Psychological Well-Being: Evidence Regarding its Causes and its Consequences.* London: Foresight Mental Capital and Wellbeing Project.

Igbaria, M., & Baroudi, J. J. (1993). A short-form measure of career orientations: a psychometric evaluation. *Journal of Management Information Systems, 10*(2), 131–154.

Inkson, K., Gunz, H., Ganesh, S., & Roper, J. (2012). Boundaryless careers: bringing back boundaries. *Organization Studies, 33*(3), 323–340.

International Labour Organisation (2016). *World Employment and Social Outlook.* Geneva: International Labour Organisation.

Iyengar, S. S., & Lepper, M. R. (2000). When choice is demotivating: can one desire too much of a good thing? *Journal of Personality and Social Psychology, 79*(6), 995.

Jacobsen, M. H. (2000). *Hand-Me-Down-Dreams: How Families Influence Our Career Paths.* New York, NY: Three Rivers Press.

Janeiro, I. N. (2010). Motivational dynamics in the development of career attitudes among adolescents. *Journal of Vocational Behavior, 76*(2), 170–177.

Johnson, S. M., & Greenberg, L. S. (1985). Emotionally focused couples therapy: an outcome study. *Journal of Marital and Family Therapy, 11*(3), 313–317.

Jones, G. I. (2012). Using drama therapy techniques in secondary education. Doctoral dissertation, University of Akron.

Judge, T. A., & Bono, J. E. (2001). Relationship of core self-evaluations traits—self-esteem, generalized self-efficacy, locus of control, and emotional stability—with job satisfaction and job performance: a meta-analysis. *Journal of Applied Psychology, 86*(1), 80.

Judge, T. A., Heller, D., & Mount, M. K. (2002). Five-factor model of personality and job satisfaction: a meta-analysis. *Journal of Applied Psychology, 87*(3), 530–541.

Judge, T. A., Piccolo, R. F., Podsakoff, N. P., Shaw, J. C., & Rich, B. L. (2010). The relationship between pay and job satisfaction: a meta-analysis of the literature. *Journal of Vocational Behavior, 77*(2), 157–167.

Kahneman, D. (2011). *Thinking, Fast and Slow.* New York, NY: Macmillan.

Kalliath, T. J., Bluedorn, A. C., & Strube, M. J. (1999). A test of value congruence effects. *Journal of Organizational Behavior, 20*(7), 1175–1198.

Kanfer, R., Wanberg, C. R., & Kantrowitz, T. M. (2001). Job search and employment: a personality–motivational analysis and meta-analytic review. *Journal of Applied Psychology, 86*(5), 837–855.

Karas, D., & Spada, M. M. (2009). Brief cognitive-behavioural coaching for procrastination: a case series. *Coaching: An International Journal of Theory, Research and Practice, 2*(1), 44–53.

Karst, T. O., & Trexler, L. D. (1970). Initial study using fixed-role and rational-emotive therapy in treating public-speaking anxiety. *Journal of Consulting and Clinical Psychology, 34*(3), 360–366.

Kearns, H., Forbes, A., & Gardiner, M. (2007). A cognitive behavioural coaching intervention for the treatment of perfectionism and self-handicapping in a nonclinical population. *Behaviour Change, 24*(3), 157–172.

Kearns, H., Gardiner, M., & Marshall, K. (2008). Innovation in PhD completion: the hardy shall succeed (and be happy!). *Higher Education Research & Development, 27*(1), 77–89.

Kelly, G. (1955). *Personal Construct Psychology.* New York, NY: Norton.

Kelly, K. R., & Lee, W. C. (2002). Mapping the domain of career decision problems. *Journal of Vocational Behavior, 61*(2), 302–326.

Kidd, J. M. (2008). Exploring the components of career well-being and the emotions associated with significant career experiences. *Journal of Career Development, 35*(2), 166–186.

Killingsworth, M. A., & Gilbert, D. T. (2010). A wandering mind is an unhappy mind. *Science*, *330*(6006), 932–932.

Kirkpatrick, K. L. (2005). Enhancing self-compassion using a Gestalt two-chair intervention (Doctoral dissertation). Austin, TX: University of Texas.

Kirschenbaum, H., & Jourdan, A. (2005). The current status of Carl Rogers and the person-centered approach. *Psychotherapy: Theory, Research, Practice, Training*, *42*(1), 37.

Klein, M. H., Kolden, G. G., Michels, J., & Chisholm-Stockard, S. (2002). In: J. C. Norcross (Ed.), *Psychotherapy Relationships That Work* (pp. 191–211). Oxford: Oxford University Press.

Klonek, F. E., Wunderlich, E., Spurk, D., & Kauffeld, S. (2016). Career counseling meets motivational interviewing: a sequential analysis of dynamic counselor–client interactions. *Journal of Vocational Behavior*, *94*(1), 28–38.

Kolb, D. A. (2014). *Experiential Learning: Experience as the Source of Learning and Development*. Upper Saddle River, NJ: Pearson/FT Press.

Kristof, A. L. (1996). Person-organization fit: an integrative review of its conceptualizations, measurement, and implications. *Personnel Psychology*, *49*(1), 1–49.

Kristof-Brown, A. L., Zimmerman, R. D., & Johnson, E. C. (2005). Consequences of individuals' fit at work: a meta-analysis of person–job, person–organisation, person–group and person–supervisor fit. *Personnel Psychology*, *58*(2), 281–342.

La Lopa, J. M., Beck, J., & Ghiselli, R. (2009). The role of biodata and career anchors on turnover intentions among hospitality and tourism educators. *Journal of Culinary Science & Technology*, *7*(2–3), 196–206.

Lambert, M. J. (1992). Psychotherapy outcome research: implications for integrative and eclectical therapists. In J. C. Norcross & M. R. Goldfried (Eds), *Handbook of Psychotherapy Integration* (pp. 94–129). New York, NY: Basic Books.

Langer, E. J. (1989). *Mindfulness*. Reading, MA: Addison-Wesley/Addison Wesley Longman.

Lent, R. W., Brown, S. D., & Hackett, G. (1994). Toward a unifying social cognitive theory of career and academic interest, choice, and performance. *Journal of Vocational Behavior*, *45*(1), 79–122.

Leong, F. T., & Chervinko, S. (1996). Construct validity of career indecision: negative personality traits as predictors of career indecision. *Journal of Career Assessment*, *4*(3), 315–329.

Lietaer, G. (2002). The united colors of person-centred and experiential therapies. *Person-Centred and Experiential Psychotherapies*, *1*(1&2), 4–13.

Lindstrom, L., Doren, B., Metheny, J., Johnson, P., & Zane, C. (2007). Transition to employment: role of the family in career development. *Exceptional Children*, *73*(3), 348–366.

Litman-Ovadia, H., & Davidovitch, N. (2010). Effects of congruence and character-strength deployment on work adjustment and well-being. *International Journal of Business and Social Science*, *1*(3), 137–146.

Locke, E. A., & Latham, G. P. (2002). Building a practically useful theory of goal setting and task motivation: a 35-year odyssey. *American Psychologist*, *57*(9), 705.

Loffredo, D. A., Harrington, R., Munoz, M. K., & Knowles, L. R. (2004). The ego state questionnaire-revised. *Transactional Analysis Journal*, *34*(1), 90–95.

Lundahl, B. W., Kunz, C., Brownell, C., Tollefson, D., & Burke, B. L. (2010). A meta-analysis of motivational interviewing: twenty-five years of empirical studies. *Research on Social Work Practice*, *20*(2), 137–160.

Luoma, J. B., Hayes, S. C., & Walser, R. D. (2007). *Learning ACT: An Acceptance & Commitment Therapy Skills-Training Manual for Therapists*. Oakland, CA: New Harbinger Publications.

Luthans, F., Avey, J. B., Avolio, B. J., Norman, S. M., & Combs, G. M. (2006). Psychological capital development: toward a micro-intervention. *Journal of Organizational Behavior*, *27*(3), 387–393.

Malott, K. M., & Magnuson, S. (2004). Using genograms to facilitate undergraduate students' career development: a group model. *The Career Development Quarterly*, *53*(2), 178–186.

Marcic, D., Aiuppa, T. A., & Watson, J. G. (1989). Personality type, organizational norms and self-esteem. *Psychological Reports*, *65*(3), 915–919.

Marko, K. W., & Savickas, M. L. (1998). Effectiveness of a career time perspective intervention. *Journal of Vocational Behavior*, *52*(1), 106–119.

Markus, H., & Nurius, P. (1986). Possible selves. *American Psychologist*, *41*(9), 954.

Maslow, A. H. (1943). A theory of human motivation. *Psychological Review*, *50*(4), 370.

Mason, M. F., Bar, M., & Macrae, C. N. (2008). Exploring the past and impending future in the here and now: mind-wandering in the default state. *Cognitive Sciences*, *3*, 1–19.

Matos, P. S., Neushotz, L. A., Griffin, M. T. Q., & Fitzpatrick, J. J. (2010). An exploratory study of resilience and job satisfaction among psychiatric nurses working in inpatient units. *International Journal of Mental Health Nursing*, *19*(5), 307–312.

McKenna, D. D., & Davis, S. L. (2009). Hidden in plain sight: the active ingredients of executive coaching. *Industrial and Organizational Psychology*, *2*(3), 244–260.

McMahon, M. (Ed.) (2016). *Career Counselling: Constructivist Approaches*. Abingdon: Routledge.

McMahon, M., & Watson, M. (2015). Qualitative career assessment. In M. McMahon & M. Watson (Eds), *Career Assessment* (pp. 257–262), Career Development Series (Connecting Theory and Practice). Rotterdam: SensePublishers.

McMurtrey, M. E., Grover, V., Teng, J. T., & Lightner, N. J. (2002). Job satisfaction of information technology workers: the impact of career orientation and task automation in a CASE environment. *Journal of Management Information Systems*, *19*(2), 273–302.

Meglino, B. M., & Ravlin, E. C. (1998). Individual values in organizations: concepts, controversies, and research. *Journal of Management*, *24*(3), 351–389.

Metcalfe, C., Winter, D., & Viney, L. (2007). The effectiveness of personal construct psychotherapy in clinical practice: a systematic review and meta-analysis. *Psychotherapy Research*, *17*(4), 431–442.

Miller, J. (2017). Solution-focused career counselling. In M. McMahon (Ed.), *Career Counselling: Constructivist Approaches* (pp. 127–138). Abingdon: Routledge.

Miller, W. R., & Moyers, T. B. (2006). Eight stages in learning motivational interviewing. *Journal of Teaching in the Addictions*, *5*(1), 3–17.

Miller, W. R. & Rollnick, S. (1991). *Motivational Interviewing: Preparing People to Change Addictive Behaviour*. New York, NY: Guilford.

Miller, W. R., & Rose, G. S. (2009). Toward a theory of motivational interviewing. *American Psychologist*, *64*(6), 527.

Mongrain, M., & Anselmo-Matthews, T. (2012). Do positive psychology exercises work? A replication of Seligman et al. *Journal of Clinical Psychology*, *68*(4), 382–389.

Moran, D. J. (2011). ACT for leadership: using acceptance and commitment training to develop crisis-resilient change managers. *International Journal of Behavioral Consultation and Therapy*, *7*(1), 66.

Mulawarman, U. (2014). Brief counselling in schools: a Solution-Focused Brief Counselling (SFBC) approach for school counsellor in Indonesia. *Journal of Education and Practice*, *5*(21), 68–80.

Munyon, T. P., Hochwarter, W. A., Perrewé, P. L., & Ferris, G. R. (2010). Optimism and the nonlinear citizenship behavior—job satisfaction relationship in three studies. *Journal of Management, 36*(6), 1505–1528.

Muscat, A. C. (2005). Ready, set, go: the transtheoretical model of change and motivational interviewing for "fringe" clients. *Journal of Employment Counseling, 42*(4), 179–191.

Myerhoff, B. (1990). The transformation of consciousness in ritual performances: some thoughts and questions. In R. Schechner & W. Appel (Eds), *By Means of Performance: Intercultural Studies of Theatre and Ritual* (pp. 245–283). Cambridge: Cambridge University Press.

Myers, I. B. (1962). *The Myers-Briggs Type Indicator*. Palo Alto, CA: Consulting Psychologists Press.

Nau, D. S., & Shilts, L. (2000). When to use the miracle question: clues from a qualitative study of four SFBT practitioners. *Journal of Systemic Therapies, 19*(1), 129–135.

Neimeyer, G. J. (1989). Personal construct systems in vocational development and information-processing. *Journal of Career Development, 16*(2), 83–96.

Neimeyer, G. J. (1992). Personal constructs in career counseling and development. *Journal of Career Development, 18*(3), 163–173.

Nestel, D., & Tierney, T. (2007). Role-play for medical students learning about communication: guidelines for maximising benefits. *BMC Medical Education, 7*(1), 3.

Ng, T. W., Eby, L. T., Sorensen, K. L., & Feldman, D. C. (2005). Predictors of objective and subjective career success: a meta-analysis. *Personnel Psychology, 58*(2), 367–408.

Ng, T. W., & Feldman, D. C. (2014). Subjective career success: a meta-analytic review. *Journal of Vocational Behavior, 85*(2), 169–179.

Nordvik, H. (1996). Relationships between Holland's vocational typology, Schein's career anchors and Myers–Briggs' types. *Journal of Occupational and Organizational Psychology, 69*(3), 263–275.

Novey, T. B. (2002). Measuring the effectiveness of transactional analysis: an international study. *Transactional Analysis Journal, 32*(1), 8–24.

Office for National Statistics (ONS) (2010). *SOC Codes*. London: Office for National Statistics.

Orlinsky, D. E., & Howard, K. I. (1986). The psychological interior of psychotherapy: explorations with the Therapy Session Reports. In L. S. Greenberg & W. M. Pinsof (Eds), *The Psychotherapeutic Process: A Research Handbook* (pp. 477–501), Guilford Clinical Psychology and Psychotherapy Series. New York, NY: Guilford Press.

Osipow, S. H. (1987). *Career Decision Scale*. Odessa, FL: Psychological Assessment Resources, Incorporated.

Osipow, S. H., & Gati, I. (1998). Construct and concurrent validity of the career decision-making difficulties questionnaire. *Journal of Career Assessment, 6*(3), 347–364.

Öst, L. G. (2014). The efficacy of Acceptance and Commitment Therapy: an updated systematic review and meta-analysis. *Behaviour Research and Therapy, 61*, 105–121.

Parsons, F. (1909). *Choosing a Vocation*. Boston, MA: Houghton Mifflin.

Paszkowska-Rogacz, A., & Kabzinska, Z. (2012). Applications of Kelly's personal construct theory to vocational guidance. *Psychology Research, 2*(7), 408.

Pelaprat, E., & Cole, M. (2011). "Minding the gap": imagination, creativity and human cognition. *Integrative Psychological and Behavioral Science, 45*(4), 397–418.

Perls, F., Hefferline, G., & Goodman, P. (1951). *Gestalt Therapy*. New York, NY: Continuum.

Peterson, C., Ruch, W., Beermann, U., Park, N., & Seligman, M. E. (2007). Strengths of character, orientations to happiness, and life satisfaction. *The Journal of Positive Psychology, 2*(3), 149–156.

Phillips, S. D. (1997). Toward an expanded definition of adaptive decision making. *The Career Development Quarterly*, 45, 275–287.
Pisarik, C. T., & Currie, L. K. (2015). Recording and interpreting work-related daydreams: effects on vocational self-concept crystallization. *The Career Development Quarterly*, 63(3), 223–237.
Pisarik, C. T., Rowell, P. C., & Currie, L. K. (2013). Work-related daydreams: a qualitative content analysis. *Journal of Career Development*, 40(2), 87–106.
Polanyi, M. (1966). *The Tacit Dimension*. Abingdon: Routledge.
Positive Futures (2005). *Positive Futures Impact Report*. London: The Home Office.
Pouyaud, J., Bangali, M., Cohen-Scali, V., Robinet, M. L., & Guichard, J. (2016). Exploring changes during life and career design dialogues. *Journal of Vocational Behavior*, 97, 3–12.
Powers, M. B., Vörding, M. B. Z. V. S., & Emmelkamp, P. M. (2009). Acceptance and commitment therapy: a meta-analytic review. *Psychotherapy and Psychosomatics*, 78(2), 73–80.
Quimby, J. L., & DeSantis, A. M. (2006). The influence of role models on women's career choices. *The Career Development Quarterly*, 54(4), 297–306.
Rahim, A. (1981). Job satisfaction as a function of personality-job congruence: a study with Jungian psychological types. *Psychological Reports*, 49(2), 496–498.
Rath, T., & Harter, J. K. (2010). *Wellbeing: The Five Essential Elements*. New York, NY: Simon and Schuster.
Reid, H., & West, L. (2011). "Telling tales": using narrative in career guidance. *Journal of Vocational Behavior*, 78(2), 174–183.
Rilling, J., Glenn, A., Jairam, M., Pagnoni, G., Goldsmith, D., Elfenbein, H., & Lilienfeld, S. (2007). Neural correlates of social cooperation and non-cooperation as a function of psychopathy. *Biological Psychiatry*, 61(11), 1260–1271.
Robinson, B. S., Davis, K. L., & Meara, N. M. (2003). Motivational attributes of occupational possible selves for low-income rural women. *Journal of Counseling Psychology*, 50(2), 156–164.
Rochat, S., & Rossier, J. (2016). Integrating motivational interviewing in career counseling: a case study. *Journal of Vocational Behavior*, 93, 150–162.
Rodrigues, R. A., & Guest, D. (2010). Have careers become boundaryless? *Human Relations*, 63(8), 1157–1175.
Roelen, C. A., Koopmans, P. C., & Groothoff, J. W. (2008). Which work factors determine job satisfaction? *Work*, 30(4), 433–439.
Rogers, C. R. (1957). *On Becoming a Person*. Boston, MA: Houghton Mifflin, p. 202.
Rogers, C. R. (1962). The interpersonal relationship. *Harvard Educational Review*, 32(4), 416–429.
Roth, W.-M. (2009). Realizing Vygotsky's program concerning language and thought: tracking knowing (ideas, conceptions, beliefs) in real time. *Language and Education*, 23(4), 295–311.
Rotter, J. B. (1966). Generalized expectancies for internal versus external control of reinforcement. *Psychological Monographs: General and Applied*, 80(1), 1.
Rousseau, C., Benoit, M., Gauthier, M. F., Lacroix, L., Alain, N., Viger Rojas, M., ... & Bourassa, D. (2007). Classroom drama therapy program for immigrant and refugee adolescents: a pilot study. *Clinical Child Psychology and Psychiatry*, 12(3), 451–465.
Ryan, R. M., & Deci, E. L. (2000). Self-determination theory and the facilitation of intrinsic motivation, social development, and well-being. *American Psychologist*, 55(1), 68–78.

Saka, N., Gati, I., & Kelly, K. R. (2008). Emotional and personality-related aspects of career-decision-making difficulties. *Journal of Career Assessment, 16*(4), 403–424.

Saks, A. M., & Ashforth, B. E. (2000). Change in job search behaviors and employment outcomes. *Journal of Vocational Behavior, 56*(2), 277–287.

Sampson, J. P. (2009). Modern and postmodern career theories: the unnecessary divorce. *The Career Development Quarterly, 58*(1), 91–96.

Santos, P. J. (2001). Predictors of generalized indecision among Portuguese secondary school students. *Journal of Career Assessment, 9*(4), 381–396.

Savickas, M. L. (1991). Improving career time perspective. In D. Brown & L. Brooks (Eds), *Techniques of Career Counseling* (pp. 236–249). Boston, MA: Allyn & Bacon.

Savickas, M. (2015). *Life-Design Counseling Manual*. Rootstown, OH: Mark L. Savickas, p. 88.

Savickas, M. L., Nota, L., Rossier, J., Dauwalder, J. P., Duarte, M. E., Guichard, J., . . . & Van Vianen, A. E. (2009). Life designing: a paradigm for career construction in the 21st century. *Journal of Vocational Behavior, 75*(3), 239–250.

Savickas, M. L., Silling, S. M., & Schwartz, S. (1984). Time perspective in vocational maturity and career decision making. *Journal of Vocational Behavior, 25*(3), 258–269.

Scheier, M. F., & Carver, C. S. (2003). Self-regulatory processes and responses to health threats: effects of optimism on well-being. In J. Suls & K. A. Wallston (Eds), *Social Psychological Foundations of Health and Illness* (pp. 395–428). Oxford: Blackwell.

Schein, E. H. (1978). *Career Anchors (Revised)*. San Diego, CA: University Associates.

Schön, D. A. (1987). *Educating the Reflective Practitioner: Toward a New Design for Teaching and Learning in the Professions*. San Francisco, CA: Jossey-Bass.

Schuitema, J., Peetsma, T., & van der Veen, I. (2014). Enhancing student motivation: a longitudinal intervention study based on future time perspective theory. *The Journal of Educational Research, 107*(6), 467–481.

Schultheiss, D. E. P., Kress, H. M., Manzi, A. J., & Glasscock, J. M. J. (2001). Relational influences in career development: a qualitative inquiry. *The Counseling Psychologist, 29*(2), 216–241.

Seligman, M. E., & Csikszentmihalyi, M. (2000). Special issue on happiness, excellence, and optimal human functioning. *American Psychologist, 55*(1), 5–183.

Serling, D. A., & Betz, N. E. (1990). Development and evaluation of a measure of fear of commitment. *Journal of Counseling Psychology, 37*(1), 91.

Sexton, T. L., & Whiston, S. C. (1994). The status of the counseling relationship: an empirical review, theoretical implications, and research directions. *The Counseling Psychologist, 22*(1), 6–78.

Sheehan, M. J. (1981). Constructs and 'conflict' in depression. *British Journal of Psychology, 72*(2), 197–209.

Shimizu, E., So, M., Noguchi, R., Yamaguchi, S., & Sekizawa, Y. (2017). Effects of five-minute internet-based cognitive behavioral therapy and simplified emotion-focused mindfulness on depressive symptoms: a randomized controlled trial. *BMC Psychiatry, 17*(1), 85.

Simmons, B. L., & Nelson, D. L. (2001). Eustress at work: the relationship between hope and health in hospital nurses. *Health Care Management Review, 26*(4), 7–18.

Simonneaux, L. (2001). Role-play or debate to promote students' argumentation and justification on an issue in animal transgenesis. *International Journal of Science Education, 23*(9), 903–927.

Singh, R., & Greenhaus, J. H. (2004). The relation between career decision-making strategies and person–job fit: a study of job changers. *Journal of Vocational Behavior, 64*(1), 198–221.

Slade, P. (1955). *Child Drama*. Philosophical Library. London: Cassell.

Slayton, S. C., D'Archer, J., & Kaplan, F. (2010). Outcome studies on the efficacy of art therapy: a review of findings. *Art Therapy, 27*(3), 108–118.

Smith, K. A. (2008). Restructuring metaphors: using mental re-mapping in cognitive coaching. *Journal of Rational-Emotive & Cognitive-Behavior Therapy, 26*(1), 16–29.

Soelberg, P. O. (1967). Unprogrammed decision making. *Industrial Management Review, 8*(2), 19–29.

Spence, G. B., Cavanagh, M. J., & Grant, A. M. (2008). The integration of mindfulness training and health coaching: an exploratory study. *Coaching: An International Journal of Theory, Research and Practice, 1*(2), 145–163.

Stawarczyk, D., Majerus, S., Van der Linden, M., & D'Argembeau, A. (2012). Using the daydreaming frequency scale to investigate the relationships between mind-wandering, psychological well-being, and present-moment awareness. *Frontiers in Psychology, 3*, 1–12.

Steele, C., & Francis-Smythe, J. (2007). Career anchors: an empirical investigation. *Proceedings of the British Psychological Society's 2007 Occupational Psychology Conference, Bristol, England*. ISBN: 9781854334671. Available at: https://eprints.worc.ac.uk/265/1/CareerAnchorsEmp.pdf.

Steiner, C. (2005). Transactional analysis: an elegant theory and practice. *The Script, 35*(2), 4–5.

Stevenson, H. (2004). *Paradox: A Gestalt Theory of Change*. The Gestalt Therapy Network. Available at: www.gestalttherapy.net/writers/herb2.pdf.

Stokoe, E. (2011). Simulated interaction and communication skills training: the 'conversation-analytic role-play method'. In C. Antaki (Ed.), *Applied Conversation Analysis* (pp. 119–139). Basingstoke: Palgrave Macmillan UK.

Stoltz, K. B., & Young, T. L. (2013). Applications of motivational interviewing in career counseling: facilitating career transition. *Journal of Career Development, 40*(4), 329–346.

Strauss, K., Griffin, M. A., & Parker, S. K. (2012). Future work selves: how salient hoped-for identities motivate proactive career behaviors. *Journal of Applied Psychology, 97*(3), 580.

Suddendorf, T., & Corballis, M. C. (1997). Mental time travel and the evolution of the human mind. *Genetic, Social, and General Psychology Monographs, 123*(2), 133–167.

Super, D. E. (1953). A theory of vocational development. *American Psychologist, 8*(5), 185.

Super, D. E., & Sverko, B. (1995). *Life Roles, Values, and Careers*. San Francisco, CA: Josey-Bass.

Swain, J., Hancock, K., Hainsworth, C., & Bowman, J. (2013). Acceptance and commitment therapy in the treatment of anxiety: a systematic review. *Clinical Psychology Review, 33*(8), 965–978.

Szentagotai, A., & Jones, J. (2010). The behavioral consequences of irrational beliefs. In: D. David, S. J. Lynn, & A. Ellis (Eds), *Rational and Irrational Beliefs in Human Functioning and Disturbances*. Oxford: Oxford University Press.

Taber, B. J., & Blankemeyer, M. (2015). Future work self and career adaptability in the prediction of proactive career behaviors. *Journal of Vocational Behavior, 86*, 20–27.

Tausch, R. (1990). The supplementation of client-centered communication therapy with other valid therapeutic methods. In G. Lietaer, J. Rombauts & R. Van Balen. *Client-Centered and Experiential Psychotherapy in the Nineties* (pp. 447–456). Leuven: Leuven University Press,.

Taylor, K. M., & Betz, N. E. (1983). Applications of self-efficacy theory to the understanding and treatment of career indecision. *Journal of Vocational Behavior, 22*(1), 63–81.

Taylor, J. M., & Savickas, S. (2016). Narrative career counseling: my career story and pictorial narratives. *Journal of Vocational Behavior, 97*, 68–77.

Tokar, D. M., & Subich, L. M. (1997). Relative contributions of congruence and personality dimensions to job satisfaction. *Journal of Vocational Behavior, 50*(3), 482–491.

Tranberg, M., Slane, S., & Ekeberg, S. E. (1993). The relation between interest congruence and satisfaction: a meta-analysis. *Journal of Vocational Behavior, 42*(3), 253–264.

Van Hasselt, V. B., Romano, S. J., & Vecchi, G. M. (2008). Role playing: applications in hostage and crisis negotiation skills training. *Behavior Modification, 32*(2), 248–263.

Van Hoye, G., Van Hooft, E. A., & Lievens, F. (2009). Networking as a job search behaviour: a social network perspective. *Journal of Occupational and Organizational Psychology, 82*(3), 661–682.

Van Iddekinge, C. H., Roth, P. L., Putka, D. J., & Lanivich, S. E. (2011). Are you interested? A meta-analysis of relations between vocational interests and employee performance and turnover. *Journal of Applied Psychology, 96*(6), 1167–1194.

Varra, A. A., Hayes, S. C., Roget, N., & Fisher, G. (2008). A randomized control trial examining the effect of acceptance and commitment training on clinician willingness to use evidence-based pharmacotherapy. *Journal of Consulting and Clinical Psychology, 76*(3), 449.

Verquer, M. L., Beehr, T. A., & Wagner, S. H. (2003). A meta-analysis of relations between person–organization fit and work attitudes. *Journal of Vocational Behavior, 63*(3), 473–489.

Viney, L. L., Clarke, A. M., Bunn, T. A., & Benjamin, Y. N. (1985). Crisis-intervention counseling: an evaluation of long-and short-term effects. *Journal of Counseling Psychology, 32*(1), 29.

Vygotsky, L. S. (1986). *Thought and Language*, 2nd Edition. Boston, MA: MIT Press.

Wanberg, C. R., Kanfer, R., & Banas, J. T. (2000). Predictors and outcomes of networking intensity among unemployed job seekers. *Journal of Applied Psychology, 85*(4), 491.

Wells, K., & McCaig, M. (2016). The magic wand question and recovery-focused practice in child and adolescent mental health services. *Journal of Child and Adolescent Psychiatric Nursing, 29*(4), 164–170.

Whiston, S. C., & Keller, B. K. (2004). The influences of the family of origin on career development: a review and analysis. *The Counseling Psychologist, 32*(4), 493–568.

Whiston, S. C., Li, Y., Mitts, N. G., & Wright, L. (2017). Effectiveness of career choice interventions: a meta-analytic replication and extension. *Journal of Vocational Behavior, 100*, 175–184.

Whiston, S. C., Sexton, T. L., & Lasoff, D. L. (1998). Career-intervention outcome: a replication and extension of Oliver and Spokane (1988). *Journal of Counseling Psychology, 45*(2), 150.

Willis, G. W. (2012). The impact that career anchors and job compatibility of professional nurses has on job satisfaction – a predictor of turnover. Doctoral dissertation, University of Pretoria.

Yates, J. (2013). *The Career Coaching Handbook*. Abingdon: Routledge.

Yates, J. (2015). The heart has its reasons which reason knows not: the role of the unconscious in career decision making. *Journal of the National institute of Career Education and Counselling, 35*, 28–35.

Yates, J. (2016). A meta-theoretical framework for career practitioners. *The Indian Journal of Career and Livelihood Planning, 5*(1), 15–25.

Yontef, G., & Simkin, J. (1993). *An Introduction to Gestalt Therapy*. Behavior on Line. Available at: www.behavior.net/gestalt.html.

Zaman Bin Ahmad, K. (2008). Relationship between leader–subordinate personality congruence and performance and satisfaction in the UK. *Leadership & Organization Development Journal, 29*(5), 396–411.

Zepf, S. (2011). The relations between language, consciousness, the preconscious, and the unconscious. *Scandinavian Psychoanalytic Review, 34*(1), 50–61.

Zimbardo, P. G., & Boyd, J. N. (2015). Putting time in perspective: a valid, reliable individual-differences metric. In M. Stolarski, N. Fieulaine & W. van Beek (Eds), *Time Perspective Theory; Review, Research And Application* (pp. 17–55). New York, NY: Springer International Publishing.

Zittoun, T., & Gillespie, A. (2015). *Imagination in Human and Cultural Development*. Abingdon: Routledge.

# Index

ABCDE model 83, 86–89
abstract conceptualisation 166
acceptance 124, 127, 133–135
acceptance and commitment therapy (ACT) 1, 123, 132–142
active, being 129, 130, 132
active experimentation 166
active listening 102–103, 104, 105
adaptability 93, 95
adult ego state 112–113, 114–115, 116
affective impediments 8
agency 26, 92
agreeableness 13
all or nothing thinking 90
ambiguity, tolerance for 10
Anuszkiewicz, T. M. 156
anxiety 9, 10, 137; acceptance and commitment therapy 134, 141; art tools 41; choice anxiety 8–9; cognitive behavioural therapy 85; personal constructs 47
appreciation 58–59
appreciative inquiry 54
art therapy 33, 38–41
artistic types 76, 77, 79
Asadnia, S. 101
aspirations: drawing 33, 41; perceptual positions 117; role models 151; self-esteem 123, 131
attention 124, 127, 147
attentional bias 25–26
attitudes: empty chair technique 97; personal constructs 42; role models 151
attributes 7
autonomy 34, 61–62, 63, 128, 152
awareness 124, 127
Azar, F. S. 101

Bandler, Richard 117
barriers 74, 93
Beail, N. 47
Beck, Aaron 84
behaviour: cognitive behavioural therapy 84–85, 86; miracle question 159; personality questionnaire 13; role models 151
beliefs 85, 86–88, 101
Bem, S. L. 165
Berne, Eric 112
Bimrose, J. 95
Bishop, S. R. 124
Blankemeyer, M. 72
Bohart, A. C. 109
bosses 34
boundaries 3, 123, 172–173; drawing 40; empty chair technique 98; perceptual positions 119
Bourdieu, Pierre 91
brain 116
breathing exercises 125–127
Brecht, Bertolt 121
Brown, D. 141
Buzan, Tony 167

Cable, D. M. 59
capital 91–92
career anchors 48, 60–65
career choices 6–7, 48; ABCDE model 89; acceptance and commitment therapy 140; career anchors 64, 65; career construction interview 25; career genogram 31; career time perspective 155; change talk 164; choosing between options 143–151; daydream journal 74; drawing 40; empty chair technique 99; family influences 27–32, 111; five ways to well-being

131; head and heart 147; Holland's hexagon of career interests 80; imaginary conversations 150; job satisfaction 36; life design 21; mindfulness 127; miracle question 159; motivational interviewing 165; perceptual positions 120; person-centred dialogue 107; personal work constructs 46; personality questionnaire 17, 18, 20; possible selves 70; psychological capital 94; role models 151; self-efficacy 95; strengths 54; transactional analysis 115; values 57, 58, 59; *see also* decision making; jobs
career construction interview 12, 21–27
Career Decision Scale 8
career drivers 48, 60–65
career factors inventory 8
career genogram 12, 27–32
career planning 12, 72, 155, 156; *see also* planning
career success 36–37
career time perspective 153–156
Cavanagh, M. J. 128
challenge, pure 62, 63
change, paradoxical theory of 100
change talk 153, 161–165
Chartrand, J. M. 8
Chen, D. J. 95
child ego state 112–113, 114–115
choice anxiety 8–9
circles test 154
client as expert 102
cognitive behavioural therapy (CBT) 83–86, 87, 89, 133, 141
cognitive defusion 133–134, 135–136
cognitive dissonance 164–165
cognitive distortions 83
collaboration 24
Collard, P. 128
colleagues 34
Colozzi, E. A. 55–56
comments 106
committed action 133–134, 138
communication: ego states 113; value congruence 59, 60
competence 152
competition 16
conceptualised self 137
concrete experience 166
confidence 7; acceptance and commitment therapy 139; art tools 41; lack of 32, 83, 123; mindfulness 125; personal constructs 47; psychological capital 92; thinking errors 91; *see also* self-esteem
confidentiality 3, 172
conflict 111; *see also* disagreement with others
congruence 19, 21; acceptance and commitment therapy 133; career anchors 61; job satisfaction 34, 81; person-centred approach 107–108; values 59, 60
connection 129, 130, 131–132
conscientiousness 13
constructivism 160
contact with the present moment 133–134, 137
contest mobility 36–37
continuity 12
contracting 172–173
conventional types 76, 78, 79
Cooperrider, D. L. 54
core conditions 107–108, 109, 110
Costa, P. T. 13
counselling 3, 109, 110, 119, 172
creativity: entrepreneurial 61, 63; mindfulness 127, 128; positive emotions 95
Csikszentmihalyi, Mihaly 49
Currie, L. K. 75
CVs 166–167

daydream journal 66–67, 72–75
De Haan, Eric 4
de Shazer, Steve 160
debriefing: career construction interview 23–24, 25; empty chair technique 98
Deci, E. L. 152
decision making: career construction interview 27; choosing between options 143–151; difficulties 7–10; positive well-being 41; self-efficacy 9; skills 7; *see also* career choices
dedication to a cause 62, 63
defusion 133–134, 135–136
depression 55, 85, 101, 127, 132, 137
Depth Oriented Values Extraction 55–56
development opportunities 34
Di Fabio, A. 27
dialogue: empty chair technique 97–98; person-centred 96, 102–110
disagreement with others 8, 9, 111, 119–120
Donnellan, Brent 13, 20

drama therapy 121, 122
drawing 28, 33, 38–41
dual processing 144–148

educational opportunities 34
Edwards, J. R. 59
ego states 111, 112–116
Elliott, R. 109
Ellis, Albert 84, 86
Emmelkamp, P. M. 141
emotional intelligence 128
emotions: ABCDE model 87; acceptance and commitment therapy 140; cognitive behavioural therapy 84–85, 86; drama therapy 122; drawing 38, 39–40; empty chair technique 97; generative empathic listening 104; mindfulness 125, 127; need for harmony 15–16; negative thoughts 89; positive 95, 128, 132; possible selves 67; pre-experiencing 71
empathy 15, 18, 51–52; generative empathic listening 104; perceptual positions 117; person-centred approach 103, 106, 107–108, 109
empowerment 122, 135
empty chair technique 96–102
engagement 20, 55, 95
enterprising types 76, 77, 79, 80
entrepreneurial creativity 61, 63
environment 7
Epictetus 84
episodic future thinking 71
Erickson, Milton 160
ethical issues 3, 40, 172–173
evidence 1–2; acceptance and commitment therapy 141–142; career anchors 64–65; career construction interview 26–27; career genogram 32; career time perspective 156; cognitive behavioural therapy 85–86; daydreaming 75; drawing 41; empty chair technique 101; five ways to well-being 131–132; Holland's hexagon of career interests 81–82; imaginary conversations 151; job satisfaction 37; mindfulness 128; motivational interviewing 165; perceptual positions 121–122; person-centred approach 108–110; personal work constructs 47; personality questionnaire 20–21; possible selves 71–72; psychological capital 95; solution-focused therapy 160–161;

strengths 54–55; transactional analysis 116–117; values 60
exercise 130, 132
expectations 37, 155
expert, client as 102
expressed values 55, 57
extraversion 13, 14, 18, 20

failure, fear of 10
family: disagreement with 9, 111, 119–120; ego states 112–114; genograms 27–32
Farber, B. A. 109
faulty thinking 83, 89–91
fear 10
Festinger, L. 164
Fitzpatrick, J. J. 95
five ways to well-being 1, 129–132
flexibility 132, 133–134
flourishing 54, 129
flow 38, 49, 50
focusing on negatives 91
fusion 135
future thinking: career time perspective 153–156; change talk 162, 164; daydream journal 66–67, 72–75; episodic 71; miracle question 157–161; possible selves 66, 67–72, 150

Gati, I. 7–8, 9–10
genograms 12, 27–32
gestalt therapy 96, 100–101
getting started 171–172
giving 129, 130, 132
goals: ability to set 7; acceptance and commitment therapy 136, 138, 139; career time perspective 155; change talk 162, 163; cognitive behavioural therapy 86; empty chair technique 101; mindfulness 128; miracle question 158, 159, 160; possible selves 70–71, 72; psychological capital 92, 93; values 59, 60
González-Ramírez, E. 101
Google Scholar 174
Grant, A. M. 128
Grant, B. 108
Greenbank, P. 156
Greenberg, L. S. 109
Griffin, M. T. Q. 95
Grinder, John 117
group contexts 4; career anchors 64; career construction interview 25; career

genogram 29–30, 31; career time perspective 155; daydream journal 74; drawing 40; imaginary conversations 150; job satisfaction 36; mindfulness 127; perceptual positions 119; personal work constructs 44–45, 46; personality questionnaire 18; possible selves 70; psychological capital 92–93, 94; strengths 54; values 57–58; wheel of life 170
gut instinct 144–148

Hall, D. T. 60
Hamilton, N. 138
happiness: five ways to well-being 129; job satisfaction 34, 36; mindfulness 128; personality 20
harmony, need for 15–16, 17, 19, 20
Hart, D. 128
Hart, R. 128
head and heart 144–148
Hearne, L. 95
Heller, D. 20, 37
Hepworth, S. 156
hexagon of career interests 66, 67, 75–82
Holland, John 66, 67, 75–82
hope 83, 95; future time perspective 156; learning 132; miracle question 158, 160; psychological capital 92–93
Howard, K. I. 109
humanism 96, 102, 108

identity 6–7, 9, 10; career decisions 144; expressed values 57; 'identity diffusion' 8; *see also* possible selves
imaginary conversations 144, 148–151
imagination 14–15, 17, 18, 150, 160
implicit knowledge 46
implicit values 55–60
incongruence 19
inconsistent information 8
indecision 8–9, 10
independence 61–62, 63
information: inconsistent 8; information knowledge 46; lack of 8; System 1 and System 2 processing 144–148
instrumental non-directivity 108
interaction, need for 14, 17
interests: career construction interview 22–23; five ways to well-being 130; Holland's hexagon of career interests 66, 67, 75–82; implicit values 55, 56–57
introversion 14

intuition 15
investigative types 76, 77, 78, 80
Ivtzan, I. 128

job satisfaction: acceptance and commitment therapy 142; career anchors 65; Holland's hexagon of career interests 80, 81–82; life satisfaction 54–55; mindfulness 128; personal job satisfaction model 33–37; personality 20, 21; psychological capital 92, 95; self-efficacy 95; strengths 49, 55; values 59, 60
job search: optimism 128; positive well-being 41; possible selves 72; psychological capital 95; relationships 131–132; self-esteem 131
jobs 48, 66; Holland's hexagon of career interests 67, 76, 78–82; identification of strengths 52–53; mismatch with personality 13, 17, 19; perceptions of 7; personal job satisfaction model 33–37; personal work constructs 33, 42–47; possible selves 67–72, 150; *see also* career choices
Judge, T. A. 20, 37

Kabzinska, Z. 47
Kahneman, D. 144, 148
Kelly, George 42, 47
Kelly, K. R. 8–10
knowledge 46
Kolb's learning cycle 166–167
Krausz, M. 7–8

Lane, J. S. 109
language 141, 147, 167
Lasoff, D. L. 172
learning: five ways to well-being 129, 130, 132; Kolb's learning cycle 166–167; mindfulness 128
Lee, W. C. 8–9
life design 21, 26
life satisfaction 54–55, 128
lifestyle 62, 63
Lim, V. K. 95
listening 102–103, 104, 105
locus of control 9
Luthans, Fred 92–93

magnification 91
Magnuson, S. 29
Malott, K. M. 29

managerial competence 61, 63, 64
Maree, J. G. 27
Marko, K. W. 156
Markus, H. 71
Matos, P. S. 95
McCrae, R. R. 13
McIlveen, P. 138
meaning making 21
meditation 123, 124
memories 23
metaphors 167
Metcalfe, C. 47
Meyer, Paul 170
Miller, J. 157
Miller, W. R. 161, 165
Milwaukee Brief Family Therapy Center 157, 160
mind maps 167–168
mindfulness 123, 124–128, 132, 134, 137
Mini IPIP Scale 13–21
minimisation 91
miracle question 153, 157–161
Mirvis, P. H. 60
mismatches 13, 17, 18, 19, 21
money 37
Moran, D. J. 141
motivation 152–165; career anchors 48, 60–61, 65; goals 71; intrinsic and extrinsic 161; possible selves 67, 72; values 59, 60
motivational interviewing (MI) 153, 161–165
Mount, M. K. 20, 37
Mulawarman, U. 161
Muscat, A. C. 165
Myers Briggs Type Indicator 15

narrative approaches 75
negatives, focusing on 91
Neimeyer, G. J. 47
networking 72, 123, 131
neuro-linguistic programming (NLP) 111, 117
neuroscience 116
Neushotz, L. A. 95
New Economics Foundation (NEF) 123, 129–132
non-directivity 103, 105–106, 108
non-judgemental approach 57, 104–105, 108, 124, 135, 146, 163–164, 174
notice, taking 129, 130, 132, 137
Novey, T. B. 116
Nurius, P. 71

observer exercise 137
observing self 137
older workers 70
online coaching 4
openness to experience 13, 15, 127
optimism 7; future time perspective 156; mindfulness 128; miracle question 160; psychological capital 83, 92, 95
Orlinsky, D. E. 109
Osipow, S. H. 7–8
Öst, L. G. 141

pace 104
paradoxical theory of change 100
parent ego state 112–113, 114–115
Parsons, Frank 6
Paszkowska-Rogacz, A. 47
'pauses' 173
peer group supervision 3
Peetsma, T. 156
perceptions 7
perceptual positions 111, 117–122
perfectionism 10, 86
Performance Inhibiting Thoughts to Performance Enhancing Thoughts (PITS to PETS) 83, 89–91
person-centred approach 4, 96, 102–110, 174; miracle question 159; motivational interviewing 161, 163–164; positive psychology 54
person-environment fit 19, 20–21, 34
person-job fit 81–82
personal attributes 7
personal work constructs 33, 42–47
personalisation 91
personality 12–21; career anchors 61; career indecision 8, 9; Holland's hexagon of career interests 76–81
pessimism 9
phobias 47
Pisarik, C. T. 75
placebo effect 109
planning: career time perspective 155, 156; identification of strengths 51–52; love of 16, 17, 18, 20; psychological capital 92
pleasure 54
positive psychology 49, 54, 107, 129, 159
possible selves 66, 67–72, 150
post-it notes 168
Powers, M. B. 141
pre-experiencing 67, 71
the preconscious 147

principled non-directivity 108
procrastination 86
protean career model 60
psychological capital 83, 91–95
psychological flexibility 132, 133–134
purpose 132

questioning 106, 169–170
quizzes 63

rational thinking 144–148
readiness, lack of 8
realistic types 76, 77, 78
reflection: career anchors 62–63; career genogram 28; collaborative 4; drawing 38–39; personal work constructs 43; repeating a client's word or phrase 105
reflective observation 166
reflective professional journals 173
Reid, Hazel 27
relatedness 152
relational frame theory (RFT) 141
relationships: acceptance and commitment therapy 140; connections 130, 131–132; drama therapy 122; ego states 113–114; empty chair technique 101; positive emotions 95; values 60
repertory grid 42, 47
research: keeping up to date with 174; research skills 7
resilience 7; cognitive behavioural therapy 86; psychological capital 83, 92, 93–94, 95
retirement speech exercise 138
RIASEC 76
Robbins, S. B. 8
Rogers, Carl 96, 102, 105, 107–110, 159, 161
role models 22, 149–150, 151
role play 118, 121–122
Rollnick, S. 161
Rose, G. S. 165
Rowell, P. C. 75
Ryan, R. M. 152

Saka, N. 9–10
salaries 37
Savickas, Mark 21, 23, 26, 154, 156
sayings, favourite 23
scaling 162–163, 168–169
Schein, Edgar 48, 60–64
Schön, D. A. 46

Schuitema, J. 156
security 61, 63
self-acceptance 41
self-actualising tendency 102
self-as-context 133–134, 137
self-awareness 6, 48, 63, 66; art tools 41; career construction interview 25; cognitive defusion 136; daydreams 75; empty chair technique 101; Holland's hexagon of career interests 76, 81; personal constructs 42; personality questionnaire 18
self-coaching 88
self-concept 57, 74–75
self-criticism 10, 101, 127
self-determination theory 152
self-efficacy: art tools 41; career indecision 9; lack of 83; learning 132; psychological capital 94–95
self-esteem: art tools 41; career decisions 144; continuity 12; five ways to well-being 129, 131; identity issues 10; learning 132; low 123, 125; mindfulness 125, 126, 128; personal constructs 47; personality 13, 21; relationships 130; *see also* confidence
self-instruction 165
self-regulation 128
Seligman, Martin 49, 53
service 62, 63, 64–65
setbacks 93, 94, 131
Sexton, T. L. 109, 172
silence 105
skills: acceptance 134–135; career anchors 65; decision making 7; lists of 48; person-centred dialogue 103–106; personal constructs 42; research 7
social integration 132
social justice 26
social support 31–32, 93, 95, 132
social types 76, 77, 79
socioeconomic status 156
Socratic questioning 169–170
solution-focused therapy (SFT) 107, 153, 157, 159, 160–161
Spence, G. B. 128
sponsorship mobility 36–37
Srivastva, S. 54
stability 61, 63
Stanislavski, Konstantin 121
Stoltz, K. B. 165
stories 21, 23, 74–75
strength cards 53–54

strengths 34, 48, 49–55, 158
stress: acceptance and commitment therapy 142; cognitive behavioural therapy 86; drama therapy 122; mindfulness 128
Strokes Cluster 112
stuckness 7–10, 69
success: career success 36–37; fear of 10
supervision 3, 173–174
support 31–32, 93, 95, 132
System 1 and System 2 processing 144–148

Taber, B. J. 72
tacit knowledge 46
taking notice 129, 130, 132, 137
teams 15
technical competence 61, 63, 64
thinking errors 83, 89–91
thoughts: ABCDE model 87; cognitive behavioural therapy 84–85, 86, 133; negative 89–91, 125, 135–136
time: career time perspective 153–156; mindfulness 124; time-management 86
time perspective modification intervention (TPMI) 154
Torabzadeh, N. 101
training 34, 142
trait indecision 8
transactional analysis (TA) 111–117
trust 59, 60
turnover 81

uncertainty 10, 127
unconditional positive regard (UPR) 57, 106, 108, 109

unconscious thoughts 41, 46, 66–67, 146, 147; *see also* gut instinct

values 48, 55–60; acceptance and commitment therapy 133–134, 135, 136, 138, 139, 140–141; career anchors 61, 62, 65; career construction interview 22; daydreams 75; need for harmony 15; personal constructs 42; personal job satisfaction model 34
Values in Action Inventory of Strengths (VIA-IS) 53
van der Veen, I. 156
Viney, L. L. 47
virtues 53
volunteering 130, 132
Vörding, M. B. Z. V. S. 141

Walsh, J. 128
Watson, J. C. 109
well-being: acceptance and commitment therapy 142; art tools 41; cognitive behavioural therapy 86; drama therapy 122; five ways to 1, 129–132; job satisfaction 54–55
West, Linden 27
wheel of life 170
Whiston, S. C. 109, 110, 172
Winter, D. 47
work engagement 20, 55, 95
work load 34
working alliance 107–108, 110
working conditions 34

Young, T. L. 165